Reflections on Aesthetic Judgment and other Essays

BENJAMIN TILGHMAN
Kansas State University, USA

Routledge
Taylor & Francis Group

LONDON AND NEW YORK

First published 2006 by Ashgate Publishing

Reissued 2018 by Routledge
2 Park Square, Milton Park, Abingdon, Oxon OX14 4RN
711 Third Avenue, New York, NY 10017, USA

Routledge is an imprint of the Taylor & Francis Group, an informa business

First issued in paperback 2018

A Library of Congress record exists under LC control number: 2006026856

Notice:
Product or corporate names may be trademarks or registered trademarks, and are used only for identification and explanation without intent to infringe.

Publisher's Note
The publisher has gone to great lengths to ensure the quality of this reprint but points out that some imperfections in the original copies may be apparent.

Disclaimer
The publisher has made every effort to trace copyright holders and welcomes correspondence from those they have been unable to contact.

ISBN 13: 978-0-815-39137-1 (hbk)
ISBN 13: 978-1-138-62031-5 (pbk)
ISBN 13: 978-1-351-15060-6 (ebk)

REFLECTIONS ON AESTHETIC JUDGMENT
AND OTHER ESSAYS

Contents

Foreword

The papers in this collection were written and published over a period of more than thirty years. They are the result of a long-standing interest in aesthetics and a growing interest in art. It is, needless to say, reflection on art from which philosophers derive their problems and construct their theories and it is against art and our traffic with it that the philosophy has to be measured. For want of any other obvious systematic or thematic unity the articles are arranged chronologically in the order of their publication. They treat almost entirely of issues in literature and the visual arts, especially painting. Music is scarcely mentioned. My philosophical thinking has been shaped largely by the conception of philosophy to be found in Ludwig Wittgenstein's *Philosophical Investigations* and I have sought in these papers, as elsewhere, to apply its philosophical techniques to problems in aesthetics and the philosophy of art.

Despite a lack of systematic unity, there are, nevertheless, several recurring themes to be found in these essays. In the first place, they are consistently antitheoretical. I have long been opposed to general theories and definitions of art and what it is, the kind of theorizing that so often gets started as an attempt to respond to the question, "What is art?" Likewise, I am opposed to theories of art's subspecies that seek to tell us what painting is or what poetry is, to mention only two. Ontological theories that seek to tell us what kind of object a work of art is are frequent targets and come in for their share of criticism. I have throughout kept in mind Wittgenstein's remark that ontology is best understood as grammar, that is, as observations about how certain words function in language. Also under attack are theories about aesthetic and artistic judgments. I am of the opinion that philosophical theories, of whatever stripe, will not solve the problems about art and our appreciation of art that they are intended to solve. The task is to see through and behind those theories in order to get a clear view of what those problems are and where their solutions may lie.

In the second place, I have sought to emphasize both the importance of the representation of the human in art and our human response to art. The philosophy of art cannot get on simply by "analyzing" the language in which aesthetic descriptions and judgments are expressed; that language has to be seen in the context of the life that produces it. It is reflection upon this life, which is our life, that can reveal the importance of art and the difference it can make in our lives. Philosophical aesthetics cannot be simply play with definitions and logical puzzles for that tends to obscure the importance of doing that kind of philosophy, which, after all, should aim at giving us a clear picture of our concerns about art that leads us to think seriously about it.

I want to express my thanks to Peter McCormick and Kjell S. Johannessen who have urged me to undertake such a collection and to Marilyn Tilghman for much loving encouragement and invaluable editorial assistance.

Benjamin R. Tilghman
Lawrence, KS

Acknowledgments

"The Literary Work of Art" was published in Benjamin R. Tilghman, ed., *Language and Aesthetics*, (The University Press of Kansas, Lawrence/Manhattan/Wichita, 1973) and is reprinted by permission of the University Press of Kansas. "Aesthetic Descriptions and Secondary Senses" appeared in *Philosophical Investigations*, vol. 3, no. 3 (Summer 1980). "Danto and the Ontology of Literature," was published in *The Journal of Aesthetics and Art Criticism* (Spring 1982). öbvhpt Verlagsgesellschaft mbH & Co. KG has given permission to reprint "Understanding People and Understanding Art," *Proceedings of the 8th International Wittgenstein Symposium* (Vienna: Verlag Hölder-Pichler-Tempsky, 1983), and "Perspective, Painting and the Look of the World," *Proceedings of the 18th International Wittgenstein Symposium*, Vienna: Verlag Hölder-Pichler-Tempsky, 1995). I am indebted to Oxford University Press for permission to reprint "Picture Space and Moral Space" (*The British Journal of Aesthetics*, vol. 28, 1988, pp. 317-326); "Literature, Philosophy and Nonsense" (*The British Journal of Aesthetics*, vol. 30, 1990, pp. 256-265); "Charles Le Brun: Theory, Philosophy and Irony" (*The British Journal of Aesthetics*, vol. 32, 1992, pp. 123-133); and "Reflections on Aesthetic Judgment" (*British Journal of Aesthetics*, vol. 44, 2004, pp. 248-260). "Architecture, Expression and the Understanding of a Culture," is from Michael Mitias, ed., *Philosophy and Architecture* (Amsterdam: Rodopi, 1994) and reprinted by permission of Rodopi. "A Conceptual Dimension of Art History" appeared in Richard Woodfield, ed., *Gombrich on Art and Psychology* (Manchester and New York: Manchester University Press, 1996). "Language and Painting, Border Wars and Pipe Dreams" is reprinted from Richard Allen and Malcolm Turvey, eds, *Wittgenstein, Theory and the Arts* (London and New York: Routledge, 2001) by permission of Thompson Publishing Services. "Literature, Human Understanding and Morality" is reprinted from Peter B. Lewis, ed., *Wittgenstein, Aesthetics and Philosophy* (Aldershot: Ashgate Publishers Ltd., 2004) by permission of Ashgate Publishers. "Reflections on Aesthetic Theory" is reprinted by permission from Dickie, Sclafani & Roblin, eds, *Aesthetics: a Critical Anthology*, pp. 160-170 (Copyright © 2/89 Bedford/St. Martins).

Chapter 1

The Literary Work of Art

Literary critics, in their theoretical moments, are sometimes inclined to suppose that certain philosophical preliminaries must be accomplished before their proper business of doing criticism can be gotten on with. I would claim that this is an altogether mistaken supposition; but one that wants showing in detail, and in this paper I must restrict myself to talking about only one such philosophical issue about literature and the practice of its criticism. The question I wish to investigate is the one that Wellek and Warren introduce under the heading "The Mode of Existence of a Literary Work of Art."[1] Briefly, the question can be phrased: What kind of an object is a work of literature—or "poem," to use the going abbreviation—and where is it to be found? The question, however, cannot be discussed briefly, for it involves a number of philosophical tangles. A good deal of untangling is required before we can become clear about why there is thought to be a question at all and what finding an answer is supposed to do for criticism, and become clear about the conception of the nature of criticism that is intertwined with the raising of the question.

I shall argue that this question about the "mode of existence" of works of literature is an illegitimate question that arises out of what is basically two sets of confusions. The first of these is the result of certain misunderstandings of the depth grammar of the word "poem" in general and of names of individual works of literature in particular. The second, which is no doubt more philosophically significant as well as the more difficult to deal with, is the result of a mistaken description of what literary criticism is like. In the first section of this paper I try to show how the raising of the question about the "mode of existence" of poems is connected with this particular conception of criticism; in sections II and III I review some of the answers that have been given to the question and point out how misunderstandings of the depth grammar of "poem" have permitted the question to be entertained; finally, in the last two sections, I return to a discussion of the relevant problems about literary criticism.

I

We have learned a great deal from the New Critics about reading poetry and the hard work of digging meaning out of unyielding stanzas. They have taught us to do these things by first pointing out that far too often critics had been talking about

---

1 René Wellek and Austin Warren, *Theory of Literature*, 1st edn (New York, 1949), chap. 12.

the wrong things; they had been talking about the life and loves of poets and the sighs and sobs of readers rather than about the poems themselves. But even when we turn our attention to the poem itself and read its lines closely, we are, upon occasion, puzzled over how some figure of speech is to be taken, the meaning of some now old-fashioned term, or the motivation of a character in a play, as well as how the whole poem is to be judged. Some familiar examples: Is Blake's "dark Satanic Mills" a reference to the church or the industrial revolution?; is the last line of Housman's "From Clee to heaven" to be taken ironically?; and was Hamlet really mad or only pretending? Some critics profess to answer such questions by reference to the poet's biography and intentions or by reference to the reactions of some reader. It is against these critical tendencies that the New Critics have so often argued. Much of this argument is, of course, to the point, for there are serious difficulties in both intentionalistic and impressionistic criticism. The relevant information about the poet is not always available; and even in those cases where a poet can be asked to explain his poetry, he may well prove to be a poor reader of his own poems and do a bad job of it, and the response of any reader may be evidence that he missed the point of the work in question as often as it is evidence that he understood it.

These issues are discussed in considerable detail in Wimsatt and Beardsley's now classic pair of articles "The Intentional Fallacy" and "The Affective Fallacy." I am not concerned at this point with thrashing out the role that invoking either intentions or affections should or should not play in criticism, but I am concerned with a remark made in the second of the articles that is intended to characterize the "Fallacies:" "The Intentional Fallacy is a confusion between the poem and its origins ... . The Affective Fallacy is a confusion between the poem and its *results*."[2] The remark is made almost in passing, although it is one that cannot be allowed to pass. No further reference is made in the article to the business of confusing a poem with something else; nevertheless, the notion that a poem is a kind of object liable to get confused with other things is one that runs through—I am tempted to say "infects"—a great deal of the critical theory associated with the New Criticism.

To say that a poem is neither the same as the intentions of its author nor the same as the reaction it produces in its readers is to say a curious thing. A poem cannot be confused with something else. And this is not, of course, because poems stand out so clearly and distinctly from all other things. One man can be confused with another, especially if the light is bad; a Van Megereen can be confused with a Vermeer because of the cleverness of the stylistic forgery; and one poem can be confused with another—students in literature classes do it with appalling regularity (he thought *L'Allegro* was the one that began "Hence vain deluding follies")—but there is no conceptual room for confusing a poem with either an intention or an emotional reaction. If there were any place for this, we would have to be prepared to understand going to the bookcase and mistakenly pulling down an intention or

---

2   W.K. Wimsatt, Jr., "The Affective Fallacy," in *The Verbal Icon* (Lexington, 1965), p. 21.

setting out to recite *The Charge of the Light Brigade* and coming out instead with the military pride of an invalided hussar. But such talk is clearly without sense.

In a later section I shall try to explain how critical theorists might come to suppose that a poet's intentions and experiences can intelligibly, though perhaps incorrectly, be identified with a poem rather than being what we would ordinarily be inclined to think of them as—evidence for a (possibly correct) interpretation of the poem. But first I want to try to make clear how critical questions about the meaning and interpretation of poems come to get mixed up with questions about identifying the poem as an object and distinguishing it from other objects.

It is virtually an axiom of New Critical theory that a poem is in some sense "objective."[3] This claim involves, among other things, a rejection of impressionistic criticism and the attendant notion that any response to a poem, provided it is sincere, is as good as any other. The claim is that any given interpretation can be either rejected as mistaken or accepted as correct, and it entails, I think, that every critical dispute is, at least in principle, resolvable. What this comes to, I would suggest, is that for every poem there is a single correct account, that is, a single correct reading or interpretation. Disputes frequently arise when two inconsistent accounts of a thing are offered. Such disputes can be resolved in at least two different ways. Some accounts are the result of a careless or inattentive examination of the thing in question, and disputes about these can be settled by a closer and more careful investigation. Other disputes arise because the disputants were, in fact, although unbeknownst to each other, talking about two different objects. This kind of dispute can be settled by agreeing upon the thing to be discussed. A number of literary theorists look upon critical disputes as frequently being of this latter sort. I.A. Richards, for example, cites the case of a Wordsworth sonnet that two readers interpreted differently and remarks that the two were "surprised shortly afterwards to discover that they had been reading quite different poems."[4] Richards is led to describe this as a case of talking about two different things because of his theory that a poem is an "experience" in the mind of the reader. Different ways of understanding or interpreting a poem are thought of as the result of different "experiences," and different experiences, according to the theory, must entail different poems. The problem, then, is the obvious one of identifying a single thing—in Richard's case a standard experience—to be the subject of discourse. Only then can "we have what we want, a sense, namely, in which a critic can be said to have not read the poem or to have misread it."[5]

---

3   According to T.M. Gang ("Intention," *Essays in Criticism*, April 1957, p. 175), "Professors Wimsatt and Beardsley's basic position, with which most modem critics will sympathize, is that criticism should concern itself with the poem as something existing 'objectively.'" In support of Gang, F.W. Bateson claims that a poem "exists objectively in the same way that, e.g., a chair does, the product of a poem-using as that is of a chair-using society" ("Poetry and the Positivists," ibid., October 1957, p. 474).

4   I.A. Richards, *Principles of Literary Criticism* (New York, 1952), p. 208.

5   Ibid., p. 227.

It seems altogether plausible to describe the process of interpreting and understanding a poem as a process of discovering the characteristics of the poem. As one theorist puts it, "'What is it like?' or, more fundamentally still, what *is* it?' is a question both the scholar and the critic must try to answer."[6] Now, it is impossible to determine the characteristics of a poem or anything else until we can get that poem or thing in our hands; and thus the job of the critic can be made to appear very much like that of the naturalist undertaking to discover the characteristics of a species of animal. We hear rumors of a strange beast that is said to roam the high veldt, and the only way to find out what one is really like is to catch one. An okapi in the hand is surely worth two on the high veldt when it comes to finding out what they are really like. Once we have the beast identified and in a cage, we can proceed to lay to rest all those wild rumors, guesses, and contradictory descriptions; for with him right there before us, we can determine the truth or falsity of any proffered description. And, in like manner, if we could only get hold of the "real" poem, it would become clear at once what a satanic mill is and what Hamlet is really up to.

Thus the concern to discover an object to identify as the "real" poem can be made to seem in order and, indeed, pressing, when we realize that many philosophers of literature look at criticism on the analogy of natural history: as the naturalist describes the characteristics of the birds and the beasts, so the critic describes the characteristics of poems; and in both cases an object must be located and identified before it can be studied and described. But when critics start to look for the object that is the poem, they find it an exceptionally elusive kind of object and elusive in rather different ways than is the elusive okapi.

II

The most comprehensive of the, by now, traditional discussions of the problems involved in the search for the "real" poem is that of Wellek and Warren in the chapter already referred to. In that chapter Wellek and Warren consider, and reject, four candidates for the office of "real" poem. A poem, they argue, is not a physical object such as a printed page; it is not the sounds produced when the poem is recited aloud; it is not an experience in the mind of the author; and it is not an experience in the mind of any reader. Each of these hypotheses and the arguments against them need discussion.

(1) The real poem is a physical object. Essentially two objections are brought against this hypothesis, (a) Were all the written copies of a poem destroyed, the poem would not necessarily be destroyed, because it could still exist in memory and there is, after all, a considerable oral literature that has never been written down. In this respect poems are quite unlike paintings, for a painting can be destroyed by destroying a single object. (b) A poem cannot be identified with any written manuscript or printed page, because any such particular copy could always be

---

6   John Wain, F.W. Bateson and W.W. Robson, " 'Intention' and Blake's *Jerusalem*" in *Aesthetics and the Philosophy of Criticism*, Marvin Levich, ed. (New York, 1963).

incorrect. In short, the contention of Wellek and Warren is that "the lines in black ink are merely a method of recording a poem which must be conceived as existing elsewhere."[7]

The first of these two arguments suggests the observation that although it makes perfectly good sense to speak of destroying a painting, it is not at all clear what destroying a poem, or failing to destroy one, amounts to as something in addition to destroying particular manuscripts or printed copies. We do speak of works of literature being lost when all the copies have disappeared and no one any longer remembers them. To insist that a poem cannot be destroyed by destroying manuscripts may be to suggest, misleadingly, that poems are made of more durable stuff than pages. Of course, one could also be misled by the "lost" locution into supposing that there is something other than a manuscript that can get mislaid.

One further comment on the position that Wellek and Warren are opposing. Although they claim it is a very common one, I don't believe anyone has ever held it; at least I have been unable to find it anywhere. Nevertheless their discussion of it is valuable for no other reason than for the light it sheds on the way they understand the problem.

(2) The real poem is the sounds made when the poem is recited. The principal arguments against this theory are that many of the characteristics of these sounds can differ from reading to reading without alteration in the poem—for example, individual variations of pronunciation and the like are allowable— and that the correctness of any particular reading or recitation can always be questioned. Their conclusion echoes that in (1): "Every reading aloud or reciting of a poem is merely a performance of a poem and not the poem itself."[8]

The remaining two hypotheses—(3) the real poem is an experience in the mind of the author and (4) the real poem is an experience in the mind of a reader—are perhaps of greater philosophical interest. These hypotheses are connected with the more general thesis that any work of art is essentially an experience, is mental rather than physical in nature. This kind of theory was at one time virtually a dogma of twentieth-century aesthetics and was defended in one form or another by Croce, Collingwood, C.I. Lewis, I.A. Richards, and S.C. Pepper. The theory was developed to deal with a number of philosophical problems about artistic creation and perception and the understanding and appreciation of the meaning and emotional content of art.[9]

---

7   Wellek and Warren, *Theory of Literature*, p. 142. The literature abounds in similar observations. For example, Karl Aschenbrenner says, "What makes the problem for all the genres of fiction different from the other arts of representation is that what we can point to as the literary work of art is difficult to find; the physical page is but an *aide memoire*." ["Implications of Frege's Philosophy of Language for Literature," *British Journal of Aesthetics*, (October, 1968), p. 320.]

8   *Theory of Literature*, p. 144.

9   See B.R. Tilghman, "Aesthetic Perception and the Problem of the 'Aesthetic Object,'" *Mind* (July 1966), for a discussion of such theories applied to the visual arts.

The objections urged against these theories are of the same stuff as those brought against the Intentional Fallacy and the Affective Fallacy. In the experience of any reader there may well be much that is irrelevant to the poem itself, and the theory is unable to make the requisite discrimination between proper and improper responses to the poem. The "real" poem cannot be identified with the intentions of the poet; too frequently his intentions are unknown to us, or his stated intentions do not necessarily agree with what is actually found in the poem. Nor can the poem be identified with the "total" experience of the author at the time of writing, for this would make the poem inaccessible to us. Even if the poet were accessible to us, his experience would not be; the ghost of the "other minds" problem haunts this theory.

Philosophers who are inclined to argue either for or against the theory that a poem, or any work of art for that matter, is an experience are involved in a double confusion. In the first place they tend to think of such things as intentions and meanings as mental events of some kind; and in the second place they tend to think of an experience as if it were a kind of object, and a private object at that. It is this private-object view that allows critics of the theory to raise all the familiar epistemological difficulties about our knowledge of other minds and hence about authors' intentions and readers' reactions. This is not the place to rehearse what is wrong in all of this, for plenty of work has been done on that. It is enough to point out that these confusions are at work here, adding additional snarls to an already tangled skein.

Wellek and Warren's discussion assumes the intelligibility of the hypotheses they criticize, but this must now be questioned. What sense can we attach to the supposition that a poem either is or is not identical with a printed page, spoken sounds, or an experience in someone's mind? I want to show that no sense can be given to these "hypotheses." The phrasing of the original question itself—"What is the real poem?"—suggests a way to begin to understand this. The word "real" comes into our language along with such other words as "illusion," "imitation," "stuffed," "toy," "impostor," and the like; and it has to be understood against the contrast established by these other words. As Austin insightfully pointed out, to call a thing real is not to characterize it in any positive way, but is rather to characterize it as *not* being something else.[10] A real one is *not* an illusion, or *not* an imitation, or *not* a toy, or what not. When critical theorists raise questions about the "real" poem, what kind of contrast do they have in mind? A better question to ask, however, is, What kind of contrast could they possibly have in mind? What kind of contrast makes sense? It won't do to contrast the real poem with an illusory poem, an imitation, or a toy poem, because there is nothing that counts as an illusory, fake, or toy poem. (A poem can be written in imitation of the style, etc., of another, but this is obviously not what is at issue.) These words have no application to poems. The possibility of confusing poems with such things as printed pages, spoken words, intentions, and affections, which is entertained by philosophers of criticism, suggests that perhaps the real-impostor contrast is the proper one to be drawn. Just as someone can be mistaken for

---

10 John L. Austin, *Sense and Sensibilia* (London, 1963), pp. 70-71.

Napoleon or pretend to be Napoleon, so, possibly, something can be mistaken for a poem or foisted off as the real poem. But this won't do either. Note this logical point about impostors. The kinds of questions that one can ask and the kinds of things one can say about the real man are precisely the same kinds of things that can be asked about and said about an impostor. Thus we can talk about the physical characteristics of Napoleon, his personality, where he was born, what he did, and so on; and we can talk in just these ways about anyone who pretends to be Napoleon or who gets confused with Napoleon. It is this, however, that cannot be done in the case of poems and the things that philosophers of literature have sought to identify them with. The sorts of things that can be said about poems are, in general and for the most part, not the sorts of things that can be said about printed pages, sounds, and experiences. Talk about rhyme schemes, meter, plot, and imagery is appropriate to works of literature, but has no application to those other things. I need not elaborate the obvious. The point I am making can be summarized in the fact that the language-game in which the "real-impostor" distinction has a home does not apply to literature. The same holds, of course, for the other contrasts that are drawn by the word "real;" the language that surrounds the "real-illusory" and "real-imitation" distinction does not surround the concept of a poem.

I have no intention of claiming that the word "real" has no application at all to works of literature, for we do sometimes refer to the real poem as contrasted with, say, a parody, or we deny that some performance or editing job that fails to bring out or even distorts the values of the work is the "real" thing. We are surely justified, for example, in our claims that the children's edition is not the real *Gulliver*, that the Disney version is not the real *Pooh*, and that the musical-comedy version is not the real *Hamlet*. When literary theorists such as Wellek and Warren have tried to identify the "real" poem, they have, to be sure, wanted to distinguish good performances and versions from bad ones; but they have also wanted to do a number of other things as well. To claim that this performance is not the real thing and to mean thereby that it is one of those that distorts the work make perfectly good sense. But to claim, for example, that a printed page or an author's intention is not the real poem is, I suggest, not to make sense. In the first place, it is not established what contrast the word "real" is marking; and hence we don't know what is being claimed. In the second place, and more importantly, the contrasts that "real" regularly serves to mark in our language have no application in these cases—that is, nothing intelligible can be said here with the word "real." In other words, there is no language-game in which the expression "the real poem" can play anything like the kind of role that Wellek and Warren, as well as others, seem to think must be assigned to it.

The various theories of the "real poem" that Wellek and Warren object to are without sense. It follows, therefore, that their objections to these theories are equally without sense. What, then, makes them seem plausible? What gives them the *illusion* of sense? Their arguments against these theories contain as premises statements such as the following: "A printed text may be incorrect;" "A reading may distort literary values;" "A poet may misread his own poems;" and "A reader may misunderstand what he reads." These statements are all true if not very nearly truisms, at least for students of literature. Wellek and Warren's arguments thus do remind us of things that we all know, and this very familiarity of some of the premises no doubt can lead us to overlook the unintelligibility of the conclusions drawn from them about the ontology of literature, because under that heading there is nothing to follow.

What passes for ontology here is much better understood as grammar. Consider another of Wellek and Warren's arguments. A printed page, they say, is not the poem, because the page can be destroyed while a poem cannot. This argument makes it appear as if they have discovered a new object distinct from the page and quite unlike it in being remarkably durable. What should be said here, however, is not that poems cannot be destroyed—as if someone had tried to destroy one and was frustrated in the attempt—but that the verb "to destroy" does not come into the language-game in which poems are talked about—that is, there is no use in language for expressions like "destroying a poem," "trying to destroy a poem," "failing to destroy a poem," and the like. In this respect the depth grammar of "page" is quite different from that of "poem." There are a number of other important grammatical differences as well. Most of the terms central to the discussion of literature have no application to pages—for example, "rhyme scheme," "meter," "symbolism," and so forth. Parallel considerations hold, of course, for the other candidates for the position of "real poem:" it makes no sense to talk about the rhyme scheme of an author's intention. A cloud of philosophy has condensed into this drop of grammar: "A poem is not a page."

III

A number of the moves that Wellek and Warren make can be seen to have been dictated by a theory of meaning that they undoubtedly hold despite never explicitly articulating it. It is the theory that the meaning of a word is what it denotes or names. The search for the "real" poem can thus be seen as the search for an object to be the denotation of the word "poem." This something, they argue, cannot be a printed page, for that is only a copy of the poem and not the poem itself; and neither can it be a recitation, for that is only a performance of the poem and not the poem itself; and so on. This kind of distinction is just the kind of distinction that is familiarly drawn with respect to paintings. A particular object can be pointed out as the real *Mona Lisa* and set apart from the other objects that are the various copies and reproductions of it. One result of the search for a denotation for the word "poem" is that Wellek and Warren are thereby led to assimilate the grammar of the expression "copy of the poem" to that of the expression "copy of the painting." This seems to me to involve a double error. In the first place, the meaning of a word is not what it denotes: The meaning of the name "Mona Lisa" is not the *Mona Lisa*; the meaning of "painting" is not a painting; nor is the meaning of "poem" a poem. In the second place, the word "poem" does not play a role in language analogous to that played by the word "painting." This I shall try to make clear in what follows. To suppose that the two words do play similar roles in language is to open a floodgate of confusion.

While we can locate the real painting of which this or that is a copy, in the case of poems all we can seem to be able to put our finger upon are various copies, readings, performances, and the like; there is nothing that we can identify as the "real" poem of which the others are copies. Looked at through the distorting effect of a mistaken grammatical assimilation, the "real" poem can be made to seem a curiously elusive and mysterious object, and the way is open to all those now familiar, but wrong-headed, theories.

C.L. Stevenson has suggested with explicit references to Wellek and Warren that some of these difficulties can be obviated by invoking the familiar type-token distinction in the case of works of literature.[11] The particular copies and recitations, he tells us, should be understood as tokens of which the poem itself is the type. The type-token distinction does, of course, apply to literature, and appealing to it is sometimes useful in clearing up occasional ambiguities where nothing philosophical is at stake—for example, the ambiguity that might arise when the cleaning lady exclaims while dusting the shelves, "These books are filthy!"—but it is not by itself enough to avoid the kind of muddle that philosophers of literature have conceived. This is because it is the fact that some such distinction as the type-token one can be made with respect to literature that is one of the roots of the puzzle about the real poem. Once it is recognized that there is a type-poem in addition to the various poem tokens, there is the danger of making the additional—the philosophical—move of looking for something to identify as the type, that is, the poem itself. What is called for is a diagnosis of why this is a wrong move, and this must involve a more complete account of the depth grammar of "poem" in order to dispel the temptation to suppose there must be an object corresponding to the type.

In assimilating the depth grammar of "poem" to that of "painting," Wellek and Warren are committing a kind of category mistake not altogether unlike that committed by the little boy who is shown the lions, tigers, and elephants and then demands to see the zoo. There is another example, however, that better serves to bring out the kind of mistake being made and what can be done about it. I borrow it from H.L.A. Hart.[12] Hart asks us to imagine a man watching a game of bridge who does not himself know the game. He hears the players speak of taking tricks, and he asks what a trick is. It is explained to him how each player plays a card in turn, and the one playing the card of highest value is said to have taken the trick. The relation of trick-taking to scoring might also be explained. The onlooker, however, is not content with this reply, and he retorts, "You have told me what it is to take a trick, but I want to know what the trick itself is." There is no need for anyone to be perplexed by this question and initiate a hunt for the "real" trick. What must be explained is that the word "trick" does not function as the name of an object; the meaning of the word is not taught ostensively by pointing to an object and saying the word. Rather the word is invariably used within the context of some linguistic expression such

---

11   C.L. Stevenson, "On 'What Is a Poem?'" *Philosophical Review*, July 1957.

12   H.L.A. Hart, *Definition & Theory in Jurisprudence: An Inaugural Lecture* (Oxford, 1953), pp. 14-15.

as "taking a trick" or "scoring a trick," and the word is taught by teaching such expressions; the word is not used to make identifications or as a cry of recognition. In this respect "trick" is more like "walk" or "nap" than it is like "pill." Compare taking a walk or a nap with taking a pill. It does not always make sense to ask that an object be pointed out as the one taken.

Like "trick," the word "poem" almost invariably occurs in the context of expressions such as "copy of the poem," "reading a poem," "reciting a poem," "interpreting a poem," and so on. Children are not taught the word "poem" in anything like the way they are taught the words "dog" or "cat"; there is never a question of picking out something to be labeled "the poem." Of course, we frequently do use the names of works of literature as if we were referring to a particular object, as when we say that *Evangeline* is on the top shelf next to *Fanny Hill*. But in such cases it is clear that we have an ellipsis for a reference to a copy of the work in question. To tell someone that the *Mona Lisa* hangs in my living room might be to raise false expectations and may lead to considerable disappointment when I go on to explain that of course I meant that I have a copy and not the original. There would, however, be no corresponding hopes to dash by telling someone that what I have on my top shelf is only a copy of *Evangeline*.

An account of the meaning of the word "poem" that is not altogether dissimilar to mine has been suggested by Richard Rudner.[13] Rudner claims that the names of works of art occur syncategorimatically and hence are what he calls "non-designative." He says that an expression such as "two renditions of the *Fifth Symphony*" (we could substitute "two readings of *Evangeline*" or "two performances of *Hamlet*") can be understood as short for "two musical renditions that are similar in an important respect;" and once this kind of translation is adopted, it can be seen that there is no requirement to postulate some abstract entity as the bearer of the name. To claim, however, that the postulation of an abstract entity is not required is to imply that nevertheless such a postulate is intelligible and that is one of the things I am concerned to deny. I also suspect that the important respect in which the two renditions must be similar is just that respect in virtue of which we would say that they are renditions of the same piece of music or readings of the same poem, and this should indicate that a great deal more needs to be said about the use of names of works of literature and music. Rudner's proposed way of dealing with the question smacks too much of that kind of philosophical legislation that tends to rule a problem out of existence rather than laying bare all the confusions that generate it. The concept "poem" is too devious to be caught in that kind of net.

IV

Having rejected the four theories about the "real" poem reviewed in section II above, Wellek and Warren go on to give their own account of what a poem is. "The

---

13 Richard Rudner, "The Ontological Status of the Esthetic Object," *Philosophy and Phenomenological Research*, March 1950.

real poem," they say, "must be conceived as a structure of norms, realized only partially in the actual experience of its many readers."[14] This notion of the poem as a structure or system of norms they borrow with some modification from the Polish phenomenologist Roman Ingarden. The concept of a norm in this context is by no means a clear one, and I doubt that very much can be done to make it clear, but I will venture a guess as to what it is they have in mind. Works of literature have a number of characteristic features: they have a sound pattern, the words may have a rhythm and rhyme scheme; the words organize into sentences with a syntax that present meanings; the words can tell a story, can present images, and express metaphors; and so on. Each of these features—the sounds, meanings, and so forth—is said to be a norm; and the poem itself is the entire system of these norms. Although an exhaustive list of the things that count as norms is not given, we are given a representative list. Included in this list are the subjects of the titles of the later chapters of the *Theory of Literature*: euphony, rhythm, meter, style, imagery, metaphor, symbolism, myth, forms of narrative fiction, and literary genres. These headings cover a great many of the things that critics talk about when they discuss a work of literature and are the kinds of things that professors of literature do their best to make students aware of. I would therefore suggest that what Wellek and Warren have in mind by a norm is simply any characteristic of a poem that can be called literary or poetic or artistic— in a word, any characteristic relevant to its appreciation as a work of literature.

The literary characteristics are described as "norms"—sometimes as "ideals"—as a way of emphasizing the claim that they are independent of anyone's awareness of them; the meter of a verse is there to be grasped or misread; the plot and motivation of characters in a novel are there to be understood or misunderstood; and the like. Curiously enough, at this point Wellek and Warren to all purposes abandon the ontological question that they began with. They are not prepared to tell us *how* these norms exist, but only that they have "a special ontological status."[15] This may be just as well, for it allows us to set aside the confusions that arise out of the failure to understand the depth grammar of "poem" and generate the ontological question and allows us to return to the question of the relation between criticism and identifying an object, which was raised in section one—the natural-history view of criticism. I want to return to this question by discussing two aspects of Wellek and Warren's theory: first the notion that a poem is a structure of norms, and then the matter of the objectivity of the norms.

If I have understood them correctly, what Wellek and Warren have done in defining a poem as a structure of norms is really to define it as the sum of all its poetically relevant characteristics. It might be not altogether amiss to say that perhaps they are thinking of a poem as a kind of construction out of its literary qualities. This clearly won't do. In the first place, if it were true, every statement about a poem would be a tautology and every false statement a contradiction. That is, any literary characteristic that we attribute to a poem would either be a member of the set of

---

14   *Theory of Literature*, p. 151.
15   *Theory of Literature*, p. 157.

characteristics that is the poem, or it would be excluded from that set. Every property cannot be a defining property. In the second place, although the theory seems in line with the thinking behind what I have called the natural-history view of criticism, it presumably defines the poem in such a way that all its characteristics are laid out for our inspection and all critical disputes are thereby resolvable. This definition is hopelessly circular. The search for an object to be called the real poem is the search for an object against which all descriptions and evaluations can be checked, but under the present theory the object cannot be identified independently of already knowing everything that is true about it.

Since every property cannot be a defining property of a poem, can we legitimately speak of defining properties at all? I think there is no difficulty—no theoretical difficulty—in doing this as long as we understand by the defining properties simply those properties by which we identify a poem, that is, determine that it is this poem and not some other one. The identifying property of a poem is usually the text. What must be kept in mind throughout this discussion are the actual situations in which questions of identification are raised. Imagine someone leafing through the *Golden Treasury* for a certain poem, and I help him by telling him that the one he wants is the one beginning ... , and here I quote the first couple of lines. But how much variation in the text can be tolerated before we have to say that we have another poem? Certainly no general rule can be laid down for all cases. There are variant constructions of lines here and there in Shakespeare, for example; but there is no temptation to suppose we have a different play because this edition has Falstaff tabling instead of babbling of green fields. If, however, the texts available to us differ rather radically, we may have reason to suppose that what we have are, in reality, fragments of more than one work that the passage of time has confounded.

The case is somewhat different when we come to speak not of the same poem or play but of the same *story*. A number of tales in Mallory, for example, really tell the same story, notwithstanding that it is sometimes Gawain and sometimes Gaheris of whom they are told. The criterion of the same story is not the criterion of the same sequence of words, the same text, but is, roughly, the same pattern of events despite differences of detail. Again, there is no general rule to determine how much variation is permissible before we must call it a different story.

Some philosophers have seen related problems about translations: is the translation of a poem into another language the same as the original? As one has put it: "We speak ordinarily of a translation of a poem. But we are much exercised in explaining whether the translation is the same poem as the poem before translation."[16] It strikes me that we are never "much exercised" about whether the translation is the "same poem" as the original. We are, to be sure, much exercised sometimes about whether the translation is adequate and whether it captures the spirit and flavor of the original. It would surely be misleading to deny that those of us who have read Dante only in translation have not read Dante. The point of an Italian's telling me that I have not read Dante when I have the book open before me is no doubt to make the claim,

---

16 Joseph Margolis, "The Identity of a Work of Art," *Mind*, January 1959, p. 34.

whether justified or not, that the English translation does not do poetic justice to the original. That is all that is at issue in this case; indeed, there is not anything else that could be at issue.

There are, of course, cases in which a translation is so free that one might well ask if it is not another poem. Such is no doubt how it is with the Fitzgerald *Rubaiyat*. Are we to call it an English translation of an Arabic original or call it a new work that in some respect is based on or inspired by the older poem? Here is another instance where there is no rule to tell us what to say, and one might be justified in coming down on either side of the question, depending upon whether one is more struck by the connection, in the one instance, or the lack of it, in the other.

In all of these questions about the identity and correctness of texts, the adequacies of translations, and so on, nothing philosophical, nothing ontological, is at stake. These questions are not settled by first identifying some "real poem" of whatever peculiar nature against which the various texts and translations are tested. The "real poem" talk tends to obscure the way in which these questions are actually dealt with by historians and critics. Nor is it any more help to invoke the definition of a poem as a structure of norms. Other difficulties aside, if it cannot be laid down in advance what the norms are in any particular case—that is, what characteristics the poem in fact has—the theory cannot settle any question; the theory is compatible with any conclusion about any poem and in that respect, I think, is altogether empty.

A further word about "real" as applied to versions and performances can now be said. To say that the Disney version is not the "real *Pooh*" is not to do anything like making an identification; it is, rather, to make the critical judgment that it has in some respect been badly done. In such a context, "real" is frequently, though not necessarily always, evaluative and never part of an identification. When "real" is not being used evaluatively, it may be used to call attention to the thing's being done outside the familiar tradition of performance or possibly not as it would have been done in its own time.

An implication of these last remarks is that evaluations, interpretations, meanings, and the like are not part of the defining or identifying characteristics of a work of literature. Were it otherwise, the critical disputes that generated the problem in the first place would be wholly unintelligible. A critical dispute is the result of two people reading the same poem and then disagreeing about how that poem, or some part of it, is to be understood. And this clearly presupposes that we can identify a poem independently of settling questions about its interpretation, meaning, and value.

I want to return now to the matter of the "objectivity" of the norms or literary characteristics, and this will also permit us to return to the discussion of relevant problems about literary criticism. To say that the meaning of a poem is a norm—that is, something that is "objectively" there—may be to do no more than reject Humpty Dumpty's thesis that words can mean anything one wishes them to. If this is all there is to it, the claim is, of course, correct and philosophically quite innocent; but it is, in fact, a much stronger claim than this represents it to be, for it involves a philosophical thesis about meaning, an ontology of meaning. But it is of no help to get involved in the ontology of meaning; rather, the first step in the discussion of objectivity must be to point out the necessity of disentangling the question of meaning from ontology. It gets us nowhere to ask if meanings are "really there" or "only in the mind" or the like. It is enough to recognize that words do have meaning and that people usually can be understood when they speak and write. The second step in the discussion is to point out the problems about meaning and understanding that are peculiar to literature.

It will be helpful to introduce the question of understanding by looking at the point that Wittgenstein is making in this passage:

> "After he had said this, he left her as he had the day before."—Do I understand this sentence? Do I understand it just as I should if I heard it in the course of a narrative? If it were set down in isolation I should say, I don't know what it's about. But all the same I should know how this sentence might perhaps be used; I could myself invent a context for it.[17]

What is it that Wittgenstein understands, and what is it that he fails to understand? There is a sense in which he does understand the sentence. The words of the sentence are all quite familiar, none of them need to be explained, and the syntax is straightforward and in good order. The sentence is understood in the sense that he knows how to use it. What he does not understand, when the sentence is set down in isolation, is who the people are who are being referred to, what the one had said to the other, and how he had left her the day before. Understanding could be provided by filling in the rest of the story of which the sentence is presumably a fragment. There is yet a third way in which Wittgenstein might fail to understand. He might not know what the speaker is doing in speaking that sentence. Is he, perhaps, telling a story for our amusement, reporting the latest neighborhood scandal, providing a sample sentence for grammatical analysis, babbling like a mad man, or saying something out of the blue simply in order to mystify? In this kind of circumstance, understanding may be gotten by finding out something about the speaker, his situation, his intentions, and so on. This is a matter of coming to understand not so much the sentence as the speaker.[18] Wittgenstein is showing us that understanding requires a context, a setting, in which a sentence must be heard or read. Such a context might be some human activity in which orders and instructions are given, questions asked about the tasks to be performed, and so forth; or it might involve certain social, moral, or personal relations among people that determine the import of what is spoken. The context can, I suppose, include the tone of voice with which the words are spoken, along with the facial expression and the gestures that accompany the words and that help to establish what is said as serious, joking, ironic, or the like. Without such a background we cannot understand what someone is saying, despite the fact that his words are perfectly familiar ones and his sentences perfectly well formed. Of course, we do understand such a sentence to the extent that we know the kinds of situations in which the sentence could be appropriately used; as Wittgenstein says, we could

---

17 Ludwig Wittgenstein, *Philosophical Investigations*, 2nd edn, G.E.M. Anscombe, trans. (New York, 1958), §525.

18 See G.E.M. Anscombe's discussion of this point. (*Intention* [Ithaca, 1957], §18.)

always imagine a context for it. Imagine Wittgenstein's sentence occurring in several different stories. The characters in each story are quite different, and their situations and relations are different. The sentence will then play differing roles in each of these stories, and our understanding of it will differ correspondingly. Imagine the stories to be about the following pairs of people, and the differences should become clear: Willy Loman and his wife, Bluebeard and his latest wife, and Tarzan and Jane.

It is this centrality of context for understanding that is a major source of problems about meaning in literature. In so many cases the context of the words is either lacking or only incompletely sketched in. Too often nothing is given explicitly about who the literary speaker is, what his purposes are, what his relations to others in the work are, or in what tone of voice he is speaking. This kind of problem frequently is, or at least can be, less acute in the novel than in the drama. The novelist can, if he chooses, provide any amount of detail concerning the context in which his characters speak and move. The dramatist can do this as well by way of stage directions or explanatory comment. But it is just these extradramatic explanatory details that are frequently lacking in the extant texts of dramatic literature, if they were ever there. The task of the reader, then, must be to "invent" a context that will make the affair intelligible. This, I take it, is the sort of thing that is done in such an interesting fashion by Dover Wilson in his *What Happens in "Hamlet."* Wilson speculates, for example, about the political situation in the play and shows us that if we suppose Hamlet to have thought himself the rightful heir to his father's throne and Claudius a usurper, a new dimension of understanding is added to the play scene. And if Hamlet overheard Polonius's talk about "losing" his daughter to him, the ensuing exchange between the two, not to mention the later nunnery scene, takes on quite a different significance than if we think of it as just another, a random, manifestation of an antic disposition. Again, in any everyday exchange the tone of Housman's last line "And God will save the King" would likely be established unambiguously as either fervent or ironic by the general manner of the speaker, his tone of voice and all that. It is just that setting, however, that is lacking when we encounter the poem; and the reader is left with some freedom to take it either way.

I am now in a position to draw a moral. In the case of many works of literature, poems, plays, and novels, the context requisite for full understanding is as a matter of fact not always there. In a great many cases it was never there. Furthermore, there is no a priori guarantee that the author himself could supply all the answers; and if he offers answers, there is no guarantee that we would be satisfied with them: we might be able to make better sense of the thing than he can. If a context must be supplied, there is always the possibility of supplying alternative contexts that will produce alternative interpretations. As a consequence, we can see that it is simply false to assume that there must be a single correct interpretation in the case of every critical dispute. These remarks should be sufficient to allow us to see that there is something radically mistaken about the "natural history" model of criticism. Literary criticism cannot be a matter of first identifying an object and then describing it by reading off its characteristics. As a matter of fact, the only identification that is usually relevant is that of a text; and having made the identification, we have arrived only at the beginning of the problem: we must still exercise our understanding upon the text.

There is yet another problem about poetic meaning and understanding that reveals another respect in which the natural-history model of criticism fails. In terms of that model it is impossible to make the essential distinction between different kinds of description that must be made of works of literature, and hence it is impossible, on that model, to distinguish the kinds of understanding and meaning that correspond to these different kinds of description and make those descriptions possible. A poem can be described as having so many lines and as being about the sea, and so on. We can also describe the power of its metaphor and the aptness of its imagery. Being able to give this latter kind of description calls for a certain amount of sensitivity and appreciation of poetic values that is not required to give the former type of description. I realize that in introducing this notion of poetic sensitivity, I am introducing an exceptionally complex matter; but for the present purpose it is enough merely to give the reminder that there is such a thing and that it must play an important role in understanding a very great many things in literature. Unless the reader shares a certain sensitivity, he will be unable to give an account of many lines in a poem, and he will be unable to see how, and hence describe how, various elements in a poem are linked by a common thread of imagery, and the like.

If a poet compares the waves of the sea to the strings of a harp, as Stephen Spender does in his *Seascape*, it does not follow that anyone must appreciate the image or find it particularly appropriate. Even standing on the cliff where Spender stood, a reader may be unable to see the harp figure in the waves of the sea. As a result, the poem fails for him, and he is unable to give the proper kind of critical description of it. His failure to appreciate the image may even lead to a failure to understand certain comments that might be made about the poem. To put it once more: criticism is not a matter of locating an object and then simply describing it; it is, rather, a matter of exercising one's own sensitivity and understanding upon a text.

Chapter 2

Aesthetic Descriptions and Secondary Senses

Aesthetic appreciation is to a large extent a matter of perception, of seeing and hearing, and any theory of aesthetic and artistic appreciation must take into account the nature of perception. The task of philosophical aesthetics is complicated by the fact that perception is such a complicated affair and that there are so many different uses of verbs of perception such as "to see" and "to hear." A number of these uses have been remarked and described by Wittgenstein in Part 2, section 11, of the *Philosophical Investigations*.[1] There is no question but that the notions of "seeing as" and "aspect perception" discussed there are important for aesthetics although precisely what that importance is is very much in question. In that section Wittgenstein talks about a very wide and diverse range of kinds of seeing and it strikes me that neither the range nor the diversity of the perceptual phenomena he is concerned with has been fully appreciated, whether for aesthetics or for philosophy generally. Attempts to describe aesthetic perception in terms of seeing as have doubtless suffered from the questionable assumption that the duck-rabbit figure is the paradigm of aspect perception and that what is true of how we see and describe that figure will be true, *mutatis mutandis*, of other cases of seeing as, including our experiences of works of art. I have been guilty of making this assumption and at one time had mistakenly supposed that too many problems in aesthetics could be resolved by appealing to the duck-rabbit as a paradigm.[2] Alan Tormey is correct when he points out that the seeing as model "is misleading when it suggests that seeing, or hearing, an art work as *expressive* (or garish, or sentimental) is no different from spotting the face in the cloud or the duck in the figure."[3] But Tormey's remark—as well as my own account—is misleading to the extent that it suggests that ambiguous figures and shapes in clouds are all that Wittgenstein is talking about under the rubric of seeing as. Wittgenstein does make much of the duck-rabbit, but he does not use it as the paradigm against which all experiences of aspects are to be understood. In this paper I wish to pursue some implications for aesthetics of what Wittgenstein says about these things that have, perhaps, been overlooked.

---

1   Ludwig Wittgenstein, *Philosophical Investigations*, 2nd edn (New York, 1958).
2   B.R. Tilghman, "Aesthetic Perception and the Problem of the 'Aesthetic Object,'" *Mind* (July 1966) and *The Expression of Emotion in the Visual Arts* (The Hague: 1970).
3   Alan Tormey, *The Concept of Expression: A Study in Philosophical Psychology and Aesthetics* (Princeton, 1971), p. 116.

I

In section 11 Wittgenstein begins his discussion of seeing by calling attention to the experience of seeing a likeness between two faces. He then goes on to talk about the duck-rabbit and other ambiguous figures. He mentions seeing aspects of organization such as coming to see a face in the branches of a tree in a picture puzzle and the converse experience of losing the organization as when a familiar shape looks unfamiliar seen upside down or in a mirror. There are aspects that require imagination to be seen such as the triangle that becomes this or that depending upon the objects we imagine surrounding it. There are also such experiences as associating colors with the vowels, hearing a musical passage as an ending, or as having a character or a meaning. And there is also hearing a word as full of meaning or sometimes as drained of meaning. Wittgenstein is calling attention to a whole family of cases and complexities and his remark that "there are here hugely many interrelated phenomena and possible concepts" is a necessary warning to beware of any overly simple account of perception or too facile an application of what he says about some particular case to other examples.

After he has discussed the idea of aspects and seeing aspects, Wittgenstein mentions the possibility of aspect-blindness and then introduces the notion of "experiencing the meaning of a word" and the related concept of meaning-blindness. It is in this connection that he speaks of hearing a word as full of meaning or sometimes as drained of meaning. Someone might become puzzled about this kind of experience. How can the meaning of a word be experienced if the meaning of a word is its use? This seems especially puzzling since in Part 1 Wittgenstein was at great pains to deny that the meaning of a word is an experience. Granting, however, that we do have certain experiences with words, why do we speak of these as experiences of *meaning*? Wittgenstein answers in this way: "It is the phenomenon which is characteristic of this language-game that in *this* situation we use this expression: we say we pronounced the word with *this* meaning and take this expression over from that other language-game." [PI, p. 126.]

At this point Wittgenstein suggests a distinction between a "primary" and a "secondary" sense of a word.[4] When we say that we experienced the meaning of a word or meant a word in a certain way, we are using the word "meaning" in a secondary sense. The primary sense of the word is exhibited in expressions such as "The word 'puce' means a shade of color" where the explanation tells us something about the use of the word, i.e., the post at which it is stationed. We are given two other examples of secondary senses that are labeled as such. "Given the two ideas 'fat' and 'lean,' would you be rather inclined to say that Wednesday was fat and Tuesday lean, or the other way around? I incline to choose the former," and "For me the vowel e is yellow." [PI p.216.] It is this idea of a word having a secondary

---

4   The best general account of Wittgenstein's notion of secondary sense is that of Cora Diamond, "Secondary Sense," *Proceedings of the Aristotelian Society* 67 (1966-67): 189-208.

sense that I want to investigate, for I believe it to have considerable importance for an understanding of aesthetic descriptions.[5]

Wittgenstein points out several features of these secondary senses:

(1) The words being used with their secondary senses, "fat," "lean," and "yellow," are not being used with changed meanings. "Asked 'What do you mean here by "fat" and "lean?"—I could only explain the meanings in the usual way. I could *not* point to the examples of Tuesday and Wednesday." [PI, p.216.]

(2) Although such phenomena as finding Wednesday fat may be traceable to psychological causes, childhood associations, for example—here one might think of *les jours gras et maigres*—Wittgenstein characteristically, and correctly, dismisses any causal inquiry as philosophically irrelevant. The discovery of causes or associations cannot illuminate the kind of use words have in their secondary senses nor can it explain the fittingness and aptness that secondary descriptions so often have. I need not share Wittgenstein's associations, whatever they happened to be, to agree that Wednesday is, indeed, fat.

(3) It may be tempting to suppose that secondary senses may be reduced to, or explained away as, metaphors. Wittgenstein denies this. In the absence of a general account of metaphor—and there are notorious difficulties in providing one—both the supposition and the denial may be too vague. But we don't need a theory of metaphor to understand what he is getting at. The reason Wittgenstein offers for denying that an expression such as "*e* is yellow" is metaphorical is that "I could not express what I want to say in any other way ... ." [PI, p.216.] Wittgenstein is perhaps overly sanguine in what seems to be his assumption that a metaphor can always be paraphrased, nevertheless some metaphors can be paraphrased because they have a point that can be explained in other words, despite, no doubt, some adulteration of original substance and flavor, "*e* is yellow", however, is not one of these. The point of calling that rat Lefty a rat is to direct attention to his treachery, but the point of calling *e* yellow is to express its seeming to be just that color.

One reason for supposing that secondary senses are metaphorical may be the assumption that metaphors and, hence, secondary senses, depend upon the apprehension of likenesses, similarities, or analogies. This assumption turns metaphors into similes and that won't do as an account of metaphor and it won't do as an account of secondary sense either. This can be shown in trying to work out the implied similarities in some particular case. Romeo says that Juliet is the sun. Suppose we try to explain this by pointing out that Juliet is like the sun in that she illuminates Romeo's world, she is the focus about which all his concerns revolve, and so on. This kind of explanation is perfectly

---

5 To the best of my knowledge the only application of Wittgenstein's notion of secondary sense to aesthetics is in Roger Scruton, *Art and Imagination* (London, 1974). Scruton, however, does not develop the concept in detail.

in order when our purpose is to help someone to an awareness of the literary values in Romeo's line, but it is of no use as a theory of metaphor. The key terms "illuminate," "focus," etc., are themselves metaphors and in this context demand additional explanation. We are then faced with the problem of trying to make sense of searching for properties common to the geometrical focus of an ellipse on the one hand and the lure of a maidenhead on the other.

Much light is shed on this matter in Part 2 in *The Brown Book*. There Wittgenstein presents several different cases in which we use a common description:

> A man holds a weight with out-stretched arm; his arm, his whole body is in a state of tension. We let him put down the weight, the tension relaxes. A man runs, then rests. He thinks hard about the solution of a problem in Euclid, then finds it, and relaxes. He tries to remember a name, and relaxes on finding it.[6]

He then asks immediately "What do all these cases have in common that makes us say that they are cases of strain and relaxation?" He notes the strong temptation to insist that "Surely a similarity must strike us, or we shouldn't be moved to use the same word."[7] His conclusion is, of course, that there is no necessity for there to be a similarity or for one to be struck by a similarity in order to use the same word of different things. Indeed, in some instances no sense can be made of talk about similarities. Wittgenstein's strategy in reaching this conclusion is to parade a number of examples in which it makes perfect sense to speak of different things having something in common, e.g., "The fire engine, the traffic light, and the apple all have something in common; they are all red,"[8] and to contrast them with examples in which there is no sense in speaking of having something in common, e.g., the common property that two shades of red have by virtue of which they are both red. No more sense can be made of explaining someone's calling Wednesday fat by the supposition that he has seen a likeness between Wednesday and, say, a fat man, than can be made of calling two shades of red "red" on the basis of having seen something in common. What is it that two shades of red have in common that makes us call them both "red?" The question can be answered only by the repetition of the original contention: They are both red, or: "Don't you see?" This is not a case of noticing a likeness (although we could perhaps call it a limiting or degenerate case). There is nothing that makes us call them both red, no more than there is anything that makes us call cases of both physical strain and mental strain "strain" or Wednesday as well as Falstaff "fat," that is, there are no reasons that can be given. To say that someone has seen a likeness in cases such as these is to say no more than that he uses the same word to describe

---

6   Ludwig Wittgenstein, *The Brown Book* in *The Blue and Brown Books* (New York, 1965), p. 129.

7   *Brown Book*, p. 130.

8   See *Brown Book*, p. 130.

both. Reflections such as these suggest either that metaphors frequently just are secondary senses or in the paraphrase and explanation of them we are necessarily brought back to secondary senses. Thus it seems to me that it is metaphor that depends upon secondary sense and not the other way around.

(4) The ability to use a word in a secondary sense depends upon the ability to use the word in its primary sense. This is analogous to Wittgenstein's point about the substratum of the experience of seeing aspects being the mastery of a technique. The relevant technique is usually, but not always, the ability to use the appropriate language [PI, p. 208]. Wittgenstein makes explicit that this mastery is a logical and not a causal condition for these experiences. If someone were not already familiar with the ordinary use of the word "duck," or could not make appropriate use of the figure, it would not be *intelligible* to say that he has seen the duck-rabbit figure as a duck. In like manner, the intelligibility of describing Wednesday as fat or *e* as yellow depends upon "fat" and "yellow" having primary senses that are already familiar to us.

There is always the danger in developing and adapting anything that Wittgenstein says of converting remarks intended only as suggestions and guideposts for clarifying and excising particular philosophical confusions into a theory. With my own *caveat* in mind I shall attempt to summarize Wittgenstein's suggestions about secondary senses in a way that one does no disservice to his thinking. I believe that Wittgenstein thinks of the following features as characteristic of words used with secondary senses. (1) When a word is used with a secondary sense in a description it is used to describe something that may be quite different, even categorically different, from the things it ordinarily describes. (2) The word does not change its meaning. (3) A psychological or causal explanation is irrelevant to an understanding of the use. (4) The meaning of the secondary description cannot be explained by a paraphrase. (5) The thing described in the secondary sense need have nothing in common with what the word ordinarily describes in the primary sense. (6) The use of the word in its secondary sense is conceptually dependent upon the use the word has in its primary sense. (7) No explanation, in the form of reasons, can be given for using a word this way. This can be expressed by saying that there is simply the *inclination* to offer these descriptions and that such descriptions frequently strike us as natural, fitting, and apt. It should be emphasized that this invocation of an *inclination* is neither an explanation nor an attempt to disguise the lack of one. Wittgenstein is simply calling attention to the fact that there is a range of word uses where a demand for reasons is out of order. An obvious consequence of this is that sentences containing words used in secondary senses are not subject to verification nor can truth-conditions be stated for them. That there may be an important segment of language so apparently unregulated will understandably appear puzzling and unsatisfactory, perhaps even disturbing, to someone seeing it against a background of certain other uses of words taken as paradigmatic of the operation of language. And here it may be useful to remind ourselves that with a certain shift of perspective it may appear to another as a remarkable, if not disturbing, fact that some parts of a language can approximate to a calculus.

II

There are two related problems about aesthetic description that the foregoing remarks about secondary senses will allow us to solve. The first is a problem about the meaning of these descriptions that I will discuss in this section and the second is a problem about their truth that I will discuss in section III. The problem about the meaning of aesthetic descriptions can be illustrated by a pair of overworked examples. A painting is described as having depth when it is known to be but a flat piece of canvas and a melody is described as sad. A certain range of philosophically motivated reflections can generate a species of paradox about these descriptions. It is easy to suppose that descriptions such as these, if taken "literally," are either always false, categorically inappropriate, or even nonsense. Despite the philosophy we can see that the painting has depth and hear the sadness in the melody and we would reject certain other descriptions as being the false ones, e.g., that the music is gay.

One traditional way of resolving this paradox has been to assume that these sentences do not really mean what they seem to say and to remedy this apparent logical deficiency by construing (or analyzing) them in a way that will reveal their real meaning. Theories of "empathy" and "fusion" are of this sort. Both attempt to save the logical appearances by the assumption that whenever emotions or feelings are attributed to works of art, the suspicious predicate actually refers to the feelings of the spectator. According to the theory of empathy that feeling then is "projected" into the art object while the theory of fusion has the feeling "fusing" with the perceptions of the object. These theories are tangled in a number of conceptual confusions about both emotion and perception that needn't be detailed here.[9] Suffice it to say both rely upon some theoretically postulated psychological mechanism that is supposed to do things with feelings, but of which no intelligible account can be given.

I want now to discuss two other accounts of expression in art that deserve to be taken more seriously and which show the influence of Wittgenstein. The first of these is that of Richard Wollheim and the second that of O.K. Bouwsma.

In *Art and Its Objects* Wollheim calls attention to two mistaken theories of how works of art acquire expressive properties. The first is that a work of art with a given expressive property is produced when the artist is in an appropriate emotional state and the second is that a work of art produces the emotional state in question in the spectator. There are familiar and obvious objections to both hypotheses. Wollheim, nevertheless, believes there is something to be said for them in that they insist on a close connection between artistic expressiveness and actual human feeling. This is a connection he believes must be maintained and he develops his own account

---

9   For a detailed criticism of some of these theories see B.R. Tilghman, *The Expression of Emotion in the Visual Arts*.

of expressiveness in art in terms of two notions of expression that bear some rough correspondence to the two just rejected.

The first notion of expression understands a work of art as expressive in the same way that we think of a gesture or a cry as expressive. He describes these latter as "natural expressions" of inner states. Wollheim, however, does not make clear whether he intends that we understand a work of art to be a gesture on the part of the artist or whether we regard it in some way as *like* a gesture (or posture, or face). It would surely be implausible, in the former instance, to think of a work of art as a *natural* expression. The second notion of expression understands an object as expressive because it seems to match or "correspond" with what we experience inwardly. He does not further elaborate this idea of correspondence except to say in another place that a work of art has characteristics which "mirror" inner states. This way of talking invites us to suppose that Wollheim has a picture of feelings as entities in their own right—"private objects," perhaps—with characteristics describable independently of "outer" manifestations. That picture notwithstanding, Wollheim summarizes his position this way:

> When we endow a natural object or an artifact with expressive meaning, we tend to see it corporeally: that is, we tend to credit it with a particular look which bears a marked analogy to some look that the human body wears and that is constantly conjoined with an inner state.[10]

What Wollheim says is reminiscent of Suzanne Langer's contention that "Music is the tonal analogue of emotive life."[11] The view that feelings are "inner states" only conjoined with outer expressions is doubtless incoherent, but if that aspect of Wollheim's theory—if, indeed, it is an aspect of his theory—is set aside, there is a substantial remainder that deserves consideration. The substance of the view, then, is that there are analogies, likenesses, between the facial expressions of people, their postures, gestures, and the like, and works of art and the other things we find expressive. This does seem to be true of at least some instances. There is a genuine similarity between the configuration of, say, a weeping willow and characteristic human postures; and the head lamps and radiator grill of some automobiles seen head on can make a face with a quite particular expression. Mrs. Langer, however, has been notoriously unsuccessful in detailing the analogy that is supposed to obtain between music and "emotive life" and one must wonder whether Wollheim's position fares any better when it comes to making good on the likeness that is supposed to exist in the case of the sad music, the emotional quality of colors, or the "atmosphere" that pervades some paintings. It may well be a mistake to suppose that all these troubling predicates can be understood in the same way by the assumption of an analogy between art and people.

I suggest that when we describe the music as sad we are using "sad" in a secondary sense. Such descriptions are natural and occur to us without reflection or investigation.

10 Richard Wollheim, *Art and its Object* (New York, 1968), p. 28.
11 Suzanne Langer, *Feeling and Form* (New York, 1953), p. 27.

There need be no analogies or likenesses to be noticed between the music and human beings to justify the description. Such a characterization of the music nevertheless retains its connection with human feeling because the word "sad" is being used with its usual meaning and it is, of course, the mastery of that usual meaning that makes the secondary aesthetic description intelligible. Wollheim's theory, along with the others mentioned, seems to share the assumption that aesthetic descriptions employ words only in primary senses so that when an emotion word is used of a work of art it must refer either to the feelings of the artist or audience or to something sufficiently like (analogous to) these to justify the description. It is this assumption that creates the demand for an explanation of the workings of aesthetic descriptions and sends one in search of dubious psychological mechanisms or analogies that can never be made good. If we regard at least some aesthetic descriptions as using words in secondary senses, then the need for theories like these disappears.

Bouwsma's article, "The Expression Theory of Art,"[12] has had a great influence on philosophical aesthetics. Its importance lies in its making clear that the problem about aesthetic descriptions is conceptual rather than psychological and in its directing attention to the flexibility of our language and thereby making us more aware of the many subtleties in it.

Bouwsma's essay, despite its familiarity, has not been looked at with the kind of sympathetically critical eye it deserves. I believe there are certain mistakes in it and in uncovering these we learn something about both Wittgenstein and aesthetics.

Bouwsma diagnoses the problem as the result of trying to understand the sentence "The music is sad" on the model of "Cassie is sad" when Cassie has just gotten the bad news about her beloved cat and bursts into tears. With Cassie as the model, the music surely does seem categorically unfit to be a subject of sadness, nevertheless we hear the sadness in the music and want to describe it that way; therein lies the puzzle. Bouwsma says that "The puzzling is relieved by discerning the similarity between the offending use and some other use or uses."[13] His strategy for discerning the similarity is to offer a series of additional sentences of the form "... is sad" to close the conceptual gap between the description of Cassie and the description of the music. He offers the following examples:

---

12 O.K. Bouwsma, *Philosophical Essays* (Lincoln, 1965).
13 *Philosophical Essays*, p. 33.

(1) Cassie is sad. (She got the news about her cat.)
(2) Cassie's cousin is sad. (Disappointed in love, she lived out the rest of her maiden life with neither tears nor voiced regrets.)
(3) Cassie is sad reading the book. (She sheds tears over the fate of the characters, all the while munching popcorn and petting the cat.)
(4) Cassie's reading is sad. (Now the mature actress, she reads with controlled expression.)
(5) Cassie's dog is sad. (He mopes while his mistress is away.)
(6) The book is sad. (It is the passage about Alyosha and the boys.)
(7) Cassie's face is sad. (A permanent character trait.)
(8) The music is sad.

It is questionable whether these examples are in fact all examples of different uses of "sad." There is a distinction to be made between different *uses* of a word and the different *things* to which the word might apply under one of those uses. Wittgenstein showed that the word "game" can apply to a wide variety of activities linked only by overlapping strands of similarity, a family resemblance, but he was not thereby describing different uses of the word. Both chess and football can be called games without any reason for supposing the word is being used differently. To say, however, that a boy played a game of football and then made a game of his chores is undoubtedly to use the word differently. The former describes the *kind* of activity he was engaged in while the latter describes the *spirit* in which the activity was undertaken. There are, of course, connections between the two: that spirit is characteristic of the way many people play games, and so on.

Bouwsma's examples do not always distinguish sufficiently between different uses of "sad" and the variety of different circumstances in which someone, or something, can be called sad. I don't think, for example, that (1) and (5) are different uses. (1) and (2), on the other hand, may well be; (1) characterizes a rather brief episode in someone's life while (2) refers to a permanent character or even to an entire life. Nor does Bouwsma's concern really seem to be in showing how the *use* of one of his sentences is like that of another; his actual strategy, rather, is to show the likenesses (as well as differences) between the *people* and *circumstances* described by his sentences. Thus we are shown how the situations of Cassie and her cousin are similar—there is the bad news, the want of a beloved, perhaps loss of appetite, and so on—and how they are different—tears here, but not there, and, so on. The sadness of the Alyosha passage has connections with Cassie and her cousin for all share a range of human relationships and concerns, loves, hopes, and losses, despite the one being only a story about these things.

Bouwsma contends that "The music is sad" is to be understood in terms of its resemblances to (4), (6), and (7) rather than by any direct connections to the other sentences. But a problem begins to emerge here. We understand "The book is sad" because the story leads us into the same web of human concerns that includes Cassie, her cousin, and even, by extension, her dog. Why, however, should we speak of either Cassie's face or her reading as sad? The reading, after all, is not like the speech of someone overcome with sadness for the reading is calm and controlled. To be sure, there are similarities between the music and the reading. The passage can be read with or without feeling just as the music can be played with or without feeling and in neither case is there anything that can be identified as the feeling apart from the reading or the playing. Bouwsma succeeds in giving us only differences between this set of examples and the others, e.g., no sobs, no tears, no loss of a beloved. When we want the similarities laid out for us so we can understand these to be instances of sadness along with the others, Bouwsma does not oblige, but instead instructs us, in seemingly enigmatic fashion, "Look and you will see."[14]

Bouwsma's failure to come up with the requisite similarities is, I suggest, the result of the failure of his strategy of tracing similarities. It just might be that there are no relevant similarities to be described; indeed, it becomes difficult to imagine what might count as a relevant similarity. This failure of his strategy at the critical juncture can be explained if "The reading is sad" and "The music is sad" employ the word "sad" in a secondary sense. If that is so, then there is no need to look for the required connections because there needn't be any such connection at all. Bouwsma's instruction to look and see can now appear in quite a different light. Instead of seeming enigmatic it comes across as exactly the right one, only not for the reason he thought. It is not an instruction to look for similarities; in the absence of reasons for the description, by way of similarities, the only thing to do is to look or listen, and let yourself be struck by the thing before you and then you will be inclined to describe the reading or the music that way. The only feature common to both Cassie and the music is the description.[15]

III

The current controversy over the truth and justification of aesthetic descriptions revolves around the question whether there are criteria for the correct application of aesthetic terms. Frank Sibley has claimed—if not exactly argued—that aesthetic terms are not conditioned-governed."[16] He says that although reasons and explanations can be given for the use of these terms, these do not constitute criteria in the shape of either necessary or sufficient conditions for their application. He cites as examples of this kind of reason giving describing a painting as delicate because of its pastel shades and the judgment that a painting lacks balance because one group of figures is so far off to the left. There is surely something right about what Sibley says of

---

14 *Philosophical Essays*, p. 32.

15 Richard Scheer has told me that Professor Bouwsma once mentioned to him that his essay was mistaken in supposing that there are criteria for sadness in music. Scheer was not sure what Bouwsma had in mind, but I surmise he meant that the mistake was essentially the one I pointed out, that there must be similarities between sad music and other sad things to justify calling it sad. I regret never having spoken to Professor Bouwsma about this. When the difficulty in the essay finally did occur to me it was too late.

16 "Aesthetic Concepts," *The Philosophical Review* (October 1959).

these examples. Talk of necessary and sufficient conditions suggests the possibility of there being rules and recipes for achieving delicacy and balance in painting, but the notion that these artistic accomplishments might be reached by recipe cannot help but strike us as intuitively repugnant. The use and understanding of aesthetic descriptions are supposed by Sibley to depend upon what he calls taste and sensitivity and he goes on to connect the exercise of taste and sensitivity with a kind of seeing. His remarks about seeing suggest that he has Wittgenstein's discussion of seeing as in mind, but his views are not worked out in the detail required to make them clear and coherent.

Peter Kivy charges that on Sibley's view aesthetic terms would become "ungovernable" and argues against Sibley that at least some aesthetic terms are condition-governed. He offers the musical term "stretto" as a counterexample and cites part of the definition of the word from the *Harvard Dictionary of Music*: " ... the imitation of the subject in close succession, with the answer coming in before the subject is complete."[17] He is certainly correct in pointing out that the word is applied on the basis of the criteria specified in the definition despite a certain vagueness in what is to count as the subject and the answer. It seems to me that there are a number of other important words in the artistic vocabulary of which this is also true. Art historians seek to establish criteria for style and period designations such as "Mannerist" and "Baroque" although there is considerable disagreement over just what these criteria should be.

The work of Roger Scruton allows this controversy to be seen from a slightly different perspective. Scruton proceeds from the commonly held assumption that concern for the meaning of any word has to involve concern for the truth of the sentences in which that word occurs. Meaning is thus a function of truth conditions.[18] He is not concerned with truth conditions as they figure in formal semantical theory, but in what he calls the "strong epistemological" sense of the observable features of the world by means of which empirical statements are verified. Scruton contends that aesthetic terms do not denote properties of things and hence aesthetic descriptions do not have truth conditions of the kind noted. Instead, aesthetic terms denote *aspects*—in Wittgenstein's sense—and have *acceptance* conditions. Scruton thus follows Wittgenstein in saying that aspects are not properties of things. The acceptance conditions for aesthetic descriptions are *experiences* of the sort ultimately to be elucidated in terms of various notions of seeing as.

There are no truth conditions for the sentence "It's a duck" said of the duck-rabbit figure. We can, however, *accept* the description if, and only if, we see the figure as a duck. There are, of course, truth conditions for "He sees it as a duck."

The situation can be summarized this way. Sibley denies that aesthetic descriptions have truth conditions, but can offer no convincing way of showing why they are not therefore hopelessly arbitrary and subjective. Kivy says that at least some aesthetic descriptions have truth conditions and that aesthetic terms do denote genuine

---

17 Peter Kivy, *Speaking of Art* (The Hague, 1973), pp. 38-39.
18 *Art and Imagination*, especially "Introduction" and chap. 4.

properties of things. Scruton agrees with Sibley that aesthetic descriptions lack truth conditions, but goes on to rescue Sibley's position from complete subjectivism by introducing acceptance conditions. The controversy resolves itself into one between Kivy and Scruton.

Both Kivy and Scruton have valuable insights to contribute, but their positions must be gotten into the proper relationship. At one place Scruton suggests that aspect descriptions use words in secondary senses and adds that "... in their use to describe aspects, terms need have *no* criteria for their applications." This remark leaves open the possibility that at least some aspect descriptions might have criteria for their application. This, however, would be inconsistent with the supposition that words denoting aspects are used in secondary senses, but Scruton says no more about it. But clarification requires that something more be said about it.

I see no objection to supposing that whenever a word is used with a secondary sense that it refers to an aspect. I shall argue, however, that the converse is not true; not every aspect description entails a secondary sense. If this is true, then there is the possibility that at least some aspect descriptions are governed by criteria. Indeed, I shall try to show that there is logical room within the context of aspect perception and aspect description for truth conditions. In order to show this, it will be useful to parade in some detail Sibley's examples of pastel shades and compositional balance, Wittgenstein's duck-rabbit, and finally Kivy's example of the stretto.

Pastel colors are defined as soft and subdued colors. The description of a color as soft offers a clear instance of a secondary sense of "soft" where the primary sense is found in speaking of soft pillows or perhaps soft voices. The ground of the ascription of softness to a color is, of course, the way it looks. Seeing a color as soft is very much like finding the vowel *e* yellow. In neither case does the description change its meaning and in neither case are there criteria for the truth of the description. Just as we do not take *e* into a better light to determine whether it really is yellow rather than green, so we do not subject the color to anything like a scratch test to determine its relative hardness. Here it is evident that there are no truth conditions for the sentence "This color is soft" and we can speak only of the acceptance condition of seeing it as soft which can be evidenced not only by the inclination to use the word "soft," but also by an appropriate tone of voice and relevant gestures.

Balance is obviously a more complex notion. The aesthetic use of the word to describe a composition is derivative from its primary use in referring to mechanical equilibrium. Any understanding of aesthetic balance presupposes this primary sense. In art appreciation text books balance is sometimes explained as a principle of composition by means of a schematic representation of the design of a painting where the figures are shown as if standing on a see-saw whose fulcrum is on the vertical axis of the painting. Indeed, there seems to be no other way to introduce the concept of artistic balance than by reference to see-saws and their kin. The usual criteria for mechanical equilibrium cannot, of course, apply to paintings. There are reasons and explanations for why a painting has or lacks balance: "This smaller figure balances the larger one because of its stronger color," "This figure is too far off to the left," and so on. In this respect balanced paintings are unlike soft colors, but these reasons do not constitute truth conditions.

The fact that there is considerably more to talking about balance in a painting than there is to talking about a color as soft might suggest the possibility of *aesthetic* criteria for balance distinct from the criteria for physical balance. The possibility has to be ruled out and the example of another use of "balance" can help show why. We speak of balancing the account books. The use of the word is plainly borrowed from descriptions of see-saws and laboratory scales; when the books are balanced there is the same quantity on both sides of the ledger. There are, however, precise and technical criteria for determining when the books balance that have nothing to do with physics and the analogy with physical equilibrium is no help at all in teaching the concepts and procedures of accounting; another term to denote that condition would do just as well. This is not a secondary sense of "balance;" the distinct criteria and ways of teaching the word would be justification for saying that the word now has a different meaning. In like manner, if there were independent aesthetic criteria for compositional balance the connection with the original notion would be broken. This rupture could be expressed by thinking of the word as having taken on a different meaning. In that case, however, the aesthetic description would not have the point that it in fact does.

The duck-rabbit figure provides an interesting contrast to both the preceding examples. When we say we see the figure as a duck, I do not believe "duck" is being used in a secondary sense. We see in the picture many of the same features we see in a real duck, head, eyes, bill, and in some versions even feathers. That is to say, we find the very features that serve as truth conditions for the sentence "It's a duck" said of the creature on the pond. We can even imagine someone seeing the figure only as a bird or fowl of some kind or another and then coming to identify it as a duck rather than a goose or even as a particular species of duck. Kivy is aware of this possibility and has pointed out that at least some aspect descriptions are "condition-governed," i.e., have truth conditions.[19] Scruton was thus mistaken in denying a place for truth conditions in aspect describing. There is, however, something more to be said about this that puts the matter in a better perspective. The truth conditions for the aspect description "It's a duck" are themselves aspects which do not emerge until the dot is seen as an eye and these lines as a bill. There are no truth conditions for these latter descriptions, only acceptance conditions. Any discussion of the figure and its characteristics must therefore presuppose the context of aspect perception.

These reflections can show us something about the notion of a stretto. The term "stretto" does have truth conditions, as Kivy pointed out, but the recognition of these conditions depends upon being able to apply the words "subject," "answer," and "complete." These words, I strongly suspect, are being used here in secondary senses. One has to be able to hear a series of tones as a theme and then find it appropriate to call that theme a "subject" and then to hear a variation on it as an "answer" and finally to hear the answer as seeming to interrupt the original statement. The word

---

19 *Speaking of Art*, pp. 101ff.

"stretto" itself, however, is not used here in a secondary sense. In this respect it is like "balanced" as an accounting term. It has come rather far from its original sense in which it meant something like "strict" or "compressed." It is not at all necessary to refer to that in order to explain stretto as a device within the fugue.

I wish to conclude with a hypothesis about aesthetic descriptions. It seems obvious that some aesthetic terms have criteria for their application and the sentences in which they occur have truth conditions and others do not. The hypothesis is that these criteria and truth conditions are aspects which can only be denoted by words employed in a secondary sense. I can offer no proof for this nor any argument to the general conclusion. I suspect the best that can be done is to try to show it case by case. If my hypothesis is true, then all discussion of aesthetic and artistic character presupposes a context of aesthetic perception and understanding which must be explained in terms of the extended family of concepts that Wittgenstein talks about under the general heading of seeing as; and this context is one in which aspects themselves can play the role of criteria and truth conditions.

Chapter 3

Danto and the Ontology of Literature

In his recently published book, *The Transfiguration of the Commonplace*,[1] Arthur Danto believes he finds a problem in the fact that of two objects, alike in all respects, one may be a work of art and the other not. Danto imagines an artist, whom he calls J., exhibiting a mirror, a most commonplace mirror. J. denies that his mirror makes any allusion to the hoary metaphor for art and so the fact that his work of art happens to be a mirror is of no moment; it might as well have been a breadbasket just like the one on Danto's breakfast table. How can an ordinary, commonplace object, be it mirror or breadbasket, become a work of art, and other commonplace objects just like it remain just what they are? This problem reveals in part the point of the title of the book. How do commonplace objects become "transfigured" into works of art? Danto wants to know "wherein lies the logic of such feats."[2] Before we inquire into the wherefore of a feat, however, we must be sure that there is a feat to inquire into. So far we have only Danto's word that the mirror, breadbasket, or any number of other objects that can easily be supplied, are, indeed, works of art. I am not singling out *Danto*'s word to question since many other natives of the artworld have also called the like art. It is, nevertheless, worth reminding ourselves that there is no demand grounded either in logic or in sensibility that obliges us to the same. That these things are art must remain a claim that wants making good.

Not only does Danto believe that indiscernible objects can differ with respect to their status as works of art, but also that there can be indiscernible works of art; that is, it is possible that there can be two or more distinct works of art that are to all appearances just alike. He imagines a number of identical canvases consisting of identical squares of red paint produced by different hands.[3] One is supposed to represent the Israelites crossing the Red Sea, another is entitled *Kierkegaard's Mood*, another *Red Square*, another *Untitled*, and so on. The centerpiece of Danto's discussion of this latter possibility, however, is drawn from Jorge Luis Borges's teasing little tale, "Pierre Menard, Author of Don Quixote,"[4] that he curiously (or carelessly) mentions as "Pierre Menard, Symbolist Poet." Borge's fictional author— a much more interesting fiction than Danto's artist J.—was a contemporary and a close friend of Paul Valéry; he also undertook to compose *Don Quixote*. He actually succeeded, Borges tells us, in producing two complete chapters and part of a third.

---

1   Arthur C. Danto, *The Transfiguration of the Commonplace* (Cambridge, 1981).
2   Ibid., p. 7.
3   Ibid., pp. 1ff.
4   Jorge Luis Borges, *Ficciones* (New York, 1962).

We must be very careful in making clear exactly what the nature of Menard's accomplishment is supposed to be. His project was not at all simply to copy Cervantes's text word for word nor did he propose a new version of the unfortunate knight's adventures; no modern dress *Don Quixote* would do for him; the thing itself would have to be *written*. And what he wrote was not by some miraculous coincidence to match the original nor was it to be a chance product like the *Don Quixote* turned out by the monkeys at the typewriter. No, he set out deliberately to write that book; as Borges puts it, to compose *the Don Quixote*. His first thought was to shed his twentieth-century identity and his heritage of three hundred years of culture and history and become a seventeenth-century Spaniard, become Cervantes himself. He rejected that strategy, however, as unworthy. It would be too easy to create *Don Quixote* out of the life and mind of Cervantes himself. What Menard set out to do, and in part succeeded in doing, was the far greater feat of composing *Don Quixote* out of his own, twentieth-century experience.

What are we to make of all this? Borges tells us almost nothing about the life of Menard; in the matter of these details he defers to the work in progress of the Baroness de Bacourt. He does, nevertheless, provide us with a bibliography of Menard's writings, both published and unpublished, and in his "Prologue" to *Ficciones* informs us that this bibliography "constitutes a diagram of his mental history ... ."[5] This bibliography is very instructive.

Menard began his literary career as a symbolist poet. He later became interested in formal logic and attempts to construct ideal logical languages. An interest in chess is also manifested and there are works relating to his "friend" Paul Valéry. There is a final return to poetry. There is in this the hint of a possibly suggestive parallel with the career of Valéry himself who began as a symbolist poet and became interested in mathematics and the natural sciences before taking up poetry once again. Several of the entries in Menard's bibliography are worth looking at in detail.

His interest in ideal logical languages led him to write about Leibnitz's *Characteristica Universalis*, Lull's *Ars Magna*, and the work of one John Wilkins, a seventeenth-century English ecclesiastic who had a hand in such things and who dabbled in perpetual motion as well. Parallel to this interest was a proposal for constructing an ideal poetic language whose vocabulary would not be derived from ordinary language, but would consist of "ideal objects created by means of common agreement and destined essentially to fill poetic needs." There is a proposal to enrich the game of chess by eliminating one of the rook's pawns; Menard eventually rejects this proposal. And he undertakes to transpose Valéry's *Le Cimetière Marin* into alexandrines.

To work out all the implications, interconnections, and allusions packed into this fictional bibliography would be a fascinating, but lengthy and taxing job of work for the literary scholar. A number of them, I confess, escape me, but then I make no pretense to literary scholarship. One thing about the list, however, is more than obvious. The greater number of Menard's projects are chimerical or, should we say,

---

5   Borges, p. 15.

quixotic? That the very idea of a logically perfect language, even one grounded in *PM* syntax, is misbegotten scarcely needs arguing for these days. If that is bad enough, then the thought of a "poetically perfect" language disconnected from ordinary language, despite its resemblance to good symbolist theory, is confusion compounded. Menard's project is, in fact, reminiscent of things that Mallarmé said, but the purified and ideal language of poetry that Mallarmé envisioned was simply the result of the poet's craft of using ordinary words in extraordinary and fresh ways, a technique that trades upon words retaining their ordinary senses and familiar connections. We are again twitted with the proposal to "enrich" the game of chess by eliminating one of the rook's pawns. I, and no chessman I, am led to believe that this step could only result in making the game less subtle and, consequently, the description of it as an "enrichment" is contradictory. Finally the transposition into alexandrines of Valéry's poem can be set down as another self-refuting task. We have Valéry's own testimony that *Le Cimetière Marin* began life as only a wordless rhythm that obsessed him. This rhythm was that of a line of ten syllables and the development of it into the finished poem demanded a deliberate rejection of the traditional alexandrine pattern.[6] Valéry's poem can be understood as an instance of the symbolist notion that the meaning of a poem must be essentially connected with its formal structure. To tamper with that structure and to restructure it into a form explicitly rejected by its author could be no less, in this case, than to write another poem; there could be no justification for describing the result as a transposition of *Valéry*'s poem.

There is generally a method in Borges's madness. Out of all the possible examples of classical literature that Borges could have set his Menard to work on, why did he pick *Don Quixote?* That's an easy one and you might as well ask me another. Like the rest of Menard's projects, that, too, is in its own way quixotic, one that has somehow gone very wrong. The other one is to ask me how it has gone wrong.

We do not know how Menard succeeded in writing that part of *Don Quixote* that he did. He destroyed all his rough drafts without letting anyone inspect them. At this point a certain species of skeptic will want to know how we are to distinguish the case of Menard's actually having written the stuff from the case in which he merely copied it or reproduced it from memory while claiming otherwise. Such a verificationist objection, although not conclusive, at least arouses suspicions. I recall the case of the doctoral candidate who submitted a dissertation with the title *Üfber die vierfache Wurzel des Satzes vom zureichenden Grunde.* He was about to be dishonorably sent down when it was recalled that he had not really done all that well on his history exams and further investigation showed that he had never read a word of, or about, Schopenhauer. The matter was set down as a Baffling Unexplained Phenomenon and although the charges of plagiarism were withdrawn, the dissertation was not accepted.

---

6   Paul Valéry, "Au Sujet du *Cimetière Marin*," reprinted in *Le Cimetière Marin*, Graham Dunstan Martin, ed. and trans. (Austin, 1971), p. 86.

We can distinguish the case in which someone merely copies or plagiarizes another's work from the case in which, as the result of an astounding coincidence, he produces the same thing quite on his own. One of the criteria for doing this, as I believe my academic example shows, is that the person be ignorant of the work in question. If he did know the work, as Menard did, some very extraordinary explanation would be required to escape the charge of plagiarism and I am not sure what that would have to be. Admitting the hypothesis of the astounding coincidence, what would be the reception of the new "work?" I see no reason at all why anyone should think of it as a new work. It would simply be remarked that it had been done before. The "author" himself, on the other hand, would likely be the one noticed and might well be exhibited as a curiosity, perhaps along with his "original" manuscript. The work itself would continue its own career in the usual way.

Setting all that aside, there is a further difficulty in Borges's narrative. Menard is supposed to have written *Don Quixote out of his own experience.* In order to make that intelligible a clear connection would have to be demonstrated between the text and the particulars of Menard's twentieth-century existence and literary practice. As Borges described Menard, he was "a symbolist poet from Nimes, essentially devoted to Poe, who engendered Baudelaire, who engendered Mallarmé, who engendered Valéry, who engendered Edmond Teste." The line of descent from Poe to M. Teste is an uneasy passage from personal and peculiar reactions to sights and sounds to an original's intellect abstractly concerned only with itself and within that line of descent the sensuous and the intellectually abstract dispute the rights of inheritance. Borges tells us that although Menard could not imagine the universe without Poe, Baudelaire, and such things as *Le Bateau Ivre*, he could imagine it without *Don Quixote*; the latter was in fact an "accidental" and "unnecessary" book. The force of these remarks, I take it, is to point out that Poe and Baudelaire are part of the tradition in which Menard writes and understands literature; Cervantes is not part of that tradition. If Menard is to write *Don Quixote* out of his own experience, he must be prepared to bring it into his tradition and make a symbolist work of it and we must, consequently, be prepared to read it as a symbolist work.[7] The trick, then, is to find some reasonable measure of symbolism in Cervantes and that surely is another quixotic project.

One part of *Don Quixote* that Menard did complete was Chapter XXXVIII in which Don Quixote offers us a disquisition on the superiority of arms to letters and voices his knightly disdain for firearms. These views cannot by any stretch of the imagination be accommodated in the Mallarmé-Valéry-Teste spectrum of opinion, not to mention style. Valéry may, for all I know, have despised firearms, but he could not have scorned them for motives arising out of chivalry. Borges, nevertheless, does attempt to accommodate what the Don says to modern times, but in characteristically Borgesian fashion: Menard was in the habit of "propounding ideas which were the

---

7   I owe this and several other observations about Borges's story to Jim Hamilton whose comments and discussions have been invaluable.

strict reverse of those he preferred." (After all, he had done the same thing in a published invective against Valéry, his good and much admired friend!)

In *Le Cimetière Marin* Valéry presents us with an image of the calm sea, all shimmering surface, fixed under a motionless noonday sun where time and life are stopped like Zeno's arrow, an image of eternity. The surface of the sea, however, hides an abyss where who knows what forces of change are mustering that will break the spell of the poet's reverie and call him back to life and participation in the vitality of the world. In Valéry's poem all is irony and tension between the surface and depth, contemplation and action, appearance and reality. There is none of that in Cervantes. Don Quixote means what he says about arms and letters, no more and no less. There are no ironies and hidden meanings there. *Don Quixote* cannot be read as one reads *Le Cimetière Marin*; no text is that malleable.

When Borges tells us that Menard succeeded in writing (a part of) *Don Quixote*, he has not succeeded in telling us anything at all. And that, of course, is Borges's joke. Menard's project has gone wrong because it is a piece of nonsense, and I mean "nonsense" in the strict interpretation of that word as "without meaning" or "unintelligible." This joke is paralleled by another piece of Borgesian nonsense when we are told that Menard's original intention had been to write the book by becoming Cervantes. Note that this does not mean that he proposed simply to become an Hispano-philic antiquarian and affect the manners and morals of Cervantes's day; he was to become Cervantes himself—just as it that were a something to be understood. The joke, thus, belongs to the species of conceptual joke in which the point turns upon a deliberate misuse, or misconstrual, of some piece of language. Borges's joke has a kinship with Gracie Allen's response to George Burns when he remarked that since it was very late and they had to get up quite early in the morning, they could get only four hours' sleep. "Then we will have to sleep twice as fast," said Gracie.

Conceptual jokes frequently have a point that is deeper than mere surface play with words. Gracie's response serves to remind us of the grammar of "to sleep," that it does not function in our language like, for example, "to run." Misunderstandings of the grammar of "to sleep" have not, to the best of my knowledge, generated any philosophical perplexities unless one wishes to include Descartes's straight-faced assertion that he was deceived during sleep, but misunderstandings of the role of various literary and artistic concepts certainly have. The point that Borges wants to make, however, by way of his joke is not essentially philosophical; it concerns, rather, the appreciation and criticism of literature.

Borges's critical conclusions can, I believe, be understood as a special application of a more general observation about language. Our understanding of a grammatically well formed sentence is a function of at least two things, our knowledge of the language and our knowledge of the circumstances in which the sentence is spoken or written. It is this latter that determines what the words are being used to do, establishes their tone, and so on. Borges has seen that something similar may apply to a work of literature as a whole. It is possible to read and understand the same text—within limitations—in different ways and how a text is read and understood is in part a function of the reader's knowledge of the circumstances in which the text was produced. Among these circumstances is the present state of literature as well as its history and traditions. Thus, had *Don Quixote* been written by a twentieth-century Frenchman *instead* of a seventeenth-century Spaniard, we would be inclined to find the use of a foreign language in an archaic style affected and the matter anachronistic and likely would probe the text for twentieth-century ideas and if symbolist ironies and devices were not forthcoming, we might yet insist upon regarding the poor Don as an allegory of modern alienation. Conversely, of course, it is possible to find motifs in the literature of the past that strike us as characteristically contemporary and one is free to indulge his fancy in that regard on Cervantes. What Borges is doing here, he has done in other places. In a brief essay on Kafka he called attention to Kafkaesque themes in earlier writers and added that:

> Kafka's idiosyncrasy, in greater or less degree, is present in each of these writings, but if Kafka had not written we would not perceive it; that is to say, it would not exist. The poem "Fears and Scruples" by Robert Browning is like a prophecy of Kafka's stories, but our readings of Kafka refines and changes our reading of the poem perceptibly .... The fact is that each writer *creates* his precursors. His work modifies our conception of the past, as it will modify the future.[8]

Now what does Danto make of all this? He takes Borges quite seriously and sees no joke in what Menard did—as if there was a something that he did and for which a description could be given. This is what he says:

> It is not just that the books are written at different times by different authors of different nationalities and different literary intentions: these facts are not external ones; they serve to characterize the work(s) and of course to individuate them for all their graphic indiscernibility. That is to say, the works are in part constituted by their location in the history of literature as well as by their relationship to their authors, and as these are often dismissed by critics who urge us to pay attention to the work itself, Borges' contribution to the ontology of art is stupendous: you cannot isolate these factors from the work since they penetrate, so to speak, the *essence* of the work.[9]

Danto believes that a work of literature has an *essence*, although it is a curiously qualified "so-to-speak" one, but at any rate he thinks that works of literature are "constituted" by various facts that some other people—Intentional Fallacyites, for example—believe are only "external" to "the work itself." Borges, I have suggested, was saying something about criticism, that is, about how we read and describe works of literature. Danto has converted this piece of criticism into a piece of philosophy with Borges's contribution showing up, not as criticism, but as ontology. How are we to understand what Danto has done in this transfiguration of Borges and with his talk of "the work itself?"

---

8   "Kafka and his Precursors," *Other Inquisitions:*1937-1952, L.C. Sims, trans. (Austin, 1964), p. 108.
    9   Danto, pp. 35-36.

An expression such as "the work itself" has a perfectly straightforward use. Suppose we are discussing a poem and the conversation strays to its initial critical reception. Someone may admonish us to get back to the work itself, the poem itself, rather than simply reviewing what some other people thought of it. We are being admonished to return to considering such things as why April is the cruelest month and whether the meter really does contribute to the general tone the poem seems to want to establish. In this use "the work itself" is philosophically innocent and has nothing to do with ontology and hence is of no help in understanding what it is that philosophers have wanted to mean by the expression. The question is whether there is another, philosophical, use of such expressions.

If we are to understand what Danto means by "the work itself," then we must be prepared to understand the terminology of "constitutive" and "external." What is constitutive of a work of literature and what is only external to it and how, in any case, do we decide? Danto has not provided any answer to this latter question. It is initially tempting to suppose that a work is constituted by its text or that the text is at least one important constituent of the work. Texts, of course, must be read and understood and there are notorious problems associated with the understanding of some texts and some texts can be understood and interpreted in different ways. Danto is correct to point out that our knowledge of the relation of the text to its author and its place in literary history—the circumstances in which the work was produced—have much to do with how we understand and interpret it. It is one thing to insist upon the relevance of authorial relations and historical loci for literary understanding; it is quite another to assert that these are constitutive of literature, especially when no criteria of constitution have been specified.

Ordinarily we identify and individuate literary works by their texts—one of the Qumran scrolls was identified as part of *Isaiah* because the text matched in large part that book—and here I am overlooking certain problems about textural variations, translations, and the like, but, then, so does Danto. The criterion of the same text will not do for Danto, however, since he admits the possibility that there can be more than one work with the same text, e.g., the two *Don Quixotes*. Danto's admission is wonderfully ironic since Borges tells us that Menard wanted to compose *the Don Quixote* and not a different one. The criterion that Danto seems to use to individuate the different works among his arrays of indiscernibles is the fact that different descriptions, e.g., of their relations to their authors and their place in literary history, can be true of them. Indeed, he says that these relations and loci "seem to characterize the work(s) and ... to individuate them." But this is to beg all the questions by the assumption that such relations and loci are constitutive, because the only ground for saying that Borges has contributed to literary ontology by discovering that these things are constitutive is the claim that Menard has really written a new work. The connection between individuation and constitution either rests upon a blatantly circular argument or it is a package to be bought without argument.

Danto has not succeeded in giving sense to his talk of the work itself and what is constitutive of it. If it is true that we identity and individuate works of literature on the basis of texts, it does not follow that we have to yield to temptation and suppose that the text is a, perhaps the, constituent of a work of literature; after all, we have no hint of what constitutes constituency. The facts about literary history that Danto finds significant are, of course, significant and figure significantly in our descriptions and understanding of literature. Had *Don Quixote* been a twentieth-century product, it would no doubt be characterized as a stylistic *tour de force*, and so on, but there would remain a considerable logical gap between that fact, that anyone of sensitivity can recognize, and the philosophical hypothesis that it is—or perhaps is not—*constitutive* of the novel. Philosophical discussions of what constitutes the "real" work of art have been in large part motivated by the desire to determine what is relevant to the understanding and appreciation of works of art. This question of criticism and appreciation, however, can be approached in any particular case without raising the ontological question of constitution at all, on the assumption that there is such a question to raise. Nor do I see any reason to suppose that differing descriptions, even apparently logically exclusive ones, of what we are inclined to take as the same thing must entail that these are really different things. Danto's assertions about ontology and individuation seem to amount to no more than the observation that the same work of art can be given different descriptions.

In a private collection near Wolverhampton hangs Sir Edwin Landseer's *Portrait of a Duck*. The Hungarian émigré painter Segrob Ennazec recently created quite a furor in the artworld when he exhibited his latest painting. It looked exactly like the Landseer. "An exact copy!" exclaimed some in amazement; "A forgery!" cried others in horror. "On the contrary," retorted Ennazec, "it is an altogether original painting. I call it *Portrait of a Rabbit*." I don't think there is any problem at all about how to describe this case and, consequently how to deal with Ennazec. There is no need to say that Ennazec has created a new work of art and accord him the measure of glory that goes with that; he has simply given us a duplicate of one we already have. His originality lies in recognizing that the Landseer can be seen in another way and that it has an unsuspected aspect. His picture is akin to those that psychologists use for Thematic Apperception Tests that are drawn in such a way that they can be taken as illustrations of many different stories. Nothing is gained by the claim that each tale individuates a different picture. To be sure, works of art are only rarely flip-flop ambiguities like the duck-rabbit or as bland as some TAT pictures, but nevertheless they are open to fresh interpretations and different ages will treat them differently; we can find Kafkaesque themes in Browning that the nineteenth century, of course, could not. The cases of *Don Quixote* and the red squares of paint on canvas that answer variously to the descriptions *The Israelites Crossing the Red Sea*, *Kierkegaard's Mood*, *Untitled*, and so on are different. Talk of Menard's writing *Don Quixote* is nonsense, but the idea of different people knowingly and intentionally turning out identical canvases with different titles is not nonsense. The question is whether anything is served by describing them as different works of art. The examples of Ennazec and the TAT pictures suggested that nothing is so served. As a matter of fact, the art world has not had to face the contingency of the identical red squares. Suppose, however, that as a regular practice people (artists?) began knowingly and intentionally to produce identical canvases while giving them different titles. Someone might now argue that we can no longer treat this new wave as we treated Ennazec's caper when it was but an isolated aberration and that we do indeed have on our hands distinct works of art. We can imagine adopting this way of dealing with the matter if we are sufficiently struck by the radical differences that changes of title can reveal—following Danto's remark that a title can serve as a direction for interpretation—as opposed to regarding those differences merely as aspects of the same picture. The important thing to note is that there is nothing in the logic of the situation that demands we opt for that way of dealing with the new circumstance. The choice we make will influence our appreciative and critical practices, but it is a *choice* and that choice is not the kind of thing that can be decided either by philosophy in general or ontology in particular.

None of what I have said addresses the question of what is either constitutive of or only external to a work of art. There is, I suggest, no such question of a philosophical character. There are to be sure, for those of us who love art, pressing and sometimes perplexing questions about how to look at a painting, read a poem, or listen to a piece of music, but the answer to these questions is usually to be sought on a case by case basis by exercising our own sensibility and knowledge of art and its history, and drawing upon whatever help we can get from wiser and more experienced heads than our own. None of this entails anything about ontology and, indeed, under that heading there is nothing to be entailed.[10]

Danto wanted to know how two works of art can be—to all appearances—identical and yet be different works. He has not, however, succeeded in providing an intelligible example that demands description in these terms. That part of Danto's problem does not exist.

---

10 I have argued against the intelligibility of literary ontology in "The Literary Work of Art," in B.R. Tilghman, ed., *Language and Aesthetics* (Lawrence, 1973). Reprinted in this volume.

Chapter 4

Understanding People and Understanding Art

The collection of Wittgenstein's *Vermischte Bemerkungen*, translated by Peter Winch as *Culture and Value*, begins with this remark: "We tend to take the speech of a Chinese for inarticulate gurgling. Someone who understands Chinese will recognize *language* in what he hears. Similarly, I often cannot discern the *humanity* in a man."[1] I want to suggest that this remark is a clue to one of the central themes of section xi of Part II of the *Philosophical Investigations*. Section xi is, I believe, an extraordinarily important part of Wittgenstein's philosophy and, more importantly, is also an extraordinarily important piece of philosophy. The section begins with the notion of seeing a likeness as between two faces and ends with comments about the genuineness of human expression and the possibility of pretense. In between a number of things are talked about: various kinds of aspect perception, the possibility of aspect-blindness, experiencing the meaning of a word and meaning-blindness, words having secondary senses, thoughts and intentions as private experiences, talking lions, and understanding other people. It is surprising that all this has never been the object of a general study and that no one has undertaken to sort out the overlapping fibers that run through and connect the various topics.

I shall begin this paper by showing the relevance of some of the things that Wittgenstein says in section xi for this matter of discerning the humanity in a man, that is, for understanding another person. It is also generally recognized that there is much in the section of significance for aesthetics and the philosophy of art, the business about seeing and seeing-as is perhaps only the most obvious example, and my main concern will be to make the connection between understanding people and understanding art.

What is it not to discern the humanity in a man? The traditional philosophical account of humanity is Cartesian. In the Cartesian picture of a human being the humanity resides in the non-material soul and not in the material body itself. To the

---

1 *Culture and Value* (Chicago, 1980), p.1. Peter Winch has spoken to me of his dissatisfaction with "humanity" as a translation of "Menschen ." The latter is far more specific than "humanity" and suggests the particular character, concerns, even weaknesses, of an individual rather than some generalized notion of what it is to be human. He cited as an example Dorothea's failure to understand Casaubon when, through the eyes of her romanticized puritanism, she could not discern his self-doubts and the resentment he felt toward genuine scholars.

extent that he has a body a person is no different from an animal or a physiological automaton; his uniqueness has to reside somewhere else. To fail to discern the humanity in a person, then, is to fail to become aware of, or to have knowledge about, the real inner self. But as we all know, the Cartesian soul or mind is a private place accessible only to the one whose mind it is and mental events, thoughts, feelings, intentions, and all the rest are private objects forever inaccessible to another. The relation between the inner and the outer, the relation between a mental event and its expression in overt bodily behavior, is represented as entirely contingent. Since we can never be directly aware of the contents of another's mind, we are forced to rely upon inferences from overt behavior to inner mental states. According to this picture, what a person really is and what he is really up to are hidden from us and whether we understand a person is, therefore, a function of whether the inferences we make from the outer to the inner are correct or incorrect.

This picture is one of those philosophical ones that Wittgenstein says hold us captive and much of the *Philosophical Investigations*, including much of section xi, is dedicated to breaking the hold of it. As a *picture* Cartesian privacy has a certain intelligibility; it is in its *application* to human beings and to their understanding of themselves and others that the picture collapses and its intelligibility proves illusory. For one thing, if we take the picture seriously we see that there are no grounds whatsoever for making inferences about other minds and we are forced to say things about our own minds that make no sense. For all we know every other person may be an automaton and all possibility of understanding and, *a fortiori*, misunderstanding another is removed. The business of discerning the humanity in a man is thus put on par with the business of discerning the humanity in a lamp post.

Section xi attacks the private object picture of the mind and mental events at a number of points. "Always get rid of the idea of the private object in this way," said Wittgenstein, "assume that it constantly changes, but that you do not notice the change because your memory constantly deceives you."[2] That neat instruction undercuts any possible role a "private object" could play in mental life. Moreover, the appeal to a single object or event, private or otherwise, cannot explain many of our intentions and thoughts because our understanding of these depends upon what we say and do in appropriate contexts. This is the point Wittgenstein is making when he says "If God had looked into our minds he would not be able to see there who we were speaking of." [PI, p. 217.] The reason we could not understand a lion were he able to talk is not because leonine thoughts are private and inaccessible to us, but rather because we don't share the requisite form of life; we don't crouch in the tall grass of the High Veldt switching our tails and licking our chops while eyeing the stragglers from a herd of zebra.

All that, however, is familiar and it should be enough merely to remind ourselves of one of the main thrusts of Wittgenstein's thought. What remains to be

---

2   Ludwig Wittgenstein, *Philosophical Investigations*, 2nd edn, trans. G.E.M. Anscombe (New York, 1958), p. 207.

done is to point out some of the mistaken pictures we have of understanding and misunderstanding works of art that parallel those about people.

There is a range of aesthetic theories that deny that works of art are "physical objects" such as paintings, statues, or printed books. The "real" work of art is said to be, instead, an experience in the mind of someone or other, the artist and/or his audience.[3] This kind of theory is frequently conjoined with the assumption that art is a form of communication whose aim is to produce in the mind of the spectator an experience like that of the artist. The parallel with the Cartesian picture of the person is evident. Just as the real person is not the material body, but the non-material inner self, so the real work of art is not the material painting, but the inner experience of the artist. And just as Cartesianism pictures the relation between mind and body as contingent, so we must think of the relation between the artist's experience and the physical painting as contingent. The physical result of the artist's experience is the effect of that cause and in turn is the cause of the spectator's experience. The relation between the "inner" experience and its overt "expression" is simply another instance of the relation between Cartesian mental events as private objects and overt bodily behavior. To understand a work of art in these terms, then, is to have an experience sufficiently like the artist's and to misunderstand a work of art is to have an experience that is rather too unlike.

All the conceptual confusions that make the Cartesian theory of a person unintelligible are duplicated in this kind of philosophy of art. The other-minds problem comes home to roost with a vengeance. There is no way of determining when a spectator's aesthetic experience matches that of the artist and hence no way of knowing when a work of art has been understood or misunderstood. A picture that we can understand in its own terms once more collapses in its application.

We have reminded ourselves of a couple of philosophical fly bottles to avoid and we can now return to the question with which we began: What is it not to discern the humanity in a man? A failure here is not in any interesting way a failure of species identification nor is it to mistake someone for an automaton. The latter is a common enough science-fiction theme—and one that, by the way, is not generally very well exploited—but it is not one that *we* are liable to make. It never is the problem for us. (Cartesianism, however, requires that it be the ever-present and pressing problem.) The Brobdingnagians at first suspected that Gulliver was a piece of clockwork and that was forgivable in view of the disproportion in size. When that disproportion was the other way around Gulliver, in his turn, was hard put to take the concerns of the Lilliputians seriously; nothing that small could have serious concerns and a Lilliputian's pride had to appear to him as the most absurd kind of posturing.

To take someone for an automaton is, of course, to deny that he or she (it?) has a mental life; it is to deny thoughts and intentions. When we fail to discern the humanity in someone we do not fail to discern generally that he or she has thoughts, feelings, concerns, intentions, and so on; the real problem in our relations with other people is not that we deny them a mental life, but that either we don't know what it is

---

3   See for example, S.C. Pepper, *The Work of Art* (Bloomington, 1955).

in particular that they are thinking, feeling, doing, or that whatever it is is in some way inadequate or unworthy, e.g., Gulliver's view of the Lilliputians. It is primarily with this latter kind of misunderstanding and its analogue in art that I will be concerned.

People often have reactions similar to Gulliver's in encounters with those from other national or ethnic groups. The history of the United States affords numberless examples in the reaction of the natives to more recent immigrant groups. "Those people," it was said—and here one can fill in with the name of whatever race or nationality one wishes—"are dull of wit, lazy, lacking in ambition, fit only for the lowest form of labor, content to live in poverty, squalor, and general degradation," and the litany of impugned thoughts, feelings, concerns, and behavior goes on and on.

One of the most interesting species of the failure to discern the humanity in a person is evidenced by what was once a very common white man's view of the African slave and later of the free black; a view that was by no means confined to the Americans. The black man was seen as a primitive and even child-like creature who was simply incapable of behaving in proper civilized fashion. Moreover, when he did attempt to enter into the charmed circle of cultivated folk the result appeared to many as an *imitation* and his antics came off as a parody or a caricature of how things are properly done. This view from the white man's gallery doubtless explains one aspect of the black man's appeal as an entertainer: the darky on the stage was more than a little like the trained circus dog walking on its hind legs or the performimg chimpanzee wearing trousers, a top hat, and riding a bicycle.

A chimpanzee wearing clothes can aspire to no higher estate than to be a parody, but, to speak more carefully, that is not the chimpanzee's aspiration at all for it is someone else who is dressing him up and putting him on display. And we must also remember not to say that the poor ape hasn't the wit to be embarrassed about it all. There are occasionally individuals who have aspirations that are quite beyond their abilities and especially comprehension so that their pretensions and subsequent failures appear pathetic or sometimes are exposed to merited comeuppance. They are degraded by a fatal combination of their own will and their own misunderstanding like characters in a Molière play, M. Jourdain, for example, with his *visions de noblesse.* The truly degrading aspect of the white man's view of the black man was the imputation that what is true of the occasional individual maladroit applies across the board to the entire race.

We know that generalizations can behave in logically odd ways. The inference from "Some of my socks have holes in them" to "Therefore it is possible that all of them do" is perfectly legitimate, but the inference from "Some beliefs are false" to "Therefore it is possible that all beliefs are false" is not because the latter generalization is unintelligible. It may be true that the behavior of some members of *that* tribe is a parody of the behavior of certain other people, ours perhaps. But what sense can be made of the contention that the behavior of the entire tribe is a parody of ours? What is the nature of this kind of anthropological logic? While the latter kind of quasi-anthropological generalization does not collapse into nonsense like the skeptic's, it may nevertheless be symptomatic of something that has gone wrong.

Such remarks about people and their behavior must not be understood as merely a piece of detached theoretical observation, but as expressing and reflecting the ways we deal with them. The very description of their way of life as a parody or travesty of our's entails that our behavior toward them can only be at best condescending and at worst brutally oppressive. This result signals that something has gone morally askew and, consequently, that something may have been misunderstood. In such cases, we are better off operating under the hypothesis that the pattern of behavior in question has its own values and must be described and understood in its own terms and not in ours. It would be a hopeless misunderstanding for an Englishman to regard baseball as a corruption of cricket; all the thrills and drama of the World Series would be opaque to him. Likewise we may be missing much when we insist upon describing the black lodge parade as a parody of the thing properly done by the white man instead of looking at it as a highly inventive adaptation that exhibits a style, flair, and exuberance simply not to be found in the original.

One can, to be sure, stick to one's ethnocentric guns and insist on regarding all that as an unwitting parody of proper behavior without fear of sliding into either inconsistency or nonsense. Of course one pays a moral price for it. But one can also pay a price for trying to look at things from some other perspective. When faced with strange and unfamiliar practices and patterns of behavior we are often at a loss to know how to describe them. Do we really know what to say about the Azande practices of witchcraft and divination that Evans-Pritchard makes so much of and Peter Winch puzzles about? To see them as a deficient version of our own practices—Azande divination as inadequate science—involves describing them in terms that are familiar to us, but which may be the wrong ones. If these practices have their own values and demand to be described in their own terms, then we must learn what these terms are and that is not always easy to do. It may involve learning a whole new way of life and it is by no means obvious that can always be done.

Given that a major theme organizing section xi is the one of understanding people and that many of the things talked about there are also of enormous importance for the philosophy of art and aesthetic theory, it remains to make clear the relation between the two topics: to what extent are the problems about understanding and misunderstanding people parallel to problems about understanding and misunderstanding works of art? If I sometimes cannot discern the *humanity* in a man, may I sometimes fail to discern the *art* in a thing?

There is a consideration that arises out of this latter question that is not found in the former. When I fail to discern the humanity in a man, it is never in doubt that it is *a person* that I am dealing with despite sometimes my relegating him to the lower ranks of that condition. When I fail to discern the art in something, by contrast, it is not always evident *what* it is I am dealing with. To make the question parallel to the one about people I would have to speak of failing to discern the art in a work of art. If the item is not a work of art, then there can be no failure of discernment. After all, one cannot fail to discern the humanity in a lamp post. Sometimes, however, things are such that if I do not discern any art, then I cannot say that the item under consideration is not a work of art and whether there has been any failure of discernment then remains an open question. There are different kinds of cases here and some examples are wanted.

What do I fail to discern when I fail to discern the art in a work of art? First of all, I want to set aside questions of necessary and sufficient defining properties that constitute the essence of art. All that, I believe, results from misbegotten theorizing and has been argued elsewhere. What I fail to discern when I fail to discern the art in a work of art must be confined to various particulars that are characteristic of art. Sometimes it is skill where "I fail to see any art in that" is directed at a sketch wanting in draftsmanship, a canvas whose pigments are merely smeared about, a clumsy poem whose feet stumble and whose rhymes strain credulity, or the performance of an incompetent musician who plays out of tune and misses notes. I would not say, in this vein, that I cannot see the art in a Greek tragedy, *Oedipus Rex*, for example. The piece is constructed with extraordinary skill. The alternation of moments of hope with moments of despair is masterful and the motivation that makes the whole thing go is everywhere clear and consistent. There is, nevertheless, an important aspect of that play that I do not understand and that must remain alien to me. Although I know what the motivation is that impels the characters to do the things they do, these motives are not mine and I cannot imagine them impelling me to act; indeed, they cannot be mine because I do not share those (primitive?) Greek religious views about the cosmic consequences of incest and parricide even when, and despite the fact, they are unintentional. All these things can be explained to me by an editor's historical footnotes, but the result is rather like having to have a joke explained to you when the joke turns around circumstances and concerns to which you are not privy. The resulting awareness of what is going on is not like getting the point for yourself.

Nor would I say of a painter such as Paul Delvaux that I cannot see the art in his work. His draftsmanship and formal composition are impeccable, yet there is something that escapes my understanding. What are these somnambulant nudes doing about the streets and walking arm in arm with those other people? It is as if it is a representation of only one scene from a play and to understand what is going on we must know the rest of the story. It is always possible, of course, that there isn't any more to the story and that the whole point of the painting is to leave us with a sense of mystery and enigma.

It goes without saying that art is much more than merely skill and that one characteristic aim of art is to present us with a certain conception of a subject or with a certain stance from which to view it. "I fail to discern the art in that" can sometimes be a comment about the failure or inadequacy of that conception or stance. Much popular art is lacking in this way even when there is no want of skill. The popular illustrator Norman Rockwell was generally agreed to be a highly skillful practitioner of his craft, but his vignettes of American life are uniformly banal and invariably make their profit by trading upon stock situations and responses to them. Likewise Leroy Anderson's *Typewriter Concerto* is skillfully, indeed cleverly, constructed, but lacking in musical significance; one can't see any art, that is, depth and character, there.

With respect to all the examples so far things are pretty clear. Their status is understood, we know their strengths and weaknesses, where the art in them is to be found and where it isn't. Now it is time to consider some problematic cases where things are not so clear and where our real problems of artistic understanding can lie. There are, to be sure, many problems in trying to understand the art of other cultures. If the speech of a Chinese could strike Wittgenstein as inarticulate gurgling, think of his reaction to Chinese music! The difficulty here is no different than that faced in trying to understand any other aspect of that culture. There are conventions, traditions, practices, in a word, a whole way of life behind it all that we do not share. But it is not the art of other cultures that I want to talk about, it is instead problems that arise in and around our own artistic traditions and practices. Let us consider some historical examples.

It has been argued that the early nineteenth-century German painter Caspar David Friedrich was misunderstood in his own time. It was said of his striking canvas *Polar Sea* that in addition to the ice being the wrong color, the iceberg was too large and the ship too little. The assumption was that the subject of the painting was supposed to be a ship caught in the arctic ice and the drama of the ensuring struggle to break free and subsequent shipwreck. Seen in this way the painting had miscarried because of the disproportion in scale of iceberg and ship. The painting is redescribed and reassessed by pointing out that Friedrich intended neither to paint a realistic polar icescape nor the drama of a shipwreck and that in fact "The pure blue of the sky with the sun in the central axis is an allegory of transcendence and eternity, since the rhythm of the times of day is absent at the North Pole. In contrast, the wreckage of the ship, whose embedment in the ice floes, recalls a grave, signifies the ephemeralness of man ... ."[4]

Another artist misunderstood in his own day was Edouard Manet. One art historian describes his situation this way. "His large Salon paintings of the 1860s looked like Old Masters, but not quite. They raised false hopes, and when they failed to live up to the standards of conventional figure painting they came to be regarded as jokes, elaborate *blagues.*"[5] That reaction, of course, misses what Manet was about and can be corrected by the realization that his "main concern was not with his subject but with the technique for realizing it."[6]

One of the most notorious examples of critical and appreciative misunderstanding was the British reaction to the first Post Impressionist exhibition that Roger Fry organized at the Grafton Gallery in London in 1910. This case is especially interesting because it concerns a reaction to an entire movement and not just a single painting or even the spectrum of work of a single artist. Cézanne and the other Post Impressionists were thought by some to be incompetent and by others to be

4   Jens Christian Jensen, *Caspar David Friederich*, trans. Joachim Neugroschel (Woodbury NY, and London, 1981), p. 180.

5   Ian Dunlop, *The Shock of the New* (New York-St. Louis-San Francisco, 1972), pp. 21-22.

6   Dunlop, p.21.

deliberately and maliciously overthrowing all the hard won artistic values developed since the Renaissance. Some even thought them obscene. Fry's defense of these painters is equally interesting. He defended them by pointing out the similarities between their work and that of Giotto and other painters of the early Renaissance. It was wrong, he thought, to compare them to later painters such as Raphael and Titian.[7]

In order to understand the nature of these various misunderstandings, whether of other people or works of art, it is, I believe, very helpful to appeal to Wittgenstein's notion of seeing likeness and, to some extent, to other notions of seeing-as as well. To take one thing as a parody or travesty of something else we must, naturally be familiar with that something else. We recognize Lewis Carroll's amusing rhyme about the crocodile as a parody only when we are familiar with the execrable verse about the busy little bee. Otherwise Carroll's remains only an amusing bit of nonsense. While familiarity with the one is a necessary condition for the recognition of parody, it is by no means sufficient; the proper connection between the two must also be recognized.

The parallel between the vocabulary and the construction of "How doth the little busy bee / improve each shining hour" and "How doth the little crocodile / improve his shining tail" is only too obvious, but the recognition of the parody depends upon appreciating the shift in the subject from bee to crocodile with all the associations and "aura" that surround the notions of these two beasts. Likewise understanding a sketch as a caricature involves not only recognizing it as a picture of a certain individual, but also in noting how certain features have been exaggerated or distorted to bring out a character or produce a flavor. The recognition of parody depends, then, not only on seeing a likeness, but also, analogously, seeing differences where *seeing* comprehends the appreciation of character and a word or a pencil stroke becomes "filled with its meaning."

With respect to parodies in verse such as Carroll's and the sketches of Max Beerbohm that so delightfully caricature well known people it is a matter of recognizing that they are parodies and caricatures, that they are done intentionally with that point in mind. With respect to some of our examples of failing to discern the humanity in a man, however, it is not a matter of recognizing that the behavior *is* parody or travesty, but is rather a matter of seeing *it as* a parody. We see the behavior of these other people as trying to be like our own, proper, behavior and falling short of the mark because something is exaggerated, distorted, or perhaps left out. It was in just this way that the British critics and public reacted to the Post Impressionists; they saw them as trying to do what the painters of the High Renaissance and the academic painters of the nineteenth century were doing. With Raphael or Alma-Tadema as the basis of comparison it is no wonder that they had to describe Cézanne either as incompetent or as perpetrating some kind of malicious joke. In like manner, critics tended to see Friedrich and Manet as intending to paint another kind of picture

7   See Dunlop (1972), Chapter 4, for an account of Fry and the Post Impressionists.

than the kind they were actually painting and as a result their vision was skewed and they missed the point of what they were really up to.

It is in such cases that we can speak of mistakes and misunderstandings. It may appear, however, that the way I have been characterizing the mistakes really precludes the possibility of making any. I have been talking about these things in terms of Wittgenstein's ideas about seeing, seeing-as, and seeing likenesses and other aspects of things. Can one make mistakes about aspects? If I see a likeness between these two faces, can I be wrong? The report that I see the likeness need not be a hypothesis that the two people are actually related. Am I in error in seeing the duck-aspect of the ambiguous figure or in seeing the triangle now as standing up and again as fallen over? Wittgenstein says that aspects are not properties and if that is right then no report of having seen an aspect, as long as it is an honest expression of what was seen, can be in error.

We must not deny that from a certain insular perspective baseball can be regarded as a kind of travesty of cricket nor, that from a transatlantic viewpoint, cricket as a kind of pantywaist baseball. Neither should we deny that it is possible from a certain stance to take Cézanne for an incompetent academic. The mistake and misunderstanding in such cases does not lie solely in the fact that a certain likeness or aspect is seen, but instead lies in the consequences for our dealing with people on the one hand and art on the other that follow upon viewing things in those ways.

What must be stressed here are those practical consequences. Our descriptions of people, their thoughts, feelings, motives, and, consequently, their actions are not part of some theoretical scheme nor are they in any way pre-theoretical and awaiting incorporation into a properly developed science of psychology and human behavior. They are, instead, built into our ways of interacting with people on a day-to-day basis; they are part of our form of life. And much the same is true of art as well. Our descriptions of works of art cannot be restricted merely to detached observations. Our descriptions reflect our relations to art. We are moved by art, works of art may delight us, we recognize ourselves reflected in them, they show us new ways to see the world, and so on. The foregoing are, of course, commonplaces, but commonplaces can be very useful as reminders against mistaken philosophical theories that represent art to be something that we can understand while remaining essentially indifferent. Theories of the work of art as symbolic of something external to it or that characterize art in terms of a semantic function surely misrepresent the role that art can play in our lives. Understanding an individual work of art and especially understanding an entire movement is important because we do not want to miss something that can make a difference to us.

There need be no problems of either a practical or theoretical kind in labeling the work of a single artist as incompetent and a travesty of real art, but the situation may alter when we encounter an entire movement doing deliberately and with care the same sort of thing. Here we have the parallel with the moral judgment that degrades an entire people and their way of life. When we are inclined to such a general judgment we are often wise to suspect there may be another way of looking at it all. In the matter of an entire culture there may not be another viewpoint that is available to us; there may be little in our ways and practices to use as a reference point. The problem in understanding a new artistic movement, by contrast, has to be somewhat different. Roger Fry defended the Post Impressionists by directing our attention to a likeness with an element that was already there in our own artistic traditions. Had he not been able to do so, had he shown instead a likeness to something other than art, his defense would not have been a defense of the movement as *art*.

In recent decades the problem of discerning the art in a thing has been exacerbated by what have passed for developments in art; I have in mind, obviously, such things as Dada and Conceptual art. In an earlier day when one failed to discern the art in a thing there was generally little doubt that the thing was a work of art. It may have been wanting in skill, conception, or in decorum, or even been too subtle for one's limited sensibilities, but in all other respects it was a work of art, however deficient or difficult. Only yesterday, however, we were being offered things as art, at least they were being called art, in which we could discern no art and, moreover, we could not even discern the point of calling them art. Now suddenly the question whether there has been a failure of discernment appears puzzling if not forever moot.

My intention is not to settle the question whether or no these twentieth-century phenomena are art, but rather to suggest what must be done in order to answer such a question. First off, no theory, no piece of philosophy, is going to help us understand the artistic status of an *avant garde* movement. Secondly, some relevant connection to going to have to be shown between the new and some part of the already familiar artistic tradition to give point to referring to the new as art and, thirdly, this connection is going to have make clear how the new material is to affect us, to become important to us, and to enter into our lives. Without the latter, the language of the new "art"— along with the things themselves—has gone on holiday.

Chapter 5

Picture Space and Moral Space

In 1983-84 Frank Stella delivered the Charles Eliot Norton Lectures at Harvard University. These have recently been published under the title *Working Space*.[1] Stella's aim in these lectures is to comment on the present state of painting and to propose a program for its future development. His perspective on present painting and its future is buttressed by an interesting, if somewhat idiosyncratic, view of art history since the Renaissance, a view that will allow us to raise some significant philosophical questions about painting and our understanding of it.

For Stella twentieth-century painting is abstract painting and abstract painting is the future of painting. Abstract painting today, however, is in a period of crisis, a crisis that Stella believes is analogous to the crisis in European painting at the end of the sixteenth century. He contends that it has developed a sense of pictoriality similar to that of the sixteenth century. Prior to 1600 painting had been restricted by architecture; it was confined to architectural surfaces or designed to be seen in architectural contexts as are altar pieces and the like. The heroes of Stella's art-historical tale are, first, Caravaggio, and, second, Rubens.

According to Stella, Caravaggio's achievement concerns the development of space. After all, he says, "the aim of art is to create space—space that is not compromised by decoration or illustration, space in which the subjects of painting can live. That is what painting has always been about." [Stella, p. 5.] Caravaggio painted free-standing paintings that tended to overflow the artificial boundaries of his panels. He opened up the space of the earlier Renaissance and thereby created the standard of what we think successful painting must be.

I think his point can be made by an analogy with theater although it is an analogy that he does not use. Fifteenth-century Italian painting had created the perspective box in which the subjects of painting were placed. Imagine this as the stage of the proscenium theater, the box in which the action is played and which we view from the outside as through a window.[2] Caravaggio destroyed the boundaries of the proscenium arch and opened up the stage. But he did not do this by creating a "theater in the round," a stage that extends into the audience that we can walk around and so view the action from all sides. What he did was more radical; he created a

---

1 Frank Stella, *Working Space: The Charles Eliot Norton Lectures 1983-84* (Cambridge, Mass. and London, 1986).

2 "First of all about where I draw. I inscribe a quadrangle of right angles, as large as I wish, which is considered to be an open window through which I see what I paint." [Leon Battista Alberti, *On Painting*, John R. Spencer, trans. (New Haven and London, 1966).

space that put the spectator into the midst of the action with the sense that he could see on all sides of him. Things are going on not only in front of the spectator, but beside, behind, above, and below him.

What Caravaggio inaugurated Rubens developed. Stella explains his conception of the spatial achievement of Caravaggio and Rubens with the examples of two of Rubens' paintings:

> The one thing more than anything else that *both Saint Francis Xavier and Saint Ignatius* do in Rubens' painting is to remind us that we should see ourselves on a pedestal if we want to be true viewers of painting, because elevated on a pedestal we will surely be reminded of the space all around us—the space behind us, next to us, below us, and above us—in addition, of course, to the space in front of us which we have so often taken as being the only space available to us as viewers. [p. 70][3]

This account of Caravaggio allows Stella to ask whether we can "find a mode of pictorial expression that will do for abstraction now what Caravaggio's pictorial genius did for sixteenth-century naturalism and its magnificent successors?"[p. 4].

Stella states the problem facing twentieth-century painting by reference to Picasso. Picasso is said to have abandoned Cubism because it was in danger of making everything flat. This was supposed to have already happened with the pioneering abstraction of Kandinsky and Malevich. Picasso's fear was that Kandinsky's pure painting would turn into pure paint. Stella is very much aware that there is a

---

3   The analogy drawn from theater that I imposed upon Stella's description of the spatial achievement of Caravaggio and Rubens raises the possibility that this work is subject to the criticism of "theatricality" that Michael Fried brought against literalist (i.e., minimalist) painting in "Art and Objecthood," *Art Forum* (June 1967). I think not. Both Stella's descriptions of Caravaggio's and Rubens' space and Fried's descriptions of literalist works are derivative from our experiences of things and people as we go about the world. There are, however, two important differences. The people and objects we encounter in painting are, of course, not real things, but only representations of things; we encounter them, as it were, only in imagination. By contrast, Fried speaks as if encounters with literalist works are real encounters. This is not to claim that in some way Fried's example descriptions of the work waiting for you or refusing to leave you alone are "literal" for in one way or another they are borrowed from actual relations with people and certainly not all the connections available in the one language game go through in the other. These are, nevertheless, the sorts of experiences and descriptions that can apply in encounters with objects that have nothing whatsoever to do with art; one could have the same thoughts about a tree in the woods or a packing crate left in the middle of the shop floor.

The second point of difference is that the experiences Fried notes are all in some fashion untoward or unsettling; they produce isolation rather than communion. The appeal that Stella finds in Caravaggio and Rubens, on the other hand, is precisely the appeal of a communion in which we can see the light of revelation shining in the eyes of Caravaggio's St. Paul and share in the awe and wonder of Loyola's miracles.

If my analogy with the practices of theater are at all helpful for illuminating Stella's discussion of space, the result is not a description of Caravaggio and Rubens as "theatrical" that participates in the pejorative flavor of Fried's notion.

connection of some sort between the kind of space he values and the human figure; indeed it is the human figure that is supposed to be largely responsible for creating this space. He says that:

> The glory of the human figure is precisely its spatial versatility, and nothing confirms the glory and value of the figure more clearly than Picasso's post-Cubist paintings. Yet abstraction has dared to try to get along without the human figure. Today it struggles, at least partly, because it has failed to come up with a viable substitute for human figuration, for the spatial vitality and versatility provided by the human figure. It was not so much the loss of the human figure itself as it was the loss of what the figure did to the space around itself that has been hard to replace. [p. 74]

My philosophical interest in all this lies in Stella's notion of space and its relation to the human figure. To bring out the nature of this interest it will be necessary to survey a view of earlier art history that in some ways complements Stella's. It is the view of William M. Ivins about the relation between the visual art of the Greeks and the art of the Renaissance.[4]

It is Ivins' thesis that the Greeks had no clear sense of spatial organization. He says that at important cult sites such as Delphi, Olympia, and the Athenian Acropolis the architectural spaces are not coherently organized and the buildings are stuck in wherever room can be found for them. The same lack of organization and relationship applies to the visual arts. Ivins uses this imaginary example to illustrate his point:

> The Greeks represented Jim making a single gesture such as he might use in a fight, and somewhere they represented Jack making another such gesture, but they never represented the fight *between* Jim and Jack or the way in which the gestures of the two fighters coalesced in a single continuous rhythmical movement, such that each gesture of the one had meaning through the series of related gestures of the other. [Ivins, p. 15]

Ivins says that the figures in Greek sculpture exist in "abstraction" and describes them as "aloof" or "frighteningly lonely." He goes on to say that despite an increasing knowledge of anatomy Greek art "fails to give any indication of the emotional and volitional characteristics that are the peculiar and most wonderful attributes of its subject."[p. 19.]

Interestingly enough Stella complains of Renaissance space in a way that is reminiscent of Ivins' criticism of the Greeks:

> ... Caravaggio makes us realize that Renaissance painting had a hard time putting figures together, grouping them in a convincing pictorial way. There was a tendency to make the figures appear real one at a time, to allow them to function individually, but no effort was made to make them 'real' together. The sense of figurative grouping was basically stilted, even though individual figures might appear almost natural. [Stella, p. 27]

---

4   William M. Ivins Jr., *Art and Geometry: A Study in Space Intuitions* (New York: Dover 1964). The book was originally published in 1946.

Could we say that it is a matter of comparison, of point of view? Compared to Caravaggio the fifteenth century looks awkward, but by comparison with the Greeks the quattrocento is a regular miracle?

We are handicapped, of course, in any discussion of Greek painting because virtually nothing of it survives save for vase painting. And in vase painting Ivins doesn't find any serious spatial organization; the figures represented exist, as it were, in different spaces and make no contact with one another. By the Middle Ages, however, he thinks that artists are beginning to change their relation to their subject-matter:

> Across the centuries the religious subject matter of art gradually becomes dramatic. This drama was full of action. Action implies relationships between human figures located in the same visual spaces and not in different ones. The artists began to dislike action at a distance, much as later philosophers and physicists have disliked it. [p. 62]

I think Ivins is entertaining two somewhat distinct notions here and he has not properly sorted out the relation between them. One of them is, of course, the matter of the representation of space by means of projective geometry. Clearly the Greeks had not worked out how to do this and had developed neither the idea nor the technique of perspective drawing. It would, for instance, be impossible to construct a three-dimensional model or stage set in which the figures from a Greek vase painting could be unambiguously placed. It is also clear that at another level Ivins' concern is not solely with the geometry of drawing and painting. The failure of the Greeks to provide a geometrical arena for the representation of men in action is in his eyes really a failure to provide a moral arena for human action. What needs to be worked out now is the connection between the presentation of drama, i.e., people acting and reacting with one another, on the one hand, and projective geometry on the other.

His discussion of Alberti reinforces my contention that his interest is really in what I shall call moral space, that is, a pictorial space designed to represent human beings in the fullness of their psychological nature and in their dramatic interactions with one another. According to Alberti the movements of the soul are shown by the movements of the body and so to present the psychological and emotional states of people the painter must know how to portray the body and its movements and gestures and that means he must understand their proportions and proper spatial relationships, hence the necessity and justification for perspective rendering. The implication is that Alberti's concern with the techniques of perspective rendering is ancillary to his concern to provide a moral space for human drama.

To illustrate the problem facing the early quattrocento Italian painters I want to describe and discuss a Spanish Jewish illustration (apparently fifteenth century) that lies quite outside the tradition developing during the same period in Italy.[5] The picture represents the biblical plague of locusts. On the left Pharaoh sits on his throne. On the

---

5   The Sarajevo Haggadah (Beograd and Sarajevo, 1983). This is an interesting facsimile edition of a fourteenth-century manuscript. The illustrations are assumed to have been added later.

right stands Moses holding a rod with Aaron behind him. Between them are two trees growing out of a grassy area. The trees are covered with locusts and more locusts are flying about. This miniature has no third dimension whatever. The background is a solid color like a stage curtain. We can know what the illustration represents because it either comes labeled for us or we have been told that it is a biblical scene and then the rest is obvious. We understand the dramatic confrontation between Moses and Pharaoh and what is at stake in it from the familiar literary background. Without that prior awareness, however, we could not know what is going on, we could not have any sense of a drama, of a *confrontation*. Should we confront the picture in all its charming naivety without the background knowledge of the biblical incident everything remains ambiguous. It is not clear whether the trees are between the two or whether the pair are spectators of a scene in the distance. The two trees are not drawn as tall as the standing figures and could pass more convincingly for cardboard cutouts used as stage props than for real trees in the distance. The faces of the figures are expressionless. Pharaoh has a hand raised but the nature of the gesture is not defined. Moses extends his rod apparently toward the locusts, but it is not clear what he is doing. He could be giving Pharaoh a lesson in entomology or putting the insects through their paces as if in an oversized flea circus. It would be a mistake to say that like the figures in Greek vase painting these figures exist in different spaces; rather they don't exist in any space at all. It is this lack of spatial determination that is in part responsible for the lack of dramatic character in the picture.

Art historians aplenty have talked about the development of space composition in the Renaissance, the development of perspective and all of that, but it is not obvious whether anyone has asked about the point of it all. Why was this kind of space composition important to the art of the Renaissance? Is it enough to say that artists just wanted to be able to paint things the way they look? Granted there was a new interest in nature, and nature for its own sake, but was there not also a new interest in people and, consequently, the painterly representation of people? Here it will be useful to take a closer look at Alberti.

According to Alberti the painter is concerned solely with representing what can be seen. What can be seen, of course, is to be represented by the newly developed techniques of perspective making use of geometrical optics and the visual pyramid. The human being is the standard of proportion in painting; things are large or small compared to the human figure. One third the height of a man placed arbitrarily on the picture plane is taken as the basic unit of measurement.

It is worth noting that in constructing a painting he takes as his canon of proportion a part of the human body. From the point of view of getting the projective geometry right any arbitrarily chosen object would do, a puppy dog's tail, for example. The fact that it is the human body makes clear where the interest of the art of his day really lay. He introduces this canon of proportion with a reference to Protagoras' notion that man is the measure of all things: "Since man is the thing best known to man, perhaps Protagoras, by saying that man is the mode and measure of all things, meant that the accidents of things are known through comparison to the accidents of man." [p. 55.] This can be read as a comment about something deeper than mere geometric proportion: it is their relation to people and the interests and concerns of people that give things their importance and their significance. Once more geometrical space turns into moral space.

He goes on to say "that a painted thing can never appear truthful where there is not a definite distance for seeing it." [p. 57.] I assume that this remark applies not only to the physical appearance of things, but to the representation of human action as well. With people it cannot be merely a matter of visual appearance, but must also be a matter of understanding what the person is doing, his relation to others, the significance of gestures, and all that. If we take the plague of locusts miniature as an example of a painted thing where there is not a definite distance for seeing, we may understand Alberti's comment as once more going deeper than his announced topic. The "truthfulness" of appearances points to the more fundamental notion of intelligibility. Unless the figures can be seen in the proper spatial relations we can make no sense of what they are supposed to be doing.

He adds that "The greatest work of the painter is the *istoria.*" [p.70.] (This remark is repeated more than once.) The *istoria*, I take it, is the scene portrayed, the action, the dramatic situation. In order to represent an action the intentions, emotions, and so on of the actors must be made absolutely clear. He therefore says that: "We painters who wish to show the movements of the soul by movements of the body are concerned solely with the movement of change of place." [p. 79.] Wittgenstein has shown us how a remark such as this can be taken as grammar, that is, as a reminder of how certain words are used and the role that they play in life.

Wittgenstein's arresting comment that the human body is the best picture of the human soul [PI, p. 178e] is such a grammatical remark and is, I suggest, the key to understanding the significance of what Alberti said. The movements of the body that are in question are not the motions of cartesian *res extensa* that can be plotted on a coordinate system and certainly are not the "colorless bodily movements" of behaviorist theory, but are instead the doings of people. The relevant difference can be brought out by comparing the kind of painting done by Alberti's quattrocento contemporaries with a manual illustrating, say, anatomical articulations or the physiology of gymnastic performance. Nor are these motions necessarily merely symptoms of or evidence for inner states of the soul. As elements of human action we are not dealing simply with "movements," but with gestures, postures, facial expressions, and the like that are already replete with human character, intention, and purpose.

Likewise it will be illuminating to construe as grammar Ivin's statement mentioned above that a gesture has meaning only when it is related to the gestures of another. Wittgenstein is making an analogous point in the following paragraph:

I see a picture which represents a smiling face. What do I do if I take the smile now as a kind one, now as malicious? Don't I often imagine it with a spatial and temporal context which is one either of kindness or malice? Thus I might supply the picture with the fancy that the smiler was smiling down on a child at play, or again on the suffering of an enemy.[6]

The smile requires a context for its character to become definite and so does the gesture. The requirement of context determines how we understand expressions and gestures and it determines the application of descriptions such as the "kindly" smile, or Moses' gesture as "threatening" or perhaps as "admonishing" Pharaoh. To understand what a person is doing, and hence his psychological state, he has to be seen in relation to other things and other people. We have to understand that this person is looking at another or away from someone, turning toward this or away from that, and so on. In the course of our daily lives these things are usually clear enough and if we are to understand the representation of these things in the visual arts they must be equally as clear there. A way to show relatively unambiguous spatial relations in painting can in this way be made to seem absolutely necessary.

Our failure to understand, in the absence of explanatory text, what is going on in the plague of locusts illustration is not the result of the metaphysical and epistemological privacy of mental states, but stems from an artistic tradition that was not concerned to articulate human figures and to place them in intelligible spatial relations to one another and to the landscape in which they act. The intentions of the Medieval painter of the plague of locusts miniature as well as the skills available to him and the conventions within which he operated were very different from those of later Renaissance painters who also painted biblical scenes. The miniature is a kind of symbol or reminder of the story. Our understanding of it has to presuppose the text. Now the biblical story itself is singularly devoid of any psychological details about the minds and feelings of either Pharaoh or Moses and the illustration certainly adds nothing of the sort nor embellishes the text in any way. The Jewish painter, after all, sought to remind his audience of the power of God and had little concern for the minds of his characters. A Renaissance painting of a biblical event, by contrast, adds to the text. It makes explicit psychological reactions and relations that are not supplied by the text. It is as if the text supplies only the outline or suggestion for a novel or a drama leaving it up to the painter to fill in all the details. The painter wishes to humanize the text and exploit its potential for human drama. This could be seen as a move away from the otherworldly aspect of religion and toward making the relation between God and man more concrete or simply as moving away from religion toward an interest in the human.

I have sought to show that a plausible case can be made that at least one principal aim of the development of perspective rendering and all the other techniques of Renaissance space composition was to provide a setting, a space, in which the actions of men could be clearly and unambiguously represented. In a word, Renaissance painting created moral space. We may now return to Stella and his diagnosis of the contemporary crisis in abstract painting.

---

6   Ludwig Wittgenstein, *Philosophical Investigations*, 2nd ed., (New York, 1958), §539.

Stella says that the aim of art is to create space in which the subjects of painting can live and since the human figure has always played a vital role in determining space, he laments abstraction's failure to come up with a viable substitute for human figuration. He sums up the problem in this way:

> ... the last really vibrant and exciting pictorial space was the Cubist space that Picasso left behind—Cubism—and develop it to include what Picasso went on with—a dynamic rendition of volume. That is, abstraction must go on with what painting has always had— line, plane, and volume, the basic ingredients. The problem is that in the twentieth century modernist painting has not yet been able to put all three together. [p. 77]

What kind of problem is this one of "putting all three together" that Stella has set for abstract painting in general and for his own work in particular?

Here the remark about a space in which the subjects of painting can live is significant. Traditionally the subjects of painting have been people and the space in which they can live is simply space in which they can act and relate to one another, that is, it is as much moral space as it is physical space. What would it mean to talk of a space in which the subject can live when the subject is no longer the human figure or even any recognizable object that draws its significance from its relations to living human figures? To say that the subject of a painting lives entails that we can recognize a subject in the painting and that we can talk about it "living," that is, that we can say of it at least some of the things that it is appropriate to say of human beings, that it has intentions, emotions, character, or the like. In the absence of any figuration, however, in the absence of any object represented, whether human or not, there is a very real question about whether the description of paintings in terms of space and life makes sense. And consequently there is a very real question about whether Stella's program for reanimating abstract art is an intelligible one.

He tells us that a revivified abstract art requires a dynamic rendition of volume. A characteristic Renaissance way of representing was by painting what is in effect a bit of stage scenery or a backdrop against which the subjects are portrayed. Botticelli's *Calumny* is a painting of that sort. The architectural frame within the painting defines a space—presents a stage—in which and on which any number of different actors might strut and fret their hour and any number of different dramas might be played out. It was that earlier way of Botticelli and the others with space that was surpassed by Caravaggio and Rubens as is illustrated *by The Madonna of the Rosary* and *The Miracles of Saint Ignatius of Loyola* that Stella makes much of. In neither of these paintings do the architectural features constitute a space already in place waiting for a cast of characters to make its appearance. It is the figures themselves that create the space around them and that reach out to include us, the spectators. As Stella put it, this versatility in doing things to space is the glory of the human figure. If abstract painting has abandoned the figure, then it can create neither kind of space and the second coming of Caravaggio anticipated in the late twentieth century will indeed be a miraculous event.

There is more than one way to look at the difficulty that I believe Stella has gotten himself into. Stella seems to believe that the truly important thing for painting is space itself. Although Stella is certainly a proponent of the art for art's sake doctrine, his is a rather special version of it: space for space's sake. I have argued that historically what had made space important for artists is what is in it and that is mostly the human figure. I would turn Stella's remark about the glory of the human figure around and say that the glory of space is the moral versatility of the human figure displayed in it. Doubtless some artists have explored space for its own sake, but it seems to me that the original intent of the investigation of space was to provide a place for people to interact with one another and that is what gives point to the artistic concern for space. To the extent that artists have forgotten that original intent we may have a reason to say that they have lost their way. Let us imagine a future in which there are people who cultivate the skill of kicking the ball into the goal; they become very good at it and can put the ball into the net from all distances and all angles and against any number of obstacles, but they have lost sight of the fact that this skill was once cultivated as part of a game and it was that game that gave sense and point to the skill. The practice in which that skill figured has now dropped away, the posts and net no longer constitute a *goal*, and one kicks the ball between the bars "for its own sake." Is it like that with abstract painting and space?

Stella's difficulty, however, is rather deeper than this. It is not just that the concern for space has lost its point and the artistic endeavor become idle; the difficulty is whether there is still an endeavor to be described as Stella wishes to describe it. The examples of the Botticelli, Caravaggio, and Rubens paintings just mentioned help us to realize that there is an intimate conceptual connection in the language of painting between the notion of space and the notion of the figure. In the one case the space is there in order to await the coming of the figure, not to mention the fact that the empty stage is the product of recognizable objects, whether architectural or natural; in the other case it is the figure that defines and articulates the space. Stella's talk of space, therefore, when talk of the figure has been eliminated begins to look like a kind of nonsense, the kind of nonsense that results when one tries to use a word or expression when the normal conditions of its application are absent.

It does not follow from anything I have said that abstract painting is a pointless or nonsensical enterprise or even that abstract painters have lost their way. Abstract painting can be a very interesting and exciting form of art with its own unique values and abstract art can even do much with space to the extent that it embodies forms suggestive of human figures and other objects. What has lost its way is a certain amount of *talk* about abstract painting. Frank Stella has provided us with what looks like a very striking example of language gone on holiday.

Chapter 6

Reflections on Aesthetic Theory

Questions about the nature of theories in aesthetics and the philosophy of art and skeptical doubts about whether such theories are even possible did not become serious issues until Wittgenstein's *Philosophical Investigations* began to be influential in that area of philosophy in the 1950s.[1] Wittgenstein's work suggested to a number of philosophers of art that the kinds of theories aestheticians have so often sought are either not possible or, more cautiously, of little help. Despite the considerable measure of debate, those who are skeptical about the role of theories in aesthetics have clearly been in the minority in the last thirty-five years or so. The prevailing opinion seems to be that theories are not only possible, but are essential to the philosophical enterprise of thinking about art and aesthetics. There are, nevertheless, questions about theories that still need to be raised, and I intend to raise some of them here.

What is an aesthetic theory, and what do we want of one? A good place to begin is with a distinction made by the historian of recent American art Stewart Buettner. Buettner distinguishes between two kinds of theory; on the one hand there is what he calls *aesthetics* and on the other, *art theory*:

> As opposed to aesthetics, which is the philosophic inquiry into art and beauty, art theory investigates the ideas of artists in an effort to explain a variety of phenomena in both an artist's life and work that may help to further the appreciation of an artist or a group of artists. The difference, then, between aesthetics and art theory rests almost exclusively upon the profession of the individuals concerned.[2]

It is important to make some kind of distinction along these lines between philosophical theories and those that are intended to help us understand and appreciate individual works of art, the *oeuvre* of an artist, or an artistic period or movement. Buettner, I would suggest, has mistaken the principle of the distinction, for it has nothing to do with anyone's profession. The distinction is, rather, in the broadest sense, a logical one.

If this point about Buettner's distinction is to have any interest for us, it has to amount to more than the recognition of the obvious fact that one person can wear two hats, that a professional philosopher, for example, can write for the philosophical

---

1   See, for example, Morris Weitz, "The Role of Theory in Aesthetics," *Journal of Aesthetics and Art Criticism*, (1956) and William Kennick, "Does Traditional Aesthetics Rest on a Mistake?" *Mind* (1958).

2   Stewart Buettner, *American Art Theory* (Ann Arbor, 1981), pp. ix-x.

journals on Monday, Wednesday, and Friday, and then write criticism for the art and literary magazines the rest of the week. What has to be shown is that the kind of procedure that is characteristic of the critical, the appreciative, and the art-historical discussion of particular artists and works, styles, and the like is sometimes an integral part of the philosophical investigation of the arts, and, conversely, that philosophical issues and contentions often enter into the discussion of artists, critics, and historians, even if the philosophical character of those issues and contentions is frequently not recognized. Granted that this kind of distinction is important, it remains to show why it is important and also how it resolves itself into additional distinctions of a complexity not made out by Buettner.

Before we can say much about theories in the arts, we have to say something about just what it is we are willing to call a theory. One paradigm of what a theory is or ought to be is frequently taken from the physical sciences, where we think of theory of mechanics, atomic theory, quantum theory, and so on. Aesthetic theories are only too obviously different from these; such models do not even represent all the different varieties of scientific theories, biological theories, and theories in the social sciences, for example. The examples of the paradigmatic theories of physics will, nevertheless, allow us to make three important points about theories.

In the first place, these theories aim at a high level of generality; they seek to tell us something about the nature and behavior of *all* things of a certain sort; e.g., Newtonian mechanics defines and relates the notions of velocity, acceleration, mass, and force for *all* bodies whatsoever. This is not to say, of course, that such laws and theories are generalizations arrived at inductively. In the second place, a theory involves several concepts or notions that are represented as logically interrelated. Mechanics, to use the Newtonian example once again, can be formulated with the concepts of space, time, and mass as its primitive concepts, and the ideas of velocity, acceleration, and force can then be introduced in terms of them; the familiar laws of motion then state the relations between all those concepts.

Finally, no theory is self-explanatory or carries the conditions of its application within itself. These theories exist within a context of scientific tradition and practice that determines how the theory is to be used. To make anything of classical mechanics one must know how velocities and masses are to be measured, how the appropriate mathematics is to be applied and results calculated; and one must also be aware of the limitations on the theory's application and how it does not work for velocities approaching the speed of light, for certain subatomic phenomena, and so on. One does not learn physics merely by learning the statement of its theories, for one must in addition learn something of the problems the theory was designed to solve, how the theory works to describe and explain particular phenomena, how experiments are set up in the laboratory, and, in short, how one becomes a participant in that human activity we call physical science.

Despite the great differences between physical theory and aesthetic theory, there is something to be learned about the latter from what we have just said about generality, logical structure, and practice in the former. To understand an aesthetic theory, we must know something about the human practice in which it is embedded.

This remark is no more than a reminder of what we have learned from Wittgenstein, that an expression can have a sense only in the context of an activity, that is, a language game or even a form of life, if you will. This point needs repeating only because it is so often overlooked by philosophers and aestheticians who go on as if their theories and comments can be understood in isolation from any context in which they might have a role to play.

Both Buettner's art theories and aesthetic theories are frequently encapsulated in the formula "Art is ... .," where the ellipsis is satisfied by the meat of the theory, "imitation," "expression," "significant form," or whatever it happens to be. Sometimes the theory may instead be a theory of some sub-class of art, and then we find corresponding formulas such as "Poetry is the expression of the imagination," and "Sculpture is the abstract reconstruction of the planes and volumes which determine form." We should be struck by the fact that these theories all have the same grammatical form in that they all take the form of generalizations about either the whole of art or one of the arts. But if we must understand an expression—or an entire theory—in terms of the role it plays in the context of a practice, then the fact that these theoretical expressions share a common surface grammar is not necessarily a clue to how they are actually used and hence how they must actually be understood.

How are they to be understood? Or, better, how can they be understood? Consider the contention that sculpture is the abstract reconstruction of the planes and volumes that determine form. Here we can think of several situations in which this remark could be made. Imagine this being said by a teacher to a student in the studio as a way of encouraging the student to sculpt in a certain way—perhaps the teacher is trying to wean the student away from the classicism of Canova or the beaux arts tradition of Harriet Hosmer to something more characteristically twentieth century. Now imagine the remark being made by a lecturer explaining twentieth-century developments to a popular audience where the intention is not to influence anyone's sculptural practice, but is instead to point out to the audience the significant differences between, say, Canova and Henry Moore. As a matter of fact, the statement was made by Umberto Boccioni as part of his Futurist Manifesto.[3]

We have now indicated three distinct situations or contexts that determine three distinct uses of the common formula "Sculpture is ... ." In one case it is an instruction for using hammer and chisel to achieve certain results and is roughly equivalent to "Try to get it to come out this way rather than that." In the second case it comes to the advice, "If you wish to understand and appreciate some of the more influential trends in twentieth-century sculpture, look for and concentrate on these features." In the third situation, Boccioni in his manifesto is expressing a decision or an intention to sculpt in a certain fashion.

---

3   The complete statement is, "The aim of sculpture is the abstract reconstruction of the planes and volumes which determine form, not their figurative value:" Umberto Boccioni, "Technical Manifesto of Futurist Sculpture," in *Modern Artists on Art*, ed. Robert L. Herbert (Englewood Cliffs, 1964), p. 55.

In none of these contexts does the formula carry with it any high level of generality. If the instructor finds that the students have little feel for modern abstract values, students may be encouraged in other directions or advised to seek another studio more congenial to their talents and inclinations. Art historians lecturing to their audience need not, and probably would not, commit themselves to the claim that theirs is the only thing going on in recent sculpture. Nor can we understand Boccioni to be making a truth claim about all sculptural art; his words, after all, are a *manifesto*. He may even be charitable enough to say, although disapprovingly, that others are quite free to go their own way.

It is only by sorting out the various roles that such expressions play and by getting some sense of the various contexts that determine their roles that can we begin to assess and evaluate them; needless to say, it is the context of their use that determines what is relevant to that assessment. Is the instructor giving his student good advice, and is this the most effective way to get the student to do what is wanted? This is a different question from the one we ask of the lecturer when we want to know whether he or she has focused on those features of recent sculpture that will in fact put it all in the best perspective for us and thereby help us to a better understanding of the art of this century. Our concern with the manifesto is again of a different kind: has Boccioni committed himself to a worthwhile project, and will we as artists want to follow him in that direction?

At this point in the discussion it may be tempting to suppose that what is wanted to answer these questions is some higher-level theory of aesthetic value in general, a theory about what determines significance and what is artistically worthwhile. It can thus be made to appear that an art theory presupposes a philosophical aesthetic theory. I shall return to a discussion of this point.

Boccioni's formula about sculpture is certainly one that Buettner would comprehend under the heading of art theory, for all of the uses that we have imagined for it do aim at calling our attention to particular examples of art, to particular movements within art, or the work of particular artists for the advancement of appreciation and, I would add, the practice of the art itself.

There may, however, be something a bit out of order, if not pretentious, in calling such a statement a theory; for one thing, we have seen that we can understand the formula only in particular contexts and in them we find none of the generality that characterizes other theories. Nor in Boccioni do we find his "definition" of sculpture linked to other notions so as to form a systematic network of ideas to help us in understanding his program. What we do find is a species of argument for his position that consists in pejorative descriptions of traditional sculpture that amount to the contention that the work of the past that Boccioni sees as based on the Greeks and Michelangelo has lost its vitality and that something new is needed. But this kind of reason-giving does not show the kind of logical linking of ideas characteristic of so much scientific theory.

It is certainly not the sort of thing that we find, for example, in Aristotle's *Poetics*. Aristotle maps for us a system of relationships between the plot structure of tragedy, the kinds of incidents that produce the tragic emotions of pity and fear, and the kinds of characters that can play appropriate roles in these incidents. This systematic mapping of dramatic relationships allows Aristotle to explain how a tragedy works and why some plays are better than others. Whether it is an adequate representation and explanation of what we know of Greek drama is not to the point; there is still every reason to describe it as a theory.

Should we describe the *Poetics*, in Buettner's terms, as aesthetic theory or as art theory? Aristotle, to be sure, was a professional philosopher, but the *Poetics* does not offer a general theory of art nor even a general theory of poetry; in the form that we have, it addresses only tragedy (although a lost second book may have been about comedy). There is reason to suppose that it was designed to further the appreciation of drama, at least of tragedy, and may even have been intended as a guide for authors. This is additional reinforcement of my contention that while Buettner's distinction between types of theory points to something important, the profession of the theorist is quite irrelevant to it.

Let us turn now to aesthetic theory, those philosophical theories of art and beauty. It is by no means clear just exactly what a philosophical theory of art is. One way to construe such a theory is to take it as a definition. The formula common to so many theories, "Art is ...," is thus often understood to be a statement of the properties that all works of art and only works of art have in common by virtue of which they are works of art, or to put it in the formal mode, a statement of the necessary and sufficient conditions for the application of the word "art." Conceived of as definitions, philosophical theories of art and aesthetics have frequently been supposed to allow us to distinguish art from what is not art. If we do not have a definition of art, it has been claimed, we will be unable to delimit a subject matter for art history, art criticism, and so on.[4] Theories are also required, it has been thought, to provide standards of aesthetic and artistic value and to provide philosophical justification for value judgments. It has been said in addition that theories are needed to determine what is and what is not relevant to the understanding, interpretation, and appreciation of works of art.

The standard objections to this kind of theory as definition have too often been ill-conceived. It won't do to claim that such a definition is fated to be either too wide or too narrow, admitting things as art that are not or eliminating things that clearly are art, before we have a pretty good idea of what can qualify as a viable candidate for a defining characteristic. Such a characteristic certainly cannot be anything such as rhyme scheme, space composition, or harmonic intervals. Note that it is not false to say that this painting has such and such a rhyme scheme, and consequently, the denial that at this level all works of art have something in common is simply unintelligible.

To forestall a possible objection, it should be pointed out that not infrequently works of art of one form are described in the vocabulary appropriate to another form.

---

4   This claim has been made, for example, by Lewis K. Zerby, "A Reconsideration of the Role of Theory in Aesthetics—A Reply to Morris Weitz," *Journal of Aesthetics and Art Criticism* (1957).

Thus we sometimes speak of the *rhythm* of the fenestration of an architectural facade or of the poet's use of *chiaroscuro* in the "painting" of his subject. I would suggest, however, that these appropriations or borrowings of words that have their home base somewhere else are properly understood as metaphorical, or better, as secondary uses of those bits of language, and one cannot make theory out of that.

Nor do we fare any better if we give up the search for common defining properties among such "directly exhibited" features of works of art as rhyme scheme in favor of seeking them in the background of artists' intentions.[5] The only way to understand and identify an intention is in terms of what it is an intention to do. The intention of the poet, then, is to write a poem with such and such rhyme scheme, the intention of the painter is to paint a canvas with this kind of space composition, and so on. What we find, consequently, is that the very same diversity and logical disparity among the characteristics of works of art is duplicated at the level of intentions.

As a matter of fact, theories and definitions of art have never been formulated in terms of the particulars of the various arts such as rhyme scheme, space composition, and the like. Instead we are more likely to find much broader notions such as imitation, expression, significant form, and their ilk, that are intended to have application across the full range of the arts.

Again the question is not the one of mistakenly trying to specify necessary and sufficient conditions for what is really a family resemblance concept. The theory that art is imitation is not the false generalization that all art is representational, nor is the theory that art is expression the commonplace that artists frequently are inspired by their emotional responses to situations they have lived through. The former is embedded in a whole metaphysics of reality (e.g., Plato) and the latter presupposes an entire philosophical psychology and philosophy of language and communication (e.g., Croce and Collingwood).

It is in theories such as these that we find the generality and web of logical relations typical of our paradigmatic theories. One aim of these theories is to relate art to other aspects of the world and human life and to explain the nature of artistic and aesthetic value. There nevertheless remain questions about how we are to understand and apply these theories. If we are to pursue the analogy with physical

---

5   Maurice Mandelbaum ("Family Resemblances and Generalizations Concerning the Arts," *American Philosophical Quarterly*, vol. 2, no. 3 [1965]) argued that Wittgenstein's notion of family resemblance could not be used as an objection to the search for definition in the arts on the grounds (1) that the only properties between which Wittgenstein sees a family resemblance are "directly exhibited" ones, (2) that sharing "directly exhibited" properties is not sufficient to justify calling different things by the same name, and (3) that we may need to seek the defining properties of art in the non-exhibited intentions and purposes of artists. Mandelbaum, however, has seriously misunderstood Wittgenstein. Wittgenstein does not restrict family resemblances to "directly exhibited" properties—the concept of number is a family resemblance concept—and he never uses it as a justification for calling different things by the same name, but only as a description of how it often is with our language. I have discussed Mandelbaum's paper as well other problems of definition in more detail in *But Is It Art?* (Oxford, 1984), especially Chapter 2.

theories, then we should expect, indeed demand, that these theories have a use and an application. We should expect them to help us to understand the phenomena of art. We must remember that those phenomena are simply the entirety of the human practices in which art is embedded, that is, practices of painting, writing, composition, commissioning, criticizing, appreciating, writing art history, and so on.

It seems to me that there are at least two major difficulties with these philosophical theories of art and aesthetics. The phenomena of art are diverse and, indeed, logically diverse; that is, the characteristics of painting cannot intelligibly be ascribed to poetry in a way that could serve theory, and so on. We would thus expect the terms of the theory to be just as diverse as the phenomena it is supposed to explain. But any general theory seeks to unify a range of phenomena; it seeks the unity in variety, the common form behind an apparently disparate variety of phenomena. This is certainly true of much scientific theory. Newton was not content merely to describe and catalog the various kinds of motion, e.g., that stones fall straight down, projectiles trace parabolas, planets move in ellipses, etc., but was able to show that these are all special cases of a more fundamental set of basic laws. Newton's scientific achievement was in part the result of the introduction of a new set of concepts for dealing with motion. And we must remind ourselves that a new set of concepts must bring with it a new practice; the new way of thinking about motion must bring with it new ways of measuring, predicting, conducting experiments, and so on.

When we try to apply this conception of theory to the explanation of human practices, whether artistic or otherwise, certain special problems arise. What a theory would be called upon to explain is not simply some different set of *phenomena*, but human *practices*, that is, what we do. We must remind ourselves that works of art are not just there in the world, like the planets and their motions, waiting to be investigated, but are instead the intentional products of artists and are inseparably connected with the reactions of audiences; they are part and parcel of a web of human practices. The kind of theory I have been talking about will have to understand the diversity of actual practices as surface appearance hiding some underlying unity that it is the task of the theory to reveal. In other words, it will be committed to showing that what we are doing is not what we thought we were doing, that our practices were not what we took them to be. (I thought I was just being nice to the chap, but it seems I was really manifesting latent sexual desire, or seeking ego satisfaction, or the like.)

The basic notions of Newtonian mechanics, mass, velocity, etc., are new technical terms introduced into the language together with their criteria of application as part of the theory. Sexual desire and self-interest are notions that already have a place in our language and represent only two of many possible motives with which we are familiar and between which we can discriminate. The contention that my "just being nice" is really a case of ego satisfaction can be saved from obvious falsehood only by stretching the notion of self-interest completely out of shape and draining it of all content. We have to reject the assumption that behind our practices there is a latent essence that will make everything clear once it is brought to light. With respect to human beings and human practices, we can say that nothing is hidden,[6] at least not in any philosophically significant way.

The concepts that make up the stuff of so many philosophical theories of art and aesthetics, (e.g., imitation/representation, expression of emotion, form) are notions that already have a place in the language, and we should be able to distinguish between an artist expressing his feelings in his work and one who is concerned, say, only with problems of formal design. The expression theory saves itself from empirical disconfirmation not by making the notion of expression vacuous, but by making expression into a technical notion by embedding it in a more general philosophical theory. The problem with this latter move is that the philosophical theory of art and aesthetics is precisely that, a *philosophical* theory grounded in metaphysics, epistemology, and all the rest of what we think of as the core of the philosophical tradition. As part of a general philosophical theory, the aesthetic theory shares in all the conceptual confusion that is the trade mark of that kind of thinking. A theory that results from conceptual confusion can have no use or application, no role to play in the stream of life; it is language gone on holiday, it is like an idling wheel that does no work, to parade all the familiar conceits.

Nor can aesthetic theories do for us what has been wanted of them. No theory can help us pick out works of art from things that are not art. The uses of the word "art" are more subtle and complex than most theorists have intimated and are inextricably tied to practices of evaluation and appreciation.[7] Evaluation and appreciation depend upon our reactions to works of art, and our reactions are not determined by any theory. Neither can a philosophical theory justify our value judgments—theory can't show that our ways of dealings with art and reacting to it are the correct ones.

It has to remain a curious fact, then, that philosophical theories of art and aesthetics have sometimes apparently played a role in the practical affairs of art. Clive Bell's theory of art as significant form is a case in point. It is generally recognized that Bell was influenced by G.E. Moore and, following Moore, the term "significant form" is doubtless intended to denote a simple, unanalyzable, and hence indefinable quality that not all of us are capable of apprehending. The philosophical hopelessness of all that needs no additional comment. But "significant form" nevertheless did play a role in practical criticism; Bell did put it to use in explaining and defending Post Impressionist painting. How are we to account for this?

I suggest that it can be accounted for very simply. When Bell got around to applying his theory, that is, to practical criticism, all the philosophical baggage of the theory was simply set aside, and the notion of "form" was cashed in terms of relations of line, mass, shape, and color, and the design and composition that can be constructed out of them, notions that were already perfectly familiar to artists even if their audience had never paid that much attention to them. Thus Bell could come

---

6 This expression is an invitation to refer to Norman Malcolm's recent book, *Nothing Is Hidden* (Oxford, 1986), for an extended examination of this idea in the work of Wittgenstein.

7 See *But is it Art?*, Chapter 3.

to grips with the particulars of paint and canvas when he talked about how Cézanne painted mountains, how his forms are like Giotto's, and how both painters differ from Raphael. The modifier "significant" merely trades upon our non-theoretical sense of the difference between good, bad, and better. To describe a painting as having "significant form," then, is to say that it makes good use of the formal elements of painting by contrast with one that, let us say, tries to get by solely on its historical, literary, or sentimental connotations.

Another interesting example of a philosophical theory that has had a considerable practical impact is John Dewey's theory of art as experience. Dewey's book *Art as Experience* was published in 1934 and was read and discussed by a number of American artists during the 1930s and 40s. The reception of the book and its subsequent influence has been traced in some detail by Stewart Buettner.[8] Even if the theory had no *direct* influence on the practice of American artists, it served to bring into focus many ideas that were already in the air and to articulate thoughts that artists were already thinking. Thomas Hart Benton, for one, was both thoroughly familiar with Dewey and sympathetic to his ideas, and it was thus easy enough to read *Art as Experience* as providing a justification for American Regionalism. Buettner also suggests that *Art as Experience* is consistent with Action Painting, and may have had some indirect influence on that movement. It is known, in addition, that the book did have an influence on some of the administrators of the Federal Art Project and encouraged them in their support of American artists during the Depression.

Dewey's book, like the rest of his thought, is philosophically exasperating. It is never clear how we are supposed to understand his use of the word "experience" or even whether he has provided a use for it. The word "experience" comes into our language in many different ways. I may relate the intriguing experience I had the other day ("When on my way to the university this stunning blonde in the open touring car pulled up and said ... ."), or we read the notice that says, "Dishwasher wanted, no experience necessary." "Experience" by and large does duty for things that have happened to us, events we have lived through, skills we have acquired, and the like, but Dewey's notion of experience as an entity with an ontological status all its own is a mare's nest and, I suspect, is at least partially planted in the tradition of Cartesianism that he wanted to abjure.

An ontology and metaphysics of experience fares no better than Bell's appeal to unanalyzable qualities, but it was evidently not the metaphysics of *Art as Experience* that affected American artists. Dewey's book is full of remarks to the effect that art belongs in the mainstream of life and not just museums, those "beauty parlors of civilization," and that artists should engage themselves in the fullness of life at all its levels. A remark such as "But one of the functions of art is precisely to sap the moralistic timidity that causes the mind to shy away from some materials and refuse to admit them into the clear and purifying light of perceptual consciousness" was welcomed as a justification of the artistic subjects dear to the Regionalists and to

---

8   Stewart Buettner, "John Dewey and the Visual Arts in America," *Journal of Aesthetics and Art Criticism* (Summer, 1975).

the muckraking and reforming tendencies of Depression era artists out to exalt the working classes and to portray the seamier underside of American life.

The remark just cited is a useful one for emphasizing the point that our understanding of an expression must be a function of the context of its use. We understand Dewey's statement in that we know how to use it, that is, we can describe situations in which it would have a use, but we do not understand what anyone means by it in abstraction from all specified contexts. The concerns of American artists in the 1930s provided one such context in which the statement could function as a defense of their themes and as an encouragement to go on with their artistic program. We can also easily imagine others. Such a statement—its anachronistic tone aside—could just as well have served as a defense of the introduction of Christian themes into the art of a late antiquity still dominated by paganism. Or it could have played a role in the debate about the increasing tendency to treat religious themes naturalistically in the fifteenth century by contrast to the otherworldly styles of the preceding periods. And doubtless other examples will not be wanting. Without some context that determines a use, Dewey's statement is quite empty and devoid of content.

If I am right that it was these various reflections and admonitions rather than the philosophical theory itself that made the impact on the American art scene, then it becomes clear that all those remarks are logically quite independent of any assumptions about the ontology of experience. That an artist should undertake to work in the way that he does or to concern himself with this or that subject matter neither follows from the contention that experience arises from tensions between a living organism and its environment nor presupposes it as a condition of intelligibility. Dewey's comments about the proper place and role of artists and art in society could be understood and advocated by anyone innocent of philosophical theory in general and his version of pragmatism in particular.

I have suggested that what Buettner calls art theories need have little about them that is theoretical in any interesting sense, and I have also suggested that philosophical theories of aesthetics are conceptual confusions and that when we try to untangle and apply them, they tend to turn into particular remarks and comments for particular occasions. This does not entail that there is no place for serious thinking, for rational reflection, even for philosophy, about matters of art and aesthetics; but it does mean that the kind of thinking and the kind of philosophy required must not take the form they have taken in so much of the aesthetic theory we are familiar with. What is wanted instead is, first, a closer look at the problems that a theory was generated to solve. Are these problems themselves perhaps the result of conceptual confusion, of a failure to understand something about the workings of our language? Are the problems really the kind that a theory can solve? (Do we really need a *theory* to tell us when something is a work of art or when one work is better than another?)

Along with raising questions such as these goes the need for conceptual clarification. There is, for example, a belief widely shared among philosophers that all human action and everything that is a product of intentional action requires *interpretation* if it is to be intelligible. But interpreting is something we have to do when we fail to understand what someone means or what he is up to when he speaks or acts. Interpretation has to stand in contrast to the immediate understanding, seeing, hearing, etc. of what is going on. Interpretation makes no sense unless there is a bedrock of more fundamental reaction (seeing, reading, hearing, understanding, etc.). If everything has to be interpreted, then we could never find our feet with our own cultural practices.

Examples of the importance of conceptual clarification in the philosophy of art and aesthetics can be multiplied many times over, but one of its most useful applications is in the sorting out of the different kinds of expressions found in theorizing and the different uses to which they can be put. We must be prepared to distinguish the conclusion of an argument from a grammatical remark, a conceptual issue from an empirical generalization, and expressions of advice, evaluation, intention, and so on from all the others. I have tried to do a certain amount of this in this paper, and it is in order to repeat a suggestion made earlier that it is only when such logical sorting out is done we can assess the merits of whatever is being said.

There is yet another project that may fall under the heading of philosophy, and that is taking a careful look at the place of art and its importance in our lives. What roles have the arts played in life in the past and what roles do they play now? What do we want from the arts, and what are their possibilities for entering into our lives in significant ways? These are questions that recent theory, especially analytical philosophy of art, has tended to ignore. These questions lead us into a kind of cultural criticism that is of the greatest importance, but one that must be carried out in the language that belongs to our ordinary life and functions in our day to day human relationships rather than in the jargon borrowed from some philosophical system that has no role in the very circumstances it is supposed to illuminate.

When we do aesthetics and the philosophy of art in the ways that I have just been describing, the inquiry has to begin with and eventually return to our actual commerce with art—and that includes the practices of artists and critics and all the rest of us who have any concern for that aspect of our lives. It follows from this that the philosopher doing aesthetic theory is also going to have to do a certain amount of Buettner's art theory; he is going to have to consider art in the ways that artists and critics and appreciators do.

When we look at this the other way round, we often find art theorists involved in what are really philosophical questions. Unfortunately it generally proves to be the kind of philosophy that springs from conceptual confusion rather than the kind that seeks to identify and diagnose confusion. An example of this is the critic Clement Greenberg's contention that "It seems to be a law of modernism ... that the conventions not essential to the viability of a medium be discarded as soon as they are recognized."[9] This looks suspiciously like the philosophical thesis that the various art forms have an essence, and the philosophical problems in that kind of view are well known. There is nothing to indicate that Greenberg was aware of

---

9   Clement Greenberg, "American-Type Painting," in *Art and Culture: Critical Essays* (Boston, 1961), p. 208.

his transition from explaining certain developments in the abstract painting of this century, i.e., art theory, to the move into philosophy, i.e., aesthetic theory.

I will end this paper with two pleas. The first is that discussions of art (or art theory, in Buettner's parlance) be disentangled from philosophical theory and that all who undertake to think seriously about art—artist, critic, historian, and philosopher—learn to recognize when they are taking that step into philosophy and conceptual confusion so that they can back out of it before they become trapped in whatever fly bottle they were headed into. The second plea is that all who undertake to think seriously about art be absolutely clear about what they are doing and prepare themselves to articulate it clearly, whether it be making empirical generalizations about history or styles, doing conceptual analysis, giving advice to artists or their public, or committing themselves to an artistic course of action.

Both of these recommendations chart a difficult course and call for resolve, for, as Wittgenstein pointed out, philosophy is a constant battle against the bewitchment of our intelligence by language.

Chapter 7

Literature, Philosophy and Nonsense

In this chapter I want to suggest a thesis about the relation between philosophy and literature and I will do this by an examination of the role of nonsense in some of the short stories of the French author Marcel Aymé.

Nonsense became a philosophical category only in the early twentieth century and was first introduced by, I believe, Bertrand Russell with the theory of types. It was the syntactical restrictions enjoined by the theory of types that allowed Russell to charge that many of the assertions of earlier philosophers were not simply false, but in fact made no sense. Nonsense was given a deeper dimension by Wittgenstein in the *Tractatus* with the distinction between the sayable and the unsayable: nonsense results from the attempt to say the unsayable, but, ironically, it was everything of importance in life that he believed to be comprehended under the latter. That aspect of the *Tractatus* was totally missed by logical positivism which sought to use the verification theory of meaning to distinguish the meaningful statements of empirical science from the nonsensical pseudo-statements of metaphysics. Wittgenstein went on to provide a still richer exploration of nonsense in the *Philosophical Investigations*[1] where he locates a craving for nonsense in certain deep aspects of our language and our life. It is this craving that he believes is responsible for much of traditional philosophy which, on his view, turns out to be grounded in conceptual confusion and therefore a kind of nonsense.

Given the fact that a good case can be made that the notion of meaning and all it implies for the distinction between sense and nonsense has been the primary concern of twentieth-century philosophy, at least Anglo-American philosophy, it is surprising that in their aesthetic studies the role that nonsense has played in literature has gone almost unnoticed by philosophers. Lewis Carroll's *Alice* books are, of course, the obvious exception to this, but the attention they have drawn has usually been directed toward picking out the philosophical theses and jokes rather than toward the larger possibilities of nonsense as a literary device.

It may not be so surprising that literary critics and commentators have not seen those same possibilities or have not even been aware of the existence of the kind of nonsense I want to call attention to. To be sure, literature has always recognized a garden variety of nonsense that exploits made-up words, silly situations, and unlikely juxtapositions exemplified by *Jabberwocky*, the "nonsense" verse of Edward Lear,

---

1   Ludwig Wittgenstein, *Philosophical Investigations*, 2nd edn G.E.M. Anscombe, trans. (New York, 1958.

and that American folk classic "I Was Born About Ten Thousand Years Ago."[2] What I have in mind, however, is rather different from that and can be illustrated by some of the short stories of Marcel Aymé.

Marcel Aymé (1902-1967) has not been widely read in the English-speaking world and very few of his seventeen novels, twelve plays, and eighty-three short stories have been translated into English. Aymé is generally considered to be a writer of what the French call *contes des merveilleux*, tales of the marvelous. What can be categorized generically as the marvelous has long been a staple of French literature. Since at least the twelfth century the literature of France has been populated by sorcerers, giants, ogres, fairies, and strange events. Literary historians have devised a number of ways of sorting out and classifying the various themes of these *contes des merveilleux*. Marcel Schneider, for one, distinguishes between fairy tales, horror tales, and fantasy literature.[3] In slicing up the domain of the marvelous it has not been recognized that one of its subdivisions belongs to a brand of nonsense. I want to direct attention to the literary and philosophical importance of that brand of nonsense and at the same time to call attention to an interesting author who has unfortunately been neglected by English-speaking readers.

Many of Aymé's stories clearly are *contes des merveilleux*. One of his best known is *"Le passe muraille,"*[4] "the man who could walk through walls." A clerk of modest and regular habits suddenly discovers that he has the ability to walk through walls unhindered. Worried by this derangement in his daily life, he went to the doctor who readily diagnosed his problem and prescribed two powders together with a regimen of overwork that would surely put him to rights again. He took one of the powders, but put the other aside and forgot about it. Meanwhile he began to learn that his new talent had certain advantages. He thrust his head through the wall of the office of his tyrannical boss and shouted imprecations at him. After a few repetitions of this the unfortunate man had to be taken to the mad house. He discovered that he could walk in and out of bank vaults and serve himself as he pleased. The headlines soon spoke of little else than the phantom bandit. He entered into an affair with a married woman and found it most convenient to walk directly through the wall into her bedroom. One day he suffered from a headache and so took some headache powders before going off to visit his lady love. Alas, however, it was not only a headache powder that he took, but the forgotten prescription as well. The additional dosage took effect just as he entered the wall and before he emerged on the other side. And he is still there lamenting the untimely end of his career.

---

2   I was born about ten thousand years ago, / And there's nothing in this world that I don't know. / I saw Peter, Paul, and Moses playing ring around the roses; / I can whip the guy who says it isn't so. (And so on.)

3   Marcel Schneider, *La littérature fantastique en France* (Paris, 1964). Schneider's book is a useful survey of the marvelous in French literature.

4   In *Le passe muraille* (Paris, 1943).

And then there is *Fiançailles*,[5] "The Betrothal." It seems that a woman had read so much Greek mythology that when her son was born he turned out to be a centaur. The father kept this shame hidden away from public view on his large estate and had him privately educated. One day when luncheon guests were strolling about the grounds they accidentally encountered the young centaur. The guests had a daughter—the first human female he had seen apart from his mother—and he was immediately smitten with her and she with him. An engagement was arranged on the spot and to celebrate the girl hoisted her skirts, climbed on the back of the centaur, and went for a trot around the estate. Both, needless to say, found the experience rather erotic. He seized the occasion to venture for the first time beyond the walls of the estate. Once beyond the grounds he had his first encounter with the realities of life when a passing policeman gave him a summons for indecent exposure. It was then that he spied a young mare in the pasture across the way. She was the first of her kind that he had ever seen and something deep was stirred in the other half of his nature. He threw his betrothed into the ditch and galloped off with the mare. Neither has been seen since.

Delightful as they are, it is not these stories that I want to talk about, but three others that treat, in a fast and loose manner, of the subject of time. These three are *La carte, Le décret*, and *Rechute*.[6] *La carte* is set in Paris during the German occupation. Shortages of nearly everything make life increasingly difficult and it is decided that in the interest of efficiency, time, like all else, should be rationed. Ration cards are issued. Strong and productive workers and those in necessary occupations are, naturally, given more days to exist per month than old people and those in less vital capacities. Prostitutes are allotted only seven days per month and Jews, regardless of age, sex, or occupation, are permitted to exist only a half day each month.

There are, of course, inconveniences in the new order brought about by the decree. An old man married to a young wife is in bed when his time period runs out. He returns to existence in the same place as before only to find himself between his wife and her more virile lover. In no time at all a black market in time cards has sprung up. Poor workers sell their cards to feed their families; the wealthy are buying them up and living more than their share. Some are able to amass enough tickets to live forty, fifty, even sixty days a month. Fortunately, however, another administrative decision soon cancels the program.

The story entitled *Le décret* also begins in wartime Paris. It has long been a custom each summer to set the clock ahead an hour or two to take advantage of the extra daylight, but now the authorities decide on a far bolder step. The war has become a terrible burden for all sides and so the warring powers agree—and it is a universal agreement—to set the clock ahead seventeen years in hopes that the war will have been over by that time. Once the decree takes effect it is found that the war is indeed over and fortunately another has not broken out.

---

5   In *En arrière* (Paris, 1950).

6   *La Carte* and *Le décret* are both published in *Le passe muraille*; *Rechute* is in *En arrière*.

The narrator must take a trip to a small rural town to visit an old friend who is ill. When he arrives in the town he is surprised to encounter German soldiers and upon enquiring for his friend is startled to learn that he is still a prisoner of war in East Prussia. He wonders whether the decree has somehow never been announced in this remote corner of the country, but then the truth begins to sink in and he realizes that he really is back in 1942. He returns to Paris to find it in the throes of the German occupation; he returns to an apartment house that hasn't been built yet and he must find his old place; and he returns to children that are still small and two of whom haven't been born yet. He sees people in the streets whose acquaintance he won't make for years. He remembers all the things that are going to happen. Little by little, however, these memories of the future begin to grow dim and before long all is as it was.

Rechute, unlike the other two, is not a story of the occupation. The Chamber of Deputies has just passed the "twenty-four" law making the year twenty-four months long. As soon as the law took effect everyone found himself exactly half of his previous age. Grandmother who was in her late sixties is now ready to go out on the town. The girl who is the principal character in the tale was eighteen and just engaged to be married; she wakes up to find herself nine years old and her fiancé thirteen. The army is suddenly composed of ten- and eleven-year-olds whose adult uniforms swallow them and who can scarcely carry their automatic weapons. All, however, retain the experiences and habits of mind of their former ages.

The girl's fiancé now scorns the child of nine for, as he says, between nine and thirteen there is an abyss and he reminds her that they are divided by certain physiological realities. Later on, with the aid of her brother, she forces him to reveal those physiological realities which turn out, alas for him, to be in proportion to his scrawny thirteen-year-old frame. As we should expect, the class of newly created children is restive, there is disorder in the streets, the army of children—let's not say "infantry"—cannot be relied upon, and eventually the twenty-four law is repealed and all is returned to where it was before.

Unlike the other stories, these three exploit a kind of conceptual nonsense and do not simply trade in fantasy and whimsy. It is the kind of nonsense that results from misusing the word "time" and its friends and relations by assimilating its grammar to that of some other concept. Thus time is spoken of in the way that we speak of commodities that can be bought and sold, rationed and hoarded, and so on. Or the notion of moving the clock up for summer time is assimilated to rescheduling an event or changing its venue. Or time is treated as if its dimensions were subject to legislation as the dimensions of the football pitch can be changed by action of the rules committee. What Aymé has given us in each of these tales is a *picture* of time, i.e., the word "time" is incorporated into a series of descriptions that are appropriate only for another notion.

What is perhaps the most familiar picture of time that we often make use of is that of a river upon which our life and the world is carried from past to future. As a poetic conceit this is certainly harmless and sometimes may even by apt. Gripped by this picture, nevertheless, we may be led to push the figure into doing duty for which it was not intended and begin to ask questions about it that we would ask about real rivers: how fast does time flow and might its rate change? Is there some high ground or vantage point from which we might see what is around the next bend in the future? Might we not turn the barque of our lives around and paddle back upstream? While these are exactly the questions we want to ask about rivers, they have no application to time; no sense has been given to them. An innocent trope can lead us to ask "What then is time?" and we find ourselves in nonsensical metaphysical speculation.

It is this very idea of a picture that is the basis of Wittgenstein's criticism of traditional philosophy in the *Philosophical Investigations*. Philosophical problems are said to arise when language *goes on holiday* [PI, §38] and thus is not doing its usual job, that is, when the use of certain expressions is mistakenly assimilated to that of others so that these expressions turn out to have no use, no role to play in either language or life. Thus are born those misleading analogies that are the stuff of philosophical theories, those pictures that hold us captive [PI, §109] and prevent us from seeing the world aright. In the stories I have just mentioned Marcel Aymé is exploiting—deliberately—exactly the kind of nonsense that Wittgenstein believes is the very stuff of philosophical theory.

The illusion of sense surrounds many of these events. We may think we can imagine a sudden transformation in which everyone has a body just like the one he had at half his age, or people vanishing for so many days each month and then reappearing. It is tempting to comprehend all this under the traditional category of fantasy and to think it is one with what the wicked witch does in changing the prince into a frog. We hide all the difficulties by whispering "Magic!"and think no more about it.

Whatever the intelligibility of any of that, the nonsense at work in the stories that I want to consider enters with the description of the goings-on as alterations in *time* brought about by legislative enactment. It is as if these descriptions are offered as explanations of the strange events: "Why is Josette in *Rechute* suddenly a little girl again?" we ask and are told that it is because they passed that law doubling the length of the year. It is important to focus our question on the right target. It is one thing to note that a piece of legislation cannot bring about a physical change, no act of Congress by itself can increase the length of the Mississippi River; that is an empirical truth. In addition to the legislative enactment it would require digging new channels and raising new levees. We can describe clearly what it is that the act of Congress cannot by itself bring about. Can a law nevertheless change the year? Our inclination is to say no. We can always divide the year into twenty-four rather than twelve months or decide to count two revolutions of the earth about the sun as one year instead of two, but that changes only how we count birthdays—recall the unfortunate chap in *The Pirates of Penzance* who was born on February 29 of a leap year—but that is not at issue and in any event temporal processes continue the same. (What would it be like if they didn't?) Since no other sense has been given to the expression "changing the year" we cannot say what it is that the piece of legislation is supposed not to be able to do.

That these stories of Aymé's are built around a piece of nonsense has not been recognized by his commentators. Jean-Louis Dumont, for example, says that "Aymé has found in the concept of time the possibility of a notion contrary to the one men have of it"[7] and again, "his intentions are neither to horrify nor terrify his reader; he simply wants to make him laugh by upsetting the natural order of things."[8] This is surely wrong. He has not presented us with another possibility at all nor has he upset the natural order which he would have to do by suggesting some alternative order. If he is talking nonsense, then he has removed all place for a new possibility or revised order of things. What we laugh at is the nonsense wrapped up in a picture that radiates the illusion of sense. Each of these stories is an extended conceptual joke.

Equally off the mark is Graham Lord's comment that *La carte* is in a part "a pseudo-philosophical glance at the relativity of time."[9] The relativity of time belongs to the esoteric reaches of physical theory and has nothing to do with Aymé's playing fast and loose with our ordinary ways of talking. To be sure, *Le décret* mentions several theories of time, including relativity, but that itself is all part of the joke.

Although it is not specifically about Marcel Aymé, the following remark of Marcel Schneider's is revealing:

> It is science itself which restores fantasy to the universe rationalized by the encyclopedists and from which the scientism of the 19th century had pretended to extort its secrets, not only in inventing prodigious machines and means of destruction which disorient thought, but also in rendering precarious, vacillating, and illusory all the certainties on which scientists had built their edifice and which serve as religious dogmas for modern man.[10]

Schneider is obviously referring to the replacement of Newtonian concepts of absolute space and time by Einstein's relativized ones, to Heisenberg's uncertainty principle and quantum theory with its particles that aren't anywhere or are two places at once, to Gödel's theorem, and the like. In other words, twentieth-century science is supposed to have done a great many of the very things that the fiction of fantasy has done. It is in this spirit that Graham Lord mentions à propos of Aymé, "this questioning of what is often regarded as stable and absolute." Jean Cathelin, for another, sees him as writing a kind of science fiction, only doing it better than the likes of Arthur C. Clark and Isaac Asimov.[11]

In the next paragraph after these reflections on modern science Schneider suggests that the French may have something to learn from Lewis Carroll whom they had hitherto dismissed as merely a children's writer. The juxtaposition of these topics implies that Lewis Carroll may be one of those who have put the conceptual

---

7   Jean Louis Dumont, *Marcel Aymé et le merveilleux* (Paris, 1967), p. 122. (All translations from the French are mine.)

8   Dumont, p. 177.

9   Graham Lord, *The Short Stories of Marcel Aymé* (Nedlands, 1980), p. 48.

10 Schneider, p. 391.

11 Jean Cathelin, *Marcel Aymé* (Paris, 1958), p. 145.

certitudes of our world in doubt. This has to be a misreading of the adventures of Alice. We recognize Carroll's nonsense as nonsense precisely because we see it against a background of sense. Carroll's point in playing with nonsense is not to put anything in doubt or to entertain any new conceptual possibilities, but is to remind us where sense is to be found.[12] And so it is, I think, with Marcel Aymé. His play with the nonsense about time is intended to remind us of what the conceptual restraints on our lives really are.

Everyone is agreed that something more, quite a bit more, is going on in these stories in addition to the time fantasy. By and large the critics are right about the nature of this something more—at any rate, it is not necessary to dispute any of the details of it with them. Of *La carte* Cathelin says:

> the satire here is at once social, philosophical and political; the fantasy here serves only to highlight more intensely character traits in a time of penury, of an inhuman and ferocious bureaucratism which believes that in order to find a solution to no matter what problem it is enough to regulate something.[13]

It is worth pausing to add that one of the explicit themes of *La carte* is the resentment of the narrator, a writer, at being included in the decree along with these other "useless" ones. Writers are characterized as among the "consumers whose maintenance is not compensated for by any real return." The narrator admits that he would have expected the decree to apply to painters and musicians. Aymé's playful but not quite unobtrusive proposition is that writing (and reading) are in danger of being understood as uncompensated, or improperly compensated, consumptions of time. We might reasonably take this story as making an issue, however playfully, about the importance of writing and about whether, in particular, it is worth the time that it takes.[14]

It is much the same with *Le décret*. The nonsense about remembering the future directs attention to something important about life and human relations. Think how our relation to another is altered when we know what is going to happen to him; that the company has, for example, already decided to fire him and you are bound not to tell him. The narrator's reflection that "youth which has nothing to learn is not youth" is a reminder that our concept of youth is not simply a chronological one, a

---

12 Or perhaps he should be understood sometimes as pointing out the mischief that can be occasioned by inattention to sense and conceptual restraint. The White Queen, for example, favors a system of justice in which the punishment, i.e., imprisonment, comes first, followed by the trial, with the crime coming last. And it is all the better if the crime is not committed at all. This, of course, is to make nonsense of the notion of punishment, not to mention the notion of justice, since the concept of punishment is logically linked to that of wrong doing. We can, nevertheless, imagine imprisonment for crimes not committed—actual examples unfortunately abound. This bears a suspicious resemblance to the idea of "preventive detention" advocated by some upholders of the law in the name of justice.

13 Cathelin, p. 146.

14 I owe this understanding of the story to Timothy Gould.

matter of from these years to those, but is in addition the concept of a moral, that is, a human condition, a stage on life's way, if you would. This very same reminder is what makes *Rechute* such a wonderful commentary on the nature of childhood and the logical conditions that make the relation of parent to child what it is. The authority of the parent over the child is not merely a matter of discrepancies in size and physical competence, but is in part a function of the moral incompleteness of the child who must be guided and led and pushed and prodded not only into the paths of righteousness, but also into satisfying the daily necessities of life. This is brought home to us by representing the moral competence of the adult clothed in the body of a child. The unfortunate composite being is forced to submit to the direction and correction appropriate to a child and the result can only appear as degradation to the adult in child's clothing.

Aymé's stories must not be understood as offering speculative theses about the nature of time, theses which careful examination show to be nonsense. The stories do not advance theories that could demand examination independently on their own merits. Aymé is using nonsense deliberately to say something about the human condition. What is going on in his stories must be distinguished from the inadvertent introduction of nonsense into literature where the aim is to present a piece of philosophy. Sartre's *La Nausée* is a case in point. There is little doubt that Sartre meant *La Nausée* to present metaphysical theses about the nature of the world, that everything in the world is contingent and therefore human practices have no justification, and so on. As philosophy this is elementary confusion and scarcely worth the effort of straightening out. In using his novel to state philosophical theses Sartre falls victim to all the snares and delusions of that kind of philosophy. Fortunately for his readers it is possible to take the novel as offering something other than metaphysics. When we read it carefully in order to follow the fortunes of its hero we sense that Roquentin's worries about necessity and contingency, being and becoming, may be better understood as the manifestation of his dissatisfaction with the lack of direction in his own life and his repugnance at the bourgeois culture of Bouville. What is presented as philosophy becomes instead the vehicle for the expression of what in the most general terms can be described as a mood or frame of mind and is thus not really philosophy at all.

What I have been saying about philosophical theses in literature is in direct opposition to a view of the relation between the two held by Peter Jones. In *Philosophy and the Novel* Jones says, "I do not examine the literary embodiment of the philosophical views I abstract from the text, ... I do not consider the particular contexts within the novel which occasion the philosophical utterances ... ."[15] When we look closely at the context in which those supposedly philosophical remarks occur we do not find them conveying philosophical theses at all, but instead expressing or describing some observation about the course of the world or human relations. It is only when they are taken out of context that they can appear to be *theses*.

---

15 *Philosophy and the Novel* (Oxford, 1975), p. 148.

It will be instructive to end with a comparison of Aymé's way with nonsense and the way of a philosopher who had learned much from Wittgenstein about how to expose nonsense by telling stories. I am referring to O.K. Bouwsma who raised to an art form the technique of teasing and tickling us with nonsense by telling stories intended to produce philosophical insight, a technique that others practice at their peril. Aymé never explains to us that his nonsense is nonsense. He lays out a situation with a perfectly straight face and proceeds to talk about things just as if they did make sense and were the most ordinary in the world. It must dawn on us that it is all nonsense. To get the point we must already have a nose for it, a quickened sense of the queer, as it were. Aymé, after all, is teaching us about people and not about nonsense. He is teaching us about people through the medium of the nonsense of conceptual jokes.

Aymé's literary practice is thus rather different from Bouwsma's philosophical practice, the fact notwithstanding that Bouwsma's practice is also very much a literary one. We can see this in his article "Descartes' Evil Genius"[16] where the Evil Genius undertakes to deceive the innocent and unsuspecting Tom. His first evil essay in that direction is to make everything out of paper. For a time Tom is deceived into thinking that the flowers, his beloved Millie, and even his own body are real, but before long he is undeceived by suspicious crinklings and tearings. Bouwsma makes it explicit that this story trades on our ordinary understanding and familiar use of words such as "deception," "illusion," "real," and the like; in this part of the story we find whimsy, but not nonsense.

Having failed in his first attempt the Evil Genius tries again and this time succeeds, but only too well. All conceivable tests for flowers and Millie turn out positive. The Evil Genius suggests to Tom that nevertheless he is being fooled about all those things, but Tom naturally fails to understand his evil insinuations. The criterion of reality and, consequently, of deception being invoked by the Evil Genius now proves to reside in a sense possessed only by Tom's Adversary. In other words, he does not mean what we mean when we speak of real things and deceptions and their ilk and, furthermore, by the terms of the story we can never know what he means. Now the nonsense has entered and Bouwsma can point out to us how Descartes' talk of the possibility of total illusion is the result of the misuse of language—our language—and that it is really without sense. Bouwsma has used these stories to instruct us in the nature of nonsense, how it can get started and the mischief it can work.

Bouwsma, following Wittgenstein, sees the task of the philosopher as one of turning disguised nonsense into patent nonsense [PI, §464]. The point of this exercise is not merely to remove impediments to theorizing or to permit the beauty of clarity to shine through, but is to remove impediments to seeing the world aright, to seeing other people and ourselves aright and this kind of understanding has much to do with how we are to live our lives. And, I would add, with how we are to allow literature to enter our lives.

---

16 In *Philosophical Essays* (Lincoln, 1965).

In his stories Marcel Aymé exploits patent nonsense, but it is nonsense that passes for neither philosophical theory nor philosophical therapy. Anyone who has developed a philosopher's nose for the use and misuse of language is in a position to distinguish what Aymé is doing in these tales from fantasy and the marvelous and to note its conceptual nature as well as its kinship with the confusions of traditional philosophical theory. And especially are we now in a position to appreciate how this species of nonsense can be a vehicle for conveying important insights about human beings and their lives and problems.

There may not be enough literary examples of the kind of conceptual nonsense I have been talking about to justify identifying it as a distinct genre, nevertheless there is a significant role for it to play in literature. If this recognition of this role has no other result, it should at least lead us to rethink the spectrum of possible relations between literature and philosophy.

Chapter 8

Charles Le Brun: Theory, Philosophy and Irony

The reputation of Charles Le Brun (1619-1690, *Le Premier Peintre du Roi*, theoretician, Director of the Royal Academy of Painting and Sculpture, Director of the Gobelins) has not fared well. Already by 1680 younger painters no longer found in his teaching the ideals they wished to follow.[1] Later writers criticized the theories and practice of Le Brun for their sterility. It was his views about expression and emotion that drew the greatest ire. André Fontaine, for example, said that it will be "the unpardonable error of Le Brun to give recipes for representing at one's pleasure *simple love, admiration or faith* and to freeze forever what is most mobile and most individual in the human face."[2] John Pope-Hennessy echoes this charge when he speaks of how, in the practice of the Academy, Raphael was "academicized" and how the training in the Academy was based on copying. He goes on to describe Le Brun's lecture on expression as a "harangue"[3] and adds that the line of thought about Raphael "eventuated in Lebrun's notorious handbook on the expression of emotion in the visual arts ... ."[4] The "academicizing" criticism is echoed by Louis Dimier when he says of the style of seventeenth-century classical French painting that "Vouet had introduced it, Poussin made a discipline of it, LeBrun an administration."[5]

It is not my intention nor is it within my competence to redeem the reputation of Le Brun for the present day art world. I do believe, however, that it is probable that when his work is seen in the context of the problems of his century it will be found to deserve better than it has received. I shall, then, first try to describe what that context was and how Le Brun responded to it and then I shall use Le Brun's theories as a way of calling attention to a philosophical dimension of the problem the visual arts face in the representation of human beings and human action.

---

1 For the reaction of his contemporaries against Le Brun see André Fontaine, *Les Doctrines d'Art en France: Peintures, Amateurs, Critiques, de Poussin à Diderot* (Paris, 1909), Ch. IV.

2 Ibid., p. 30. (All translations from the French are mine.)

3 John Pope-Hennessy, *Raphael: The Wrightsman Lectures* (New York U.P., 1970), p. 245.

4 Ibid., p. 246.

5 Louis Dimier, *Histoire de la peinture francaise du retour de Vouet à la mort de Le Brun, 1627 à 1690*, 2 vols (Paris and Brussels, 1926-1927), p. xii.

II

At the beginning of the seventeenth century France had known a long history of Gothic art, but the renaissance developments in Italy had passed her by. What we know as French classical painting had to be, as it were, created from scratch for it did not grow naturally out of the older tradition. Marc Fumaroli has pointed out that at the beginning of the seventeenth century there was no patronage of the arts by the wealthy and powerful, no enlightened art lovers and no fashion for collecting.[6] In 1617 Marie de Medici had to seek outside of France for a painter to decorate the Luxembourg Palace and called upon Rubens. Rubens, however, only passed through France and while he left a few paintings he left no students nor other real influence.

Painting was controlled by the masters of what were still essentially mediaeval guilds. Some of these were no more than stone polishers and decorators. If a painter could not pass the guild examinations, he could not paint and sometimes they even went so far as to confiscate the paintings of a dissident.[7] A contemporary observer expresses acidly what must have been the common view of French artists:

> In France the fine arts were given over to the opprobrium of a domination which degraded them, enslaved them to a troop of ignorant and greedy examiners, base artisans without distinction and without merit: reduced, in a word, to a point of humiliation and discouragement which could only be contrary to all aspiration and all progress.[8]

A number of French artists had gone to Rome and brought back conceptions of both the antique and what was then modern painting and many had long wanted their own school of painting to rival what was going on in Italy under the Carraci. This vision of equality with Italy was expressed by Corneille in a rather turgid poem published in 1653 with the title "La poesie à la peinture: en faveur de l'academie de peintres illustres" in which poetry addresses its sister art of painting and foresees a great future for it as the result of the founding of the academy. Painting is to follow in the footsteps of poetry and soar over the barrier of the Alps so that the Tiber will meet the Seine.

What was wanted was a *national* painting which would be the expression of a united France, not to mention the majesty of *Le Roi*, and this painting would naturally have to be centered in Paris. This was clearly part of the general movement of the century toward political centralization that was replacing both the older feudal

---

6   Pierre Rosenberg, *France in the Golden Age: Seventeenth Century French Paintings in American Collections* (New York, n.d.), "Introduction," p. 5.

7   See Dimier, Vol. II, pp. 38ff.

8   *Mémoires pour servir à l'histoire de l'Academie royale de peinture*, quoted by Jouin, p. 6. The manuscript bears no name, but Jouin surmises that Henri Testelin was the author. See Jouin, pp. 69-70 fn.

political fragmentation and regional cultural fragmentation. Louis Hourticq tells us that "the Royal Academy was one of the organs of this spiritual centralization."[9]

The Royal Academy was founded in 1648. Colbert was given the title of vice-protector in 1661 and as a result of the minister's patronage Le Brun became the director in 1663. There were really two reasons for the establishment of the Academy: to free painting and painters from the tyranny of the guilds and to establish the national painting that so many sought. As Jouin put it, "The foundation of the Academy was the charter of freedom of French art."[10] The two are, of course, connected. There can be no national painting before painters are free to pursue painting as an independent art and before there is far better instruction than was available under the old apprenticeship system of the guilds. The new teaching was to be carried on by regular lessons and would include the systematic study of anatomy and perspective.

This new charter of freedom, we might remark, did not imply that uniquely twentieth-century conception of freedom that would give leave to painters "to do their own thing." It meant, rather, that they could now paint as it was then thought that painters ought to paint even if that entailed that their art served royal purposes; there were then no other causes to tempt them into revolt against the establishment. The establishment was then barely established!

Hourticq makes an important point about the problems that faced the founders of the Academy when it came to a matter of working out a program for the new teaching:

> Our academicians were men of reflection and conscience. When, on the invitation of Colbert, they undertook to found a curriculum, they realized that they had nothing to teach. Then they applied themselves to constructing a doctrine. So much probity appears naive to us; their lectures amuse our skepticism. This zeal, however, does them honor.[11]

Fontaine makes clear the importance of the Academy as an institution for teaching and that Le Brun's concern as its director was with development of students rather then the management of the artists charged with working for the king. It was at Colbert's insistence that the monthly lectures were recorded and their results made available to serve as positive precepts for young students.[12]

It is in the context of these historical circumstances and their attendant problems that Le Brun ought to be judged. If his theories and precepts turn out to be artistic dead ends, he was, nevertheless, trying to meet very real and pressing problems in the training of artists and the practice of art; his zeal docs him honor. Objections to Le Brun and his academic curriculum such as Pope-Hennessy's mentioned above overlook the problems the French seventeenth-century painter had to face. Copying

---

9   Louis Hourticq, *De Poussin à Watteau ou des Origines de l'Ecole Parisienne de Peinture* (Paris, n.d.), p. 9.

10 Jouin, p. 6.

11 Hourticq, p. 9.

12 Fontaine, pp. 62-3.

may be ultimately sterile, but one has to start somewhere. The objection to Le Brun's account of Raphael is no more than *ad hominem*. That this is the wrong way to talk about painting can't be demonstrated by a sneer. What is wrong, after all, in being interested in expression? It is to certain aspects of those much criticized theories that I want now to turn.

III

Among Le Brun's own theoretical precepts is his recommendation that the painter take his models either from the antique or from Raphael. By borrowing the proportions of the antique nature can be improved upon and Le Brun apparently thought that it stood in need of improvement. He believed that drawing is more important than color and in the developing dispute over the relative importance of the two, the quarrel between the Poussinists and the Rubenists, he would certainly have sided with the former. What took pride of place in his thinking, however, was the concept of expression and that is the aspect of his theory that I want to discuss.

The concept of expression that concerned the artists and theorists of the seventeenth century was not the concept of expression that developed in the nineteenth and twentieth centuries out of the Romantic Movement. Le Brun was not at all concerned that the painter represent his subjects as filtered through his own emotional reactions; that would involve a conception of the artist whose time had not yet come. Expression in the earlier French context was primarily a matter of how the artist represented the emotion of the figures in his painting. Fontaine has pointed out that Poussin stressed the importance of showing the emotions that moved his characters by the way he painted their gestures, attitudes and facial expressions. He describes this concern as an "altogether French need for clarity in the exposition of the subject" and then adds that "Expression was thus particularly studied at the Academy both because it was a tradition in the art of Poussin and because it corresponded to a penchant in the national spirit."[13] Whatever we may say about Gallic needs and spirit, the influence of Poussin is evident.

Le Brun's theory of expression was presented in a lecture to the Academy in 1667 and published in 1698, eight years after his death, under the title *L'Expression générale et particulière.*[14] He characterizes expression as a:

> naive and natural resemblance of the things that we have to represent: it is necessary and enters into all parts of the painting, and a picture does not know how to be perfect without Expression, it is that which marks the true character of each thing; it is by it that we distinguish the nature of bodies; that figures seem to have movement, and all that which is feigned appears to be true.

---

13 Fontaine, p. 68.

14 The published text can be found in Henri Jouin, *Conférences de l'Academie Royale de Peinture et de Sculpture* (Paris, 1883) where it is printed in parallel columns along with Le Brun's earlier unpublished manuscript. The two are virtually identical.

Shortly after he adds that "Expression is also a part [of painting] which marks the movements [agitations] of the soul, that which renders the effects of passion visible." The organization of the lecture reflects the title: it begins with general remarks about expression and the nature of emotion and then goes on to describe in more or less detail the bodily manifestations of at least twenty two particular passions.

In addition to the lecture on expression there was another on physiognomy in which he defines that notion as "the rule or law of nature by which the affections of the soul are related to the form of the body: so that they are fixed and permanent signs that make known the passions of the soul." This seemingly curious piece, which really appeals to an old line of thought, contends that there are useful analogies between the physiognomy of animals and that of men: to the extent that we resemble animals, we can infer that we share the virtues and vices of their characters.[15]

There are two assumptions underlying Le Brun's theories of expression and physiognomy. The first is the dualist assumption that the body and the soul are two distinct things. The emotions and passions are therefore thought of as movements and agitations that occur in the soul. These inner states of the soul somehow produce movements of the body which are said to be marks or signs of the inner conditions. The second assumption is that the connection between the "inner" passion and the "outer" manifestation can be explained by principles borrowed largely from Descartes' *Passions of the Soul.* Some of Le Brun's descriptions of the particular passions are close paraphrases of Descartes' own descriptions although in places he diverges significantly from Descartes.[16]

IV

The idea that bodily movements and physiognomy are the outward signs of the emotions has a long history in thought about art. Xenophon reports a conversation between Socrates and the painter Parrhasius in which both agree that painting is the representation of visible objects. Socrates then asks whether the painter can represent the disposition of the mind of his figures and Parrhasius replies that this cannot be done because it is not a visible thing. Socrates goes on to remark that dispositions of the mind as well as states of character "show themselves both in the looks and gestures of men, whether they stand or move."[17]

In an uncharacteristic passage appended to the *Prior Analytics* Aristotle talks about how it is possible to recognize natures or states of character:

---

15 Apparently there was never a complete manuscript of this lecture. An abridgement is printed in Jouin, *Charles Le Brim.*

16 Louis Hourticq, *De Poussin à Watteau*, has juxtaposed several of Le Brun's description with those of Descartes, pp. 55ff. Stephanie Ross, "Painting the Passions: Charles LeBrun's *Conférence sur l'Expression,*" *Journal of the History of Ideas* (Jan.-March, 1984), has detailed the similarities and especially the differences between the two.

17 Xenophon, *Memorabilia of Socrates*, trans. by J.S. Watson (New York, 1886), III, x, 1. I am indebted to Göran Sörbom for bringing this passage to my attention.

Recognizing natures is possible, if someone concedes that the body and soul are altered simultaneously by such affections as are natural [i.e. such things as passions and appetites] ... Now, if this be granted, and in addition that there is a single sign of a single thing, and if we are able to grasp the affection and the sign peculiar to each kind of animal, then we will be able to recognize natures.[18]

He goes on to add the hypothetical examples of the lion possessing both courage and generosity.

Robin Smith comments on this passage:

The art of physiognomies was evidently established before Aristotle's time, in the fifth century: Alexander of Aphrodisias (*De Fato* 6) recounts an anecdote of an encounter between Socrates and the physiognomonist Zopyrus. A pseudo-Aristotelian (but probable Peripatetic) treatise with the title *Physiognomonics* has come down to us. As both this passage and that treatise make clear, the gist of this 'art' was a system of associations between anatomical characteristics and traits of character, based in large part on purported associations found in animals.[19]

In the *Physiognomonics* we read that "Mental character is not independent of and unaffected by bodily processes, but is conditioned by the state of the body; and contrariwise the body is sympathetically influenced by affections of the soul."[20] The notion of soul at work here is clearly not Aristotle's own.

The author lists three methods of investigating physiognomies. The most interesting is the third which "took as its basis the characteristic facial expressions which are observed to accompany different conditions of mind, such as anger, fear, erotic excitement, and all the other passions."[21] In remarking on this method the author suggests that the conditions of the mind in question are not so much particular feelings felt on particular occasions, but rather more or less permanent states of character. The brave man and the impudent man, however, may share a common mien and the look is therefore not a sure means of determining the character of the person. He does add that: "Gesture and the varieties *of facial expression* are interpreted by their affinity to different emotions: if, for instance, when disagreeably affected, a man takes on the look which normally characterizes an angry person, irascibility is signified."[22] The marks of character described in this curious work are not only gestures and facial expressions, but also the general build and condition of the body as well as such things as skin complexion, nature and amount of hair, muscle tone and so on. Much emphasis is also placed on the analogies between human character and animal characteristics. The various species of animals are each supposed to have

---

18 Aristotle, *Prior Analytics*, trans. by Robin Smith (Indianapolis/Cambridge, 1989), 70b, 6-14.

19 Smith, pp. 227-8.

20 *Physiognomonica*, trans. T. Loveday and E.S. Forster, in *The Works of Aristotle*, Vol. VI, W.D. Ross, ed., 805a, 1-3.

21 805a, 28-30.

22 806b, 29-32.

their own character, e.g., the lion is brave and the hare is timid. The physical and physiognomic features of these beasts have their parallels in people which thereby indicate corresponding human characters. These connections are, needless to say, extraordinarily fanciful.

Such ideas inherited from the ancient world had an obvious effect on renaissance thinking about art. Alberti, for example, expressed what was apparently a common view at the time when he said that "movements of the soul are made known by movements of the body."[23] and Leonardo seems to suggest a similar sentiment in his remark that "that figure is most admirable which by its actions best expresses the passion that animates it."[24]

When the seventeenth century takes up the matter of physiognomy what we find is not simply a catalogue of associations to be found between states of mind and bodily states, but attempts to provide theoretical explanations of the nature of the two and the associations between them.

V

The theory in question is, of course, that of Descartes as presented in his *Les Passions de L'Ame*. That treatise assumes and makes explicit reference to the ontological dualism of body and soul and one of its burdens is to explain, for the case of emotion, what the interrelationship of the two is. Descartes defines the passions as "the perceptions, or sentiments, or emotions of the soul, that we connect particularly to it which are caused, kept up and fortified by some movement of the spirits."[25] The emotions, then, have physiological causes and in their turn have effects upon the body of which the principal one is "that they incite and dispose [men's] souls to want those things for which they prepare their bodies: so that the feeling of fear incites the desire to flee, that of boldness to want to fight, and so on."[26] Consonant with this is the statement that the natural role of the passions is "to incite the soul to consent and contribute to the actions that can serve to conserve the body, or to render it in some way more perfect."[27] I shall return to this point about the connection between emotion and action.

Descartes' theoretical project of explaining the passions and correlating them with physiology and physiognomy as well as the older program of correlating character with physiognomy presupposes that states of mind and states of the body are only contingently related. If the program is to work, therefore, the physiognomy

23 Leon Battista Alberti, *On Painting*, trans. by John R. Spencer (New Haven and London, 1966), p. 77.

24 *The Notebooks of Leonardo Da Vinci*, ed. by Jean Paul Richter, II vols. (New York, 1970), Vol. I, p. 292, §584. The work was originally published in 1883.

25 *Les Passions De L'Ame*, in Charles Adam and Paul Tannery, *Oeuvres de Descartes*, Vol. XI (Paris: Leopold Cerf, 1909), Article XXVII.

26 Article XL.

27 Article CXXXVII.

has to be described in terms that are logically or conceptually independent of the description of the state of the soul. The physiognomic descriptions offered by the author of the *Physiognomonica* do not always satisfy this demand. "Grief and joy," he says, "are states of the soul, and everyone knows that grief involves a gloomy and joy a cheerful countenance,"[28] but "gloomy" and "cheerful" already carry emotional freight. Some of the other descriptions, however, do satisfy the condition, e.g., coarse hair as a mark of bravery. Nor do all of Descartes' descriptions meet the condition. We can speak of changes in the color of the skin without begging any questions, but reference to tears, groans and sighs are already emotionally laden and can hardly be independent signs of the passions.

There is a further difficulty in trying to understand how such a project is supposed to get on. The assumption is that a passion or state of character is one thing and its bodily manifestation is something else. Parrhasius says that the mind cannot be represented since it is not a visible thing. This suggests there is something like an incipient theory at work demanding that the mind and its emotional states be thought of as "private objects." It entails the claim that whether a person is experiencing a certain emotion cannot be determined empirically. This makes it impossible to know that this person is, say, angry and, consequently, to know that these facial expressions, postures and gestures are the signs of that anger. To establish any sort of correlation between emotions and their signs we must have access to both and this access is just what is ruled out by the private-object picture. Conceived in this way the project cannot get off the ground.

The confusion in that way of regarding things ought to be sufficiently well understood so that no rehearsal of it is needed here and that aspect of the question need not detain us. If we reject the philosophical picture of mental privacy as conceptual confusion, as we must, and fall back upon our actual understanding of people uncorrupted by theoretical obstructions, we can salvage the intelligibility of the project. We can thus get on with investigating characteristic expressions and gestures, looking for regularities and correlations, and the rest. Whether any useful correlations or generalizations will turn up is quite another matter.

Descartes' theory does not demand that each particular emotion in the soul generate a unique set of physiological and physiognomic responses and expressions. The principal vehicles of emotional expression (signs of the passions) are "the actions of the eyes and face, changes of color, tremblings, languor, fainting, laughter, tears, groans, and sighs."[29] In the same section he makes clear that various particular combinations of these manifestations are only the customary or usual accompaniments of a passion. Le Brun, by contrast, when he comes to detail the expressions of particular passions always does it in terms of a unique collection of eyebrow raisings, lip curls and the like. He illustrated his claim about the passions with the notorious series of paintings of faces showing how each of the emotions

---

28 *Physiognomonica*, 808b, 11-17.
29 Article CXII.

was supposed to look and how each was supposed to be represented by aspiring painters.

In another lecture at the Academy Henri Testelin criticized Le Brun on this point by stating "that it is not possible to prescribe precisely all the signs of the different passions because of the diversity of form and temperament ... ."[30] Fontaine remarks that these considerations should have refuted Le Brun, but they did not stop the publication of his lecture going through several editions.[31] A recent writer has described Le Brun's position as "preposterous."[32] It is, of course, preposterous, but its failings are not all that much worse than are those of what is taken to be the alternative. The dispute is represented as between one party who believes that there is a range of variation in the bodily expressions of a given emotion and another party claiming that there is a set of unique manifestations for each emotion. There is, however, a fundamental mistake made by both sides that reduces the details of this quarrel to lesser importance.

VI

The problem for the painter is how his figures are to be represented so that their emotional states and the actions that stem from them can be readily recognized by the viewer. It is this connection with action that Descartes had recognized, but did not develop. This problem is really parasitic upon our relations with people in real life. Our ability to recognize the emotional state of another depends upon a number of factors, only one of which involves the facial expressions and gestures that preoccupy both Descartes and Le Brun. Of equal, if not greater, importance are the idiosyncrasies of the person in question, the situation in which the person acts or reacts and the history of the person and his relation to the situation. It is this context in which the person and his expressions must be seen that is critical. Neither Descartes nor Le Brun makes any mention of context. It is this failure to take context into account rather than his uniqueness view that vitiates Le Brun's work on the passions.

We are reminded of the importance of context by the following remark of Wittgenstein's:

> I see a picture which represents a smiling face. What do I do if I take the smile now as a kind one, now as malicious? Don't I often imagine it with a spatial and temporal context which is either one of kindness or of malice? Thus I might supply the picture with the fancy that the smiler was smiling down on a child at play, or again on the suffering of an enemy.[33]

---

30 Henri Testelin, "L'expression genérale et particulière," in Jouin, *Conférences*, p. 164.

31 *Les Doctrines d'Art en France*, p. 71.

32 Stephanie Ross, "Painting the Passions," p. 25.

33 Ludwig Wittgenstein, *Philosophical Investigations*, §539, 2nd edn, G.E.M. Anscombe, trans. (New York, 1958).

So it is with several of Le Brun's faces that are supposed to represent the particular emotions. When we look at these pictures we sense that perhaps the depictions of "anger" and "fright" are quite interchangeable and that his "contemplation" might do just as well in place of "sadness." "Laughter," to be sure, could hardly take the place of "fear," but some ambiguity is bound to remain until we see the face in a definite setting.

There is a fascinating irony in the fact that when Le Brun discusses expression in the painting of others it is of the greatest importance for him to describe the figures in their contexts. The first of the lectures to the Academy was given by Le Brun in 1667 on Raphael's painting of St. Michael (*Saint Michael Overcoming the Demon*, sometimes called *St. Michael and the Devil* or simply *St. Michael*). He says that the defeated "demon, who lies as if crushed beneath [St. Michael], bites his tongue and grinds his teeth: and you see in his red and inflamed eyes the marks of his rage and his fury."[34] This makes it clear that what specifies the facial contortions as the "marks" of anger are the circumstances of his defeat at the hands of his Enemy.

In a later lecture on Poussin's *Israelites Gathering Manna in the Desert* his descriptions of the various figures always place them in some context and show how their responses are directed to some object:

> In the old man who is lying behind these two women and who looks up and extends his arms, and in the young man who is showing him where the manna is falling, the painter has sought to show two very different spiritual movements; for the young man, filled with joy in seeing the fall of this extraordinary nourishment, shows it to the old man without thinking about where it comes from. But the old man, wiser and more judicious, instead of looking at the manna, raises his eyes to heaven and adores the divine Providence that has spread it on the earth. ... .
>
> You can recognize in effect the goodness in that woman dressed in yellow in her inviting the young man who holds a basket full of manna to carry it to the old man behind her, believing that he needs to be helped.
>
> By the girl who looks up and holds her dress spread out he has expressed the delicacy and the disdainful humour of the sex which believes that everything wished for must come to it; that is why she has not taken the trouble to stoop over to pick up the manna, but receives it from heaven as if it were distributed only for her.[35]

Rensselaer Lee has spoken disparagingly of this description of the Poussin as a:

> discourse in which, it is true, some psycho-physiological commentary on expression is present, but in which the speaker is more particularly concerned with illustrating how diversely the characters in the pictorial drama react to the cause of their emotion; ... .[36]

---

34 Jouin, *Conférences*, p. 2. Le Brun's lecture is reported by Felibien.

35   Jouin, *Conférences*, p. 58.

36 Rensselaer W. Lee, *Ut Pictura Poesis: The Humanist Theory of Painting* (New York, 1967), p. 29.

Lee is calling attention to Le Brun having largely abandoned his theoretical position about physiognomy as the sign of emotion for an account in terms of context. Both the irony of the situation and the importance of it, however, escape him. If the aim of the painter is expression, that is, to show the emotions and how they move his subjects, then Le Brun's good sense takes over from his theory and his descriptions point in exactly the right direction: expression is not simply physiognomy, but physiognomy seen in context. Consequently Lee's remark about the subjects reacting to the cause of their emotion is odd. It is difficult to see what this reaction would be other than the emotion itself: the young man reacts to the cause of his joy with joy!

Painting aims at many things, but one of its aims was, and for some still is, the representation of men in action. The understanding and description of human action, what a person is doing, requires a conceptually connected web of circumstances, character, emotions, intentions, motives and the like, none of which can be understood in isolation from the others. The painter of the human must not only be familiar with the characteristic expressions, the looks, postures and gestures, of people, but must also understand how to place his personages in a context that will reveal the character of those looks. Le Brun was struggling with how to do this. Perhaps he did not succeed, but his failure serves to remind us what the artistic problem is and how the understanding of that problem demands philosophical, i.e., conceptual, clarification of the very idea of human emotion and its expression.

Chapter 9

Architecture, Expression and the Understanding of a Culture

I

Geoffrey Scott begins his classic *The Architecture of Humanism* with a quotation from that intriguing diplomat and amateur of the arts, Sir Henry Wotton, in which Wotton adapts a line from Vitruvius: "Well-building hath three Conditions: Commoditie, Firmenes, and Delight."[1] I also think that Wotton's remark makes a good place to begin.

By commodity I assume we can understand the demand that a building must be arranged so that it fulfills its function and the human activities that it was intended to shelter can be carried on there in a useful fashion. A building is firm if it can stand up and the roof doesn't leak. From our modern point of view I suppose we can adjust the idea of firmness to include the demand that the mechanical systems work, that the wiring, plumbing, heating, and ventilating are all up to snuff, the thing meets the fire codes and so on. Later writers would include Wotton's commoditie and firmeness under the general heading of utility.

Pleasure can be understood to refer to all that the eighteenth century would say makes a building beautiful and to what would eventually be called the aesthetic character of the building, including its setting and its prospects although we must remember that the term "aesthetic" was not coined until more than a century after Wotton wrote about architecture.

It was because architecture must unite delight with the utilitarian aspects of commodity and firmness that it proved somewhat recalcitrant when it came to fitting it into the new classification of *les beaux arts* developed in the eighteenth century. P.O. Kristeller tells us that the decisive step toward a system of the fine arts was taken by the Abbé Batteux.[2] Batteux divided the arts into three categories: the mechanical arts whose ends are purely practical and serve to satisfy the necessities of life; the fine arts (les beaux arts) whose aim is to produce pleasure by the imitation of beautiful nature; and eloquence and architecture which fall between the other two by combining both utility and pleasure. Of these latter Batteux says, "it is need which

---

1 Sir Henry Wotton, *The Elements of Architecture: A Facsimile Reprint of the First Edition (London, 1624)*, (Charlottesville, 1968), p. 1.

2 P.O. Kristeller, "The Modern System of the Arts," in *Renaissance Thought II* (New York, 1965), p. 199ff.

has produced them, & taste which has brought them to perfection: they maintain a kind of middle place between the two other species: they share with them pleasure and utility."[3]

Batteux defines fine art as the imitation of beautiful nature.[4] Architecture is certainly not imitative or representational in any but the most trivial sense[5] and strictly speaking cannot be fitted into Batteux's scheme of the fine arts. He was already forced to stretch things a bit to describe music as imitative and thus bring it into the fold of the fine arts. Music, he says, imitates tones of voice and it is by the tone of voice that we express our feelings. Music consequently is said to be the imitation of the feelings or passions.[6] The idea that music is imitative at least has the tradition and authority of the ancients behind it, however those worthies may have understood it. He goes on to perform an interesting piece of theoretical sleight of hand with architecture by managing to ignore part of his definition.

Architecture is said to begin with the simple necessity of providing shelter, but eventually adorns and beautifies itself to the extent that it can be placed, honorifically, beside the fine arts. Batteux evidently has a high regard for architecture, but it obviously doesn't fit in with the definition of art as imitation that he believes he gets from Aristotle. His move, in effect, is to say that since works of architecture are truly beautiful, they *deserve* to be placed along side the fine arts despite the fact that they are not imitations. He gives an analogous treatment of the art of eloquence.

One influential theme in eighteenth-century theorizing about the arts was the explanation of the notion of beauty in terms of disinterested contemplation. The analysis of beauty in terms of disinterest tended to have the consequence of sharply separating the idea of the beautiful from anything having to do with utility. Batteux did not make that kind of radical distinction for he saw some kind of connection between beauty on the one hand and the architectural virtues of utility, i.e., commodity and firmness, on the other. He speaks of

> a condition which must be regarded as the essential base & fundamental rule of all the arts: in the useful arts the pleasure takes the character of the necessity itself; everything must appear intended for the need. It is the same in the arts intended for pleasure, utility can enter only when it is of a character to procure the appropriate pleasure ... [7].

According to his view a poem or piece of sculpture cannot be justified solely on the grounds that it is true to the model followed because we do not demand truth of these arts, but rather beauty. Without beauty it is a bad poem or sculpture. A work of architecture, on the other hand, must be reproached if it appears to be designed

---

3   M. Batteux, *Les Beaux Arts Reduit A Un Même Principe*, Nouvelle Edition (Paris, 1747), pp. 6-7. Reprint edition (New York, 1970). My translation.

4   Batteux, p. 43.

5   Restaurants shaped like coffee pots and the like can be safely ignored.

6   Batteux, pp. 262ff.

7   Batteux, pp. 45-46.

solely for pleasure. Anything that is there for ornament alone is vicious because a spectacle or show is not what we want from it; what we want is service:

> If a building demands grandeur, majesty and elegance, it is always in consideration of the master who must live in it. If there is proportion, variety, unity, it is to make it more agreeable, more solid, more commodious, all the delights must appear to be useful.[8]

Batteux's remarks about the relation between utility and beauty to some extent anticipate Kant's view of architecture after Kant shifts his attention from the free beauty of nature to the beauty of art. The pure aesthetic judgment of free beauty is characterized by disinterested contemplation, freedom from concepts and the form of purposiveness without a purpose. The aesthetic character of art, by contrast, depends upon a concept. He says specifically of architecture that it is

> the art of exhibiting concepts of things that are possible *only through art*, things whose form does not have nature as its determining basis, but instead has a chosen purpose, and of doing so in order to carry out that aim and yet also with aesthetic purposiveness. In architecture the main concern is what *use* is to be made of the artistic object ... [9]

Unlike Batteux, Kant does not have to maneuver to classify architecture as art.

It is a commonplace now to recognize a connection between the aesthetic value of a work of architecture and its utility, but the nature of this connection is by no means clear. Batteux gives us no examples of what he takes to be inappropriate ornament or of what he considers a happy alliance between beauty and utility. Nor does Kant offer any specifics to help us understand the relation between the use to be made of a building and its aesthetic purposiveness. Kant does, however, say something about art, and perforce about architecture as one of its subspecies, that points in a direction that may help us to a better understanding of the relation between aesthetics and utility.

II

Kant characterizes both natural and artistic beauty as expression and describes an analogy between art and "the way people express themselves in speech so as to communicate with one another as perfectly as possible, namely, not merely as regards to their concepts but also as regards their sensations. Such expression consists in *word, gesture,* and *tone* ... ."[10]

In the wake of Kant and the Romantic Movement later nineteenth- and early twentieth-century aesthetics rejected theories of art as imitation in favor of some version of a theory of art as expression and often identified artistic beauty with expression. As a result we can understand the question for architecture shifting from

---

8   Batteux, p. 48.
9   Immanuel Kant, *Critique of Judgment*, Werner S. Pluhar, trans., §51, Ak. 322.
10 Kant, §51, Ak. 320.

the connection between beauty and utility to the connection between expression and utility.

The notion of expression in aesthetic theory is rather elastic and can be stretched to cover quite a few different things. Expression theories often followed Kant in describing expression as the communication of human feeling and emotion. In this vein one can begin, for example, by thinking of poetry as the spontaneous overflow of powerful feelings and then extend that idea to the other arts. The artist is thus said to put the feelings and emotions that arise out of his own experience into his work where they may then be perceived and experienced by his audience. In this way artistic expression as communication was thought of as the transference of the artist's experience to the audience.

The difficulties with this picture of expression are many. To use an overworked example, a composer need not be sad in order to write a piece of sad music nor must the music make the listener sad for the character of the music to be understood and appreciated. This version of the theory permits the music to have only the instrumental value of causing an experience. I hardly need mention the problem of trying to make sense of how all this causal exchange is supposed to work. These difficulties notwithstanding, there is a fundamental insight in the expression theory that can be put very simply: we attribute to works of art characteristics that are essentially characteristics of human concerns, of feeling, emotion, and action. It is just this insight that has created a puzzle for philosophers.

The puzzle can be stated very simply. Works of art, including works of architecture, are often perceived to have properties that are presumed to be inconsistent with their actual natures. Works of art are appropriately described by a vocabulary that is borrowed from descriptions of the feelings, emotions, and actions of people. We hear, for example, sadness in the music, find joy and sweetness in the very words we hear and see the tower soar into the sky.[11] In addition to being made of flesh and blood people are conscious creatures, but philosophical theory thinks of works of art as purely physical objects, as pigment on canvas or bricks and mortar. It would seem that it must be some kind of mistake to suppose that inanimate physical stuff can have the same properties as sentient beings like ourselves and it also can seem a mistake to suppose that these expressive properties can be *seen* or *heard*. Nevertheless it is surely true that we find expressive character in works of art. How can that be? It can appear that the philosophical problem is, as Bosanquet put it, "how a feeling can be got into an object."[12]

This is an exemplary philosophical puzzle. There is something that is obviously the case (i.e., works of art are expressive and are perceived to be so), but it should not be the case because it is out of joint with other things that we know (i.e., only

---

11 There are analogous problems about other kinds of aesthetic properties as well, e.g., space, mass, and motion in painting and rhythm in architecture.

12 Bernard Bosanquet, *Three Lectures on Aesthetics* (London, 1915), p. 74.

human beings can be expressive, only physical properties can be perceived).[13] In this century the puzzle has spawned a regular industry engaged in turning out philosophical theories to solve it.

One solution proposed to this problem is the theory of empathy that supposes that our feelings are somehow projected into the object. How this projection works, needless to say, is left totally unexplained. Another proposed solution is to suppose that the work of art that we find expressive is not a physical object at all, but something akin to a "perception" or "experience," something that is thought of as a mental event or state of consciousness. Our perception of the physical object is then said to combine or "fuse" with our feelings to produce a new object, the expressive work of art. Theory refers to this new object as the "aesthetic object" or the "aesthetic work of art." Empathy theory tries to get feeling into an object by a psychological mechanism that projects a bit of our consciousness into the object. Aesthetic object theories make the inverse move of importing the object into consciousness.

It is at this latter point that aesthetic theory makes its move into ontology and we enter philosophyland where things get curiouser and curiouser. The puzzle about the expressive character of art has led philosophers to ask what kind of an object a work of art is. This ought to appear an odd question to anyone who is not a philosopher. "What kind of an object is an elephant?" seems a strange way of inquiring about the beasts, but you might suppose that it would do to tell someone that it's big and grey and wrinkly all over. That kind of an answer won't do, however, for the philosopher of art. A description of a particular work of art, some genre or style, or the materials of which it is made is not what is wanted. The philosopher will accept an answer only in terms of one of the metaphysical categories of philosophical theory, e.g., physical substance, mental attribute, sense datum or the like. Aesthetic objects are supposed to belong in one or another of these metaphysical categories.

Aesthetic object theories are designed to answer at least three questions. (1) How can works of art be *perceived* to have expressive properties? How can we *hear* the sadness in the music? (2) How can the expressive properties of art that are presumably "objective" properties of the work be distinguished from various feelings and connotations only *associated* with the work? How may we distinguish between the old portmanteau which is merely a *reminder* of Florence and the joy and sweetness that can be found *in* the very words we hear? (3) How can the apparently aberrant use of language essential to aesthetic judgments be explained? How can the word "sad" which gets its meaning by referring to a human feeling also refer to *sounds*?

The theoretical answer to the first question is that the object perceived is not the physical object, but the aesthetic object which is the result of some kind of interaction between the physical object and our states of consciousness. The aesthetic object is supposed to be the locus of the union between the perceived properties of the

---

13 The air of paradox and puzzlement surrounding this question in aesthetics is charmingly invoked by O.K. Bouwsma, "The Expression Theory of Art," in *Philosophical Essays* (Lincoln, 1965).

art object and the feelings that give it its aesthetic and artistic value. The second question is answered by encouraging art criticism to confine itself to a description of the aesthetic object; in that way it can be assured of attending to what is "really" there and can avoid irrelevant "subjective" intrusions. The third question is answered by the theory's assumption that the words of the expressive vocabulary do not describe anything physical, but keep their original function of referring to the human feelings and reactions that are part of the aesthetic object.

Although theories of the special non-physical aesthetic object have been philosophical orthodoxy for most of the 20th century, they are incoherent. Suppose I am asked my view of one of the more recent buildings on our campus and I say that the thing is just a great undifferentiated block with no front or back to it, that there is no real entrance, just several doors stuck in various corners; the building makes no sense. This is the way the building looks to me; this is how I see it; this is how it strikes me. Aesthetic object theories construe this in a curious way. The "look" of the building is taken to be an object in its own right. These theories invent what are presumed to be uses for words such as "perception" and "experience" in which they are supposed to denote objects. As a consequence my account of the building is not a description of the *building*, but rather of my *experience* of the building. This, however, is to play fast and loose with the word "experience."

There are to be sure, times when we can talk about our experience of a building as opposed to talking about the building. I recall my experience of the Pantheon on my one and only visit to Rome. I was tremendously excited and thrilled to see at last the most complete remaining monument to the grandeur that was Rome. When we were told that the great bronze doors had been taken from the old senate house I felt romantic tingles to think that I was walking through the very doors where great Caesar walked. Talk about my experiences, then, is talk about me and not talk about the building. Nor was my experience an *object* of any kind. Aesthetic theory, however, has not tended to acknowledge that our understanding of the word "experience" is rooted in this garden variety use.[14] The philosopher's word makes only peripheral contact with our ordinary understanding of it.

In this incarnation the aesthetic object has to be a "private object." Indeed, the spectrum of metaphysical theories that spawned this notion conceives of all "experience," mental states and the like as private objects (or events) available only to the one who has them. It is not necessary to argue here that the private object picture of consciousness is incoherent. I will note only the following difficulty.

If we are to speak of objects, then we must be prepared to identify those objects and differentiate them from one another. Since they are private objects we cannot point to one of them; we cannot say it's the one over there. We are left, then, to identify them by description, i.e., "the sad music," "the soaring tower." But those are

---

14 We should also keep in mind that when we apply for a job we are often asked about our experience, i.e., have we done this kind of work previously and for how long?

the very descriptions the objects were introduced to explain. The introduction of the special aesthetic object gets us nowhere.[15]

These theories are in part the result of a failure to realize the remarkably complex and flexible character of our language. Aesthetic theory tends to focus upon one use of a word and then to suppose that use exhibits the essential and proper meaning of the word. It then has to regard other uses as somehow either improper or disguised instances of the proper use. This tendency is found even among sophisticated analytical philosophers such as Nelson Goodman. Writing about architecture Goodman says "A gothic building that soars and sings does not equally droop and grumble. Although both descriptions are literally false, the former but not the latter is metaphorically true."[16] Goodman thinks that the building doesn't really soar and sing so the description has to be thought of as metaphorical rather than literal. It will not do, however, to say that "the building soars and sings" is not literally true. What would it be like if it were literally true? Are we to imagine the building hang gliding or doing a music hall turn? Goodman has certainly recognized that the description uses words in a way that differs from a certain everyday use that may be thought of as standard, but it is not necessarily a metaphorical or an "as it were use." A great many, perhaps most, of the words that figure in aesthetic and artistic descriptions and judgments are borrowed from other areas of life. The connection between the aesthetic and artistic use of these words on the one hand and their employment in what we might call their home territory on the other is a complicated one, much too complicated to be encapsulated in the literal/metaphorical distinction.[17]

There is a perfectly good use of the words "to hear" and "to see" in which we can hear the music as sad and in which we can see the tower soar. There are also occasions when we may not want to say that we *see* the character in the object, but are content to remark that the object symbolizes or suggests something as, for example, the soaring spire may symbolize the aspirations of medieval men for heaven. Although we can in particular cases sometimes sort out full bodied seeing from what is only symbolized or is merely an association, the distinction may prove to be not as important as some aesthetic theory lets on. The distinction between the "objective" properties of a work of art, especially architecture and "subjective" reactions to it may not be all that interesting. The demand that we locate an object— other than the building yonder—against which aesthetic descriptions and judgments are to be measured is the result of a picture of aesthetic judgment and art criticism that I believe gets in the way when it comes to our dealings with architecture.

---

15 For a detailed criticism of aesthetic object theories see B.R. Tilghman, *The Expression of Emotion in the Visual Arts* (The Hague, 1970).

16 Nelson Goodman, "How Buildings Mean," in Nelson Goodman and Catherine Z. Elgin, *Reconceptions in Philosophy and Other Arts and Sciences* (Cambridge and Indianapolis, 1988), p. 40.

17 Some of these complexities are discussed in B.R. Tilghman *But is it Art?* (Oxford, 1984), Chaps 6-7.

The aim of this section has been to point to the conclusion that the philosophical puzzles about expression sketched here are the result of conceptual confusions about language and perception and that the metaphysics of the aesthetic object theories designed to solve those puzzles are blind alleys. Bosanquet's problem about getting a feeling into an object is no problem at all for there is nothing to be done under that heading. What is to be done is to get a clear view of the workings of the language with which we talk about these things. If we are to talk about expression in architecture we shall have to look to considerations other than the metaphysics and epistemology of aesthetic objects.

Although expression theory tended to identify beauty with expression, we can still remark differences between the purely aesthetic character of things and their expressive nature. The balance and symmetry of a facade can be appreciated along with the rhythm of an arcade and the play of contrasting textures in the materials without necessarily seeing them as embodying any specific human character. It is possible to see a building simply as a piece of abstract sculpture whose proportions and so on we find pleasing. Expression involves more than this and it is this something more that I want to consider.

III

To return to Goodman for a moment. He says that in aesthetics, the philosopher's role "is to study particular judgments made and general principles proposed on the basis of them and examine how tensions between particular judgments and general principles are resolved ... ."[18] I have no quarrel with this as a description of at least part of what philosophers of art do. But to think of this as the major part of what they do would seem to entail that the major concern about art is with judgment. Such emphasis on judgment can make it appear that in our traffic with a work of architecture the primary concern is to examine it from all sides, walk about in it and then step back and render a judgment about its value.

Goodman, however, does let on that there is more to it than simply that, for he says that "I think that a work of architecture, or any other art, works as such to the extent that it enters into the way we see, feel, perceive, comprehend in general."[19] This goes some distance toward acknowledging that architecture enters our lives in more ways than merely making judgments about it. For we want to understand how we live in it and with it and work in it and how the history of the building affects our activities and how it connects us with our traditions. In a word, we want to understand how architecture enters into a wide range of human practices.

The notion of expression keeps hovering in the background and that is understandable. We can set aside the philosophical confusions in expression theories and the attempts to explain the expressive character of art and remind ourselves that an important part of expression theory is its attempt to explain the human importance

---

18 Goodman, p. 46.
19 Goodman, p. 48.

of art by connecting works of art with human feelings and concerns. In order to bring out the human significance of architecture we need a broadened notion of expression. We can take a step toward this by replacing, or at least augmenting, the old conception of commodity with a larger notion of expression in which expression includes the sheltering and encouraging of human activities and makes clear to us the traditions and cultural heritage in which those activities are placed. We may have too narrow a view of commodity and its attendant notions of utility and the practical. The paradigm of utility that leads us may be a factory or a business office where we can evaluate the efficiency of the building that houses what are surely themselves utilitarian operations. A well designed office building or factory contributes to the efficiency and profitability of the business or manufacturing operations conducted there. There is, I will try to show, a logical connection between the artistic success of the building and the success of the activities it houses.

The situation may be different, however, when it comes to other kinds of buildings. The function of a church building is to house worship, but worship is not "utilitarian." There are, to be sure, different religious traditions with different forms of worship and churches must be built with the needs of a tradition and form of worship in mind, but to judge a church in terms of its efficiency is grotesque (as if all that mattered was crowd management). A dwelling house may be said to provide the practical needs of a family for shelter, but that hardly does justice to the family life, the home life, that it shelters. Works of architecture can be the locus of the expression of a wide range of human values. Subsuming all these under the general heading of the "practical" obscures the wealth of the human dimension. A work of architecture can bespeak an entire way of life.

IV

In *Culture and Value* we find the following remark of Wittgenstein's dating from 1940. "The house I built for Gretl is the product of a decidedly sensitive ear and *good* Manners, an expression of a great *understanding* (of a culture, etc.). But *primordial* life, wild life striving to erupt into the open—that is lacking."[20] There is no question that there was much of the romantic in Wittgenstein's views about art. Great art has to spring from primordial passions. Wittgenstein is frank about the lack of passion in his one essay into architecture. Instead of passion there is the understanding of a culture. I want to consider the idea of architecture as the understanding of a culture.

When he spoke of the house as the expression of an understanding of a culture I suspect he had something like this in mind. He understood the kind of life that his

---

20 Ludwig Wittgenstein, *Culture and Value*, G.H. von Wright, ed., Peter Winch, trans. (Chicago, 1980), p. 38. The house in question is the one Wittgenstein designed for his sister in the Kundmanngasse, Vienna, in the 1920s. A detailed description of the house is given in B. Leitner, *The Architecture of Ludwig Wittgenstein: a Documentation* (New York, 1976). A more recent account of the house is in Paul Wijdeveld, *Ludwig Wittgenstein, Architect* (Cambridge, Mass., 1994).

sister Gretl lived and the social and cultural circles in which she moved. He knew what needs there were for entertaining guests and what needs there were for privacy. He was also very much aware of the work of contemporary architects in the design of dwelling houses and also of nineteenth-century Viennese practices and traditions in house design. Some of these contemporary and traditional practices and formulae were doubtless borrowed and then modified and adapted to the specific needs of his sister. His recognition of his own shortcoming is no doubt the recognition that this understanding was too calculated.

A few years later he would say that "Architecture immortalizes and glorifies something. Hence there can be no architecture where there is nothing to glorify."[21] Given this requirement there is not much that can qualify as architecture. There is, nevertheless, a point to this remark; it does single out the great monuments and direct our attention to something important about them, but I see no reason to restrict "architecture" to this honorific use that insists upon connecting it only with high art. Wittgenstein's house in the Kundmanngasse didn't celebrate anything and so is not architecture, at least as high art. The greater part of our building is not high art, but it may be by looking at the more everyday that we can come to a better understanding of architecture as expression of the understanding of a culture.

Architecture as expression of the understanding of a culture can be construed in more than one way. There can be a retrospective understanding in which we see buildings from the past as expressions of the culture of an earlier age. Henry Adams' *Mont-Saint-Michel and Chartres* is an interesting example of this sort of retrospective understanding in which he weaves together architectural descriptions of the structures with accounts of the life that produced them and that was lived in them. After giving us a number of details of the buildings, the arrangement of the rooms and the activities that went on there, he says, in summary,

> The whole Mount still kept the grand style; it expressed the unity of Church and State, God and Man, Peace and War, Life and Death, Good and Bad; it solved the whole problem of the universe. The priest and the soldier were both at home here ... the politician was not outside of it; the sinner was welcome, the poet was made happy in his own spirit ... .[22]

Something akin to this kind of understanding can take place with respect to our own contemporary culture when we step for a moment from the stream of life and reflect upon what is going on about us as observers of the culture. Wayne Attoe describes an essay written to arouse support for the preservation of Toronto's railroad station. He says that the author

> Wants to counteract any tendency to see the station as just stones and mortar—which would be expendable—and so emphasizes the building's role as a setting for a variety of

---

21 *Culture and Value*, p. 69.

22 Henry Adams, *Mont-Saint-Michel and Chartres* (London, 1980), p. 37. It is no matter that Adams' account is overly romanticized and that perhaps he did not get it right. The important thing is that he does express an *understanding* of a culture, whether correct or not.

warm, touching human dramas. [He] discards the metaphor of building as *shelter*, and instead characterizes the building as *setting*. The human dramas he describes gives the building a "patina," a "certain aura" that makes the station "something like a home."[23]

While the railroad station in large North American cities was in fact sometimes the gesture of the railroad baron seeking to immortalize and glorify himself and his enterprise and sometimes the gesture of a growing city proclaiming itself as an expanding center of commerce, it was also very much an expression of the understanding of a culture, a culture whose people were spread over very large distances and motivated by a general desire to be someplace else where there may a better job to be had, a business deal to be made, a family to visit or a vacation to be enjoyed. The architects of the stations understood all this and arranged things accordingly, the ticket windows on this side of the vast waiting room, the baggage room there and the trains at the platforms through the great doors yonder.

There is another way, however, in which the understanding of a culture may show itself. This understanding need not be in any way reflective or retrospective, but makes itself manifest in terms of our ability to operate in our own culture and to move within it with *familiarity*.[24] We were familiar with the railroad station and knew all the procedures for buying tickets, picking up a magazine at the newsstand and making our way to the right platform to board our train. It need never have occurred to us to see the place with all its activity as somehow representative of our culture or to recall that things go quite differently in other parts of the world and thus be struck by the uniqueness of our ways.

We may understand the architect who designed the station approaching his task in much the same fashion as we made our way from the taxi stand through the concourse to the trains. He is familiar with what has to go into a station and while he may conceive of imaginative and striking ways to get it done, he need not think of what he is doing as expressing an understanding of the culture. Nevertheless, the way he sets about his work and the design he produces is an expression of his understanding.

Here it may help to think of something more commonplace and more banal, the ubiquitous fast food restaurant, for example. The architect, if we can call him that, who designs the thing understands the culture. He knows the customers and what they want, their reliance on the automobile, their desire for haste, the lack of a discriminating and adventuresome palate, the lack of interest in leisurely conversation and so on. Again, this need not be and probably is not a *reflexive* understanding of the culture. He moves around in the culture easily and with familiarity. He will say that this is, of course, just how things are.

A case can be made that the railroad station is a gesture that essays at immortality and glorification. When it comes to the fast food restaurant, however, there is nothing

---

23 Wayne Attoe, *Architecture and Critical Imagination* (New York, 1978), p. 52. The essay he cites is Pierre Berton, "A Feeling, An Echo ... ," in Richard Bébout, ed., *The Open Gate, Toronto Union Station* (Toronto, 1972).

24 It is helpful to refer to Wittgenstein's discussion of familiarity in the *Brown Book*, Part II.

to glorify or immortalize. Single out such a building and try to think of it as a great gesture. The result is more than likely to be parody. It would be one with the Pop Art of a generation ago that was sometimes claimed to be a celebration of the objects of popular culture, but if the pop artists truly thought in terms of *celebration*, then they were the parodies themselves.

The fast food restaurant is most surely a model of utility; it is designed to serve its customers as quickly as possible and to get them in and out to make room for more. The restaurant is also an expression of the understanding of a culture and we cannot understand the utility of the building without understanding it as a setting for a certain range of human activity that is in part constitutive of that culture. We cannot have a proper understanding of utility without an understanding, appreciation and evaluation of the human activities that it shelters.

V

This chapter has been a conceptual journey through a number of detours. I began with the three principles of Commoditie, Firmeness, and Delight and noted that in Wotton's thinking, as well as others, there was some kind of important connection between commodity and firmness on the one hand and delight on the other, but what the nature of this connection is was never clearly articulated. In the eighteenth century the notion of delight gave way to the notion of beauty and the aesthetic and then in the fullness of time the concept of beauty was augmented and replaced in aesthetic theory by the concept of expression. The question about architecture could now be phrased as a question about the relation between utility and expression. I then went on to point out that an important aspect of expression involves the understanding of a culture.

Part IV provides the material for what I suggest is a way to answer the question about the relation between utility and expression. The relation is, at least in part, conceptual. To understand that a building works and how it works we must understand the human activities it is intended to shelter and those activities in turn must be understood as part of a larger cultural context. We can say that the office or the factory building truly is commodious if it permits the business or the manufacturing projects to get on apace, but we must remember that we are a culture that engages in those business and manufacturing practices and that what goes on under those particular roofs reaches far out into other areas of life. The notion of utility cannot be logically sundered from an understanding of a culture and it is that understanding that permits us to see aspects of a culture, aspects of human life, in a work of architecture. A work of architecture can in this way be an expression of an understanding of a culture even though what it expresses sometimes may not be what we want to see.

Chapter 10

Perspective, Painting and the Look of the World

I want to begin by calling your attention to a philosopher that people pay little attention to these days. This is O.K. Bouwsma. Bouwsma was, I believe, one of the most sensitive users of Wittgenstein's work whom I know. I describe him as a user of Wittgenstein's work and not as an interpreter or scholar of his work. He was not inclined to speculate about what Wittgenstein "really meant" or trace the evolution of his thought from the *Tractatus* through the *Grammatik* to the *Investigations*. What he sought to do was to take Wittgenstein's conception of philosophical problems and philosophical techniques and apply them to the confusions in his own thinking and in the thinking of his students.

He was one of the few people who have taken to heart Wittgenstein's remark that what we do is to bring words back from their metaphysical to their everyday use. He was a master of this and would invent marvelous stories to remind us of the actual use of our words. If Descartes talked of being deceived in sleep, Bouwsma would talk—at a conference in Chicago—of being deceived in Chicago and thereby remind us of how talk about deception enters into the stream of life. We would then be led to realize that Descartes had given no sense to his talk of deception.

Bouwsma encouraged his students to get a nose for when something had gone wrong in the thinking of philosophers and in this connection would speak of the need for "quickening the sense of the queer." I want to follow Bouwsma in this and try to quicken in the reader the sense of the queerness of an issue in the philosophy of art and art history.

I

Historians of art have puzzled over the question whether the techniques of painting in geometrical perspective developed during the Renaissance allow the artist to represent on his canvas the world as it really appears to us. Psychologists and philosophers have shared this puzzlement as well. The controversy is usually traced to the publication of Erwin Panofsky's article "Perspective as Symbolic Form" in 1924.[1] Panofsky argued that geometrical perspective does not reproduce

---

1   Erwin Panofsky, *Perspective as Symbolic Form*, Christopher S. Ward, trans. (New York, 1991). This is a translation of the original essay "Die Perspectiv als 'symbolische Form,'" published in *Vorträge der Bibliotek Warburg* (1924-25).

the way things appear to us, but is rather a "symbolic form" by means of which the Renaissance chose to represent the world. The notion of "symbolic form" is, of course, borrowed from Ernst Cassirer who was Panofsky's colleague both at Hamburg and the Warburg Institute.[2] Art historians, psychologists, and philosophers have all joined the issue over whether Panofsky was right about perspective not capturing the look of things.

Panofsky's characterization of perspective as a symbolic form has led at least one commentator to claim that it is "little more than a system of conventions similar to the forms of versification in poetry."[3] Granted that it is not altogether clear exactly what Panofsky meant by a symbolic form, he certainly did not think of it as a *mere* convention to be used or abandoned at will but apparently supposed it to be something more like the mind set of the culture of an entire age that is connected with the whole way of regarding the world that characterizes an historical period. Thus the Renaissance painter in taking up perspective would surely not have claimed merely to have adopted a new convention, but would have vowed that he now had the correct way to paint things and that no one should dream of reverting to an older style. To read Panofsky as saying that perspective is only a convention was, however, appealing to twentieth-century artists and theorists who were inclined to abandon traditional forms of painting for the abstract and non-representational and in addition who had all the historical styles before them and could pick now this one, now that one, or abandon them all, according to purpose or whim without feeling any constraints imposed by a sense of what is supposed to be "correct."[4] It may be characteristic of an age that has no deep cultural commitments and no deep roots in traditions to regard all human practices as "mere" conventions.

The original argument in favor of perspective as the true representation of the world comes from the theorists of the Renaissance who made use of the familiar analogy of the painting as a window through which we perceive the scene beyond. Since light travels in straight lines, the light rays from the object before us that we see can be represented as forming a pyramid or cone whose apex is the eye. The "window" that forms the plane of the picture can then be represented as a section through this pyramid of sight and the correctness of the representation is thus grounded in optics.

Panofsky says that the geometrical perspective of the Renaissance makes the assumption that "the planer cross section of the visual pyramid can pass for an adequate reproduction of our optical image [Sehbild]."[5] He objects to this assumption because he believes there is a discrepancy between the geometrical construction of

2   For an account of the relation between Panofsky and Cassirer see Michael Ann Holly, *Panofsky and the Foundations of Art History* (Ithaca and London, 1984), Chap. 5.

3   M.H. Pirenne, "The Scientific Basis of Leonardo Da Vinci's Theory of Perspective," *British Journal for the Philosophy of Science* (1952-53), p. 170.

4   On this point see Samuel Y. Edgerton, Jr., *The Renaissance Rediscovery of Linear Perspective* (New York, 1975), p. 153.

5   Panofsky, p. 29.

perspective space and the space we are said really to experience and to mark this discrepancy he speaks of both *mathematical* space and *psychophysiological* space. How this expression, "psychophysiological space," is to be understood is another notion that is not at all clear as I shall show in Part II. For the time being, however, it is enough to point out that it seems to comprehend both the retinal image and a supposed somewhat he calls the "psychologically conditioned 'visual image'." He says that perspective abstracts from reality and he identifies that "reality" with what he calls the "actual subjective optical impression," an expression we may assume is synonymous with "psychologically conditioned 'visual image'." The physiological part of psychophysiological space is presumably the retinal image while the psychological part is the "actual subjective optical impression." It is his thesis that a painting in perspective reproduces neither the retinal image nor the visual impression.

He advances at least three reasons for this contention. The retinal image undergoes continual change while the visual impression maintains a remarkable degree of constancy. The geometrical space of a perspective rendering is infinite and homogeneous and represents things as seen with only one eye. Perceptual space is limited and not homogeneous and in perceptual space straight lines supposedly look curved.

Nelson Goodman, in what is undoubtedly the most influential contribution to the dispute from the side of philosophy, has tended to agree with Panofsky that perspective does not represent the world as it really looks to us. Goodman begins by stating the position that he, as well as Panofsky, is opposing, that is, "The laws of perspective are supposed to provide absolute standards of fidelity that override differences in style of seeing and picturing."[6] The argument for the thesis that perspective is the correct way to picture what is seen is that under specified conditions the picture will send to the eye the same "bundle" of light rays as the object pictured. The identity of the bundle is supposed to be scientifically determinable and that identity is the criterion of fidelity of representation. It is never made clear by Goodman, however, what this scientific determination would amount to. Presumably we would have to divide the surface of the object into incredibly small units and then measure both the wave length and intensity of the light reflected from each of these minimal areas, an operation that could scarcely be carried out. One gets the impression that the actual criterion for "bundle identity" is really "how the thing looks."

Goodman brings three empirical objections against the thesis about the correctness of perspective. (1) The light, the "bundle" of rays, that comes to the eye from the picture is the same as that from the object only under very stringent peephole conditions which cannot be maintained by the single eye. (Read: the picture looks like the object and can be mistaken for it only under very stringent conditions.) If the eye moves, as it must, the illusion is destroyed. (2) The same light stimulus can give rise to different visual experiences, and (3) pictures in correct perspective can look

_____

6   Nelson Goodman, *Languages of Art* (Indianapolis, New York, Kansas City, 1968), p. 10.

distorted. He sums up his objections by saying that "the behavior of light sanctions neither our usual nor any other way of rendering space; and perspective provides no absolute or independent standard of fidelity."[7]

In defense of perspective Michael Kubovy has charged Goodman with a number of misunderstandings of the way perspective works.[8] In addition he makes much of what he calls the "robustness" of perspective which he describes as the fact that paintings can look undistorted from different angles of sight. It is simply not true, he believes, that perspective gives a true representation only from a single position of the eye.[9]

II

It is not necessary to discuss all the details of these arguments and counter arguments because there is a problem in the positions of Panofsky, Goodman, and others who have taken sides in this debate that shows these arguments to be largely irrelevant to the issue in question. That problem can be put into focus by considering some comments that Panofsky's expositor, Michael Ann Holly, makes in describing his view:

> A painting in perspective is not just an exercise in mimesis but an expression of a desire to order the world in a certain way ... . The ideology behind spatial configuration can no longer reflect the "naive" assumption that a perspective painting is in any way isomorphic with the world it depicts.[10]

A perspective painting, then, is presumed by Panofsky not to be an exercise in mimesis, not to be isomorphic with the world and not to be an absolute standard of fidelity. Here we must ask the question: If this painting is neither an exercise in mimesis nor an absolute standard of fidelity, what would be such an exercise or standard? What would it be like for a painting to be isomorphic with the world it depicts? What kind of painting would be an absolute standard of fidelity? We are owed an account of that. Unless we have a clear description of how a painting would represent accurately how we see the world we cannot understand what we are being told when we are told that a painting in perspective does not so represent the world.

Suppose someone, a critic, art historian, or perhaps the artist himself, tells us that this painting we are looking at should not be understood as an attempt to "imitate" or represent the scene as it really is, but instead is intended to order things in a certain way. Here there must be some conception of the contrast that is being established and that means he must be prepared to tell us what the painting would be like if it

---

7   Goodman, p. 19.

8   Michael Kubovy, *The Psychology of Perspective and Renaissance Art* (Cambridge, 1986), pp. 122ff.

9   Kubovy, Chap. 4.

10   Michael Ann Holly, *Panofsky and the Foundations of Art History* (Ithaca and London, 1984), pp. 147-51.

were a representation of the scene as it really is. Erle Loran, for example, shows us by means of photographs of some of the scenes that Cézanne painted, how he did not paint things in their actual proportions and relations to one another, but rearranged them for the purpose of his composition. If you were standing there you would see that the hill does not rise as high above the houses as it does in the painting, that the wall is not that close to the road and so on. Loran described Cézanne's practice as a "process of reorganizing an unruly motif into a balanced, plastic unity."[11] Likewise we can describe, say, cubist painting as an ordering, or reordering, of things in terms of geometrical planes by contrast with how they "really" look. This need carry with it no philosophical baggage and may suggest no more than when you go to see Kahnweiler don't expect to find a man whose face is chopped up like that. Earlier in the century it may have been necessary to explain to someone put off by fauvist painting that it is not an attempt to show colors as they really are, but a rearrangement of them for certain artistic purposes. The expression "how they really are" need not be taken in reference to any ultimate reality, but may simply refer to how we find things in ordinary circumstances, e.g., grass is green and not the fauve's red, or even how they are done in the traditional painting that is more familiar to us.

These examples establish uses for the expression "how things really look" in particular circumstances—there are surely many others—and provide the contrast that makes intelligible the talk of ordering things in certain ways. Nor do these examples entail any theoretical commitments. Neither Panofsky, nor Goodman and Holly, however, have given us the materials to make sense of the general contrast they want to establish and consequently we don't know what Panofsky's theory is supposed to deny. What is lacking in their discussions is the description of any context in which we can understand talk of how things really look.

So far no sense has been given to the notion of a standard of fidelity in painting. Here are two possibilities. Assume that a photograph is the standard and the painting is to be checked against it. In a particular case a photograph may serve this purpose, e.g., the photo makes clear that the tree is to the left of the house while the painting has it on the right. What is wanted philosophically, however, is doubtless a general standard applicable to every instance. If photography is offered as that general standard, then the obvious objection, of course, is that all the questions that can be raised about geometrical perspective in painting can also be raised about photography and the distortions inherent in lenses. Or perhaps the draftsman's rendering that presents the plan and elevations with all dimensions is a candidate for such a standard. There are, after all, well understood criteria of fidelity for technical drawings. Let us note that the fidelity of the blueprint is not to how the machine *looks*—in any sense relevant to art—but to its dimensions, etc. Although we are concerned with paintings and not technical drawings, perspective renderings can play a role analogous to technical drawings.[12] If we want to know something of the

---

11 Erle Loran, *Cézanne's Composition*, 3rd edn (Berkeley, 1963), p. 47.

12 Samuel Y. Edgerton has made interesting connections between the rise of perspective painting and the development of technical drawing in the design and manufacture of machinery

architectural details, say, of a building that used to stand in Renaissance Florence the fifteenth-century perspective painting of it will surely reveal more information than an earlier medieval painting or, anachronistically, an impressionist painting of it as seen through a fog.

The question of fidelity, I take it, has to be in some sense the question of whether the painting "looks like" what it is a painting of. Here we can return to Goodman. To say that one thing "looks like" another is to say the one resembles the other and Goodman says some curious things about resemblance. Goodman is concerned with notions of representation and wants to know what it is for one thing to be a representation of another. The question about the fidelity of perspective is a question about how things are to be represented in painting. Representation, however, is a very broad notion and artistic representation is only one species of it. Goodman says that representation is not a matter of resemblance. In a very wide sense of the word this is true. An attorney represents his client, but generally does not resemble him. I may use several paper clips to represent, for example, the naval affair off the Dogger Banks, but the paper clips resemble neither *Lion* nor *Blücher*. In addition to that kind of objection he says that an object "resembles itself to the maximum degree, but rarely represents itself ... ."[13]

I want to consider that last remark along with another one of his: "A Constable painting of Marlborough Castle is more like any other picture than it is like the Castle, yet is represents the Castle ... ."[14] From these two claims we can extract the mistake that vitiates much of Goodman's thesis about fidelity in painting. That a thing resembles itself to the maximum degree is the sort of thing that could only be said by a philosopher seduced by the assumption that logic, in which we can write "x = x," sublimes our language. The exchange in *Hamlet*, "Is it not like the king? / As thou art to thyself" is closer to a joke than it is to Goodman. We look in vain for any relevant uses of "This thing looks like itself."[15] Likewise in the case of the Constable, Goodman has failed to specify any use for "resembles." Suppose someone complains that the Constable doesn't look like the Castle and goes on to point out that the windows are the wrong shape, that there is an extra tower, the stone is the wrong kind and so on. We understand that perfectly well. We also understand the person who says that the Constable resembles that other painting; there is similarity of artistic style, of composition, of use of color or the like.[16] Were someone to ask, however, whether the Constable was more like the Castle or that other painting, we

---

in his book *The Heritage of Giotto's Geometry* (Ithaca and London, 1991).

13 Goodman, p. 4.

14 Goodman, p. 5.

15 Here are two possible uses of the expression: After a debilitating illness we may say of someone restored to health that he looks like himself again. To avoid hurt feelings and family jealousies a parent may remark of a child that she doesn't resemble any of the family members, she just looks like herself. Neither, of course, is relevant to Goodman's enterprise.

16 In her book, *Ideal Landscapes* (New Haven and London, 1990), Margaretha Rossholm Lagerlöf characterizes the notion of the "ideal landscape" by using the paintings of Annibale Carracci, Poussin and Claude as paradigms. "Every picture in the group reveals a spectrum

shouldn't have the foggiest notion what to make of the question, much less what to answer.

To provide a use for "resembles," "looks like," and their friends and relations we must specify a context in which the expressions can function. Our practices of looking at, discussing, and appreciating, at least traditional, painting provides us with one such context. Given that context, we may be curious about the building pictured in this painting and we look for resemblances. Here it is intelligible to say, "This can't be Marlborough Castle; it looks more like the castle at Little Grumbly. You can tell by the extra tower and the shape of the windows."

When Goodman says that the painting looks like any other painting more than it does the castle, it is almost as if he is calling our attention to the fact that the painting is a flat piece of canvas only a couple of feet each way while the castle is a great pile of stone of vast dimensions and so on. Both descriptions are, of course, true; it is the link between them that is odd. It invites us to suppose that Goodman doesn't know what a painting is or might mistake the painting for the castle, in a poor light perhaps, and we have to tell him that the castle sits on the hill and doesn't hang on the wall. That at best is a conceptual joke.

III

The dispute about whether geometrical perspective represents the world as it really appears seems to entangle two distinct issues. One involves the old idea about the history of art as a progress toward more and more convincing representation and whether Renaissance perspective is the last step in that evolution. The other issue involves philosophical distinctions between appearance and reality. To the people of the fifteenth century the new painting in perspective surely looked more convincing, more real, we might say, than the older Medieval styles. There are still many people who will say that a painting in traditional perspective looks "more real" than typical twentieth-century expressionist or abstract works that tend to "distort" their subjects and to disorient their audience. Speaking of looking real in this connection, however, need carry no philosophical freight and may imply no more than that the painting is easier to understand, it is obvious what it is a picture of and the like.

Philosophy, however, has intruded into this issue by way of the appearance/reality distinction. This philosophical distinction turns out, in this context, to be a nest of distinctions. If art aims at an ever more accurate representation we may suppose that what it aims at is representing reality. The natural starting point of the discussion, then, ought to be reality, the world as it really is. The thrust of traditional epistemology, however, has generally been to deny that reality, the world itself, (material substance, the thing in itself or what have you) is an object of perception and to suppose instead that the true object of perception is an "idea in the mind," "sense datum," "appearance" or the like. I strongly suspect that Panofsky's *Sehbild*,

---

of attributes which, at a distance and compared with the spectrum of attributes distinguishing other groups, resembles every other picture in this group." (p. 17.)

the "subjective optical impression," takes its place in this ontological company. Given the intrusion of philosophical theory into the dispute it is not clear whether the purported aim of painting is to represent the world as it really *is* or the world as it really *looks*, where the "is" and "looks" are to be understood in terms of metaphysical and epistemological distinctions between appearance and reality.

Theorists who have concerned themselves with perspective are not unambiguous on this point. When Panofsky contrasts a perspective rendering with the "actual subjective optical impression" he suggests that the concern is only with the "looks" of things and whether the look of a painting captures the look of the thing, a conclusion consistent with the neo-Kantianism of Cassirer that influenced him. On the other hand, Ernst Gombrich, who disagrees with Panofsky about these things, says of the ambiguous duck-rabbit figure, for example, that it is impossible to see the shape of the figure itself, that is, what is "really there," apart from interpretation[17] and thereby suggests that the contrast is between how things really are and how they look.

Panofsky makes explicit that the "optical image" is the result of psychological interpretation performed upon the retinal image.[18] The notion that visual perception is the result of an interpretation of or inference from some sort of sensory raw material is a standard one among both psychologists and philosophers. Ernst Gombrich, for example, believes that the ambiguous duck-rabbit figure shows that there is no such thing as pure seeing unadulterated by the intellect. He adds that "The distinction between what we really see and what we infer through intellect is as old as human thought on perception."[19]

At this point things get rather complicated. We are led to suppose that we must sort out a hierarchy of entities. First there is the world as it really is, then the world as it appears to us unmediated by the constructions and inferences we habitually impose upon it, then the world as it appears that results from those constructions and inferences, and finally there is the appearance of the world represented in a painting. To be totally consistent we have to remember that since the painting is an object in the world we must also consider how the painting appears to us in either its mediated or unmediated condition. Since the painting is supposed to represent an appearance, we must be prepared to talk about the appearance of that appearance.

Panofsky's *Sehbild*, the subjective optical impression, the psychologically conditioned visual image, is spoken of as if it were an object in its own right. Since it is subjective, it would, of course, have to be a private object. With this in mind we can develop a picture[20] of how we could settle the question about whether perspective correctly describes the way things look: we simply compare the optical impression of the object represented with the perspective painting, that is, we compare the

---

17 E.H. Gombrich, *Art and Illusion*, 2nd edn (New York, 1961), p. 5.

18 Panofsky, p. 31

19 Gombrich, p. 15

20 I use the word "picture" in this context in Wittgenstein's sense of a misleading analogy in which language that is appropriate in one context is transferred to another where it has no application.

private subjective picture with the public one as we might compare a photograph with the painting. Lest we regret that we cannot pull out the optical impression to look at it and compare it with the painting because it is private, we should remember that the private object picture of perception is a piece of philosophical confusion and consequently there is nothing to be regretted.

To pursue the question through philosophical theories of perception and epistemology is to reach a dead end. With or without all the philosophical baggage, the dispute seems to presuppose that there must be some extra-artistic criterion that can be used to measure painting against the world. We do not know in general what that criterion is or even what such a general criterion could possibly be. Here we need to remind ourselves that the whole business of how things look is much more complex than the terms of the controversy allow. In the opening chapter of Musil's *The Man Without Qualities* there is the following description:

> Motor-cars came shooting out of deep narrow streets into the shallows of bright squares. Dark patches of pedestrian bustle formed into cloudy streams. Where stronger lines of speed transected their loose-woven hurrying, they clotted up—only to trickle on all the faster then and after a few ripples regain their regular pulse beat.[21]

This description would not be altogether inapt as a description of Kokoschka's painting of the Vienna State Opera. Kokoschka's expressionist handling of the scene may well do a much better job of capturing the flavor, the look, of cars shooting out of streets and pedestrian bustle than can a conventionally correct perspective painting.

The dispute about perspective is a result, at least in part, of the failure to recall how many different kinds of thing can count as objects of sight. The Kokoschka painting is not about the opera house, the motor-cars, the people and their dimensions and relative positions in space, but about the *bustle* of the city scene. *Bustle* can also be an object of sight as can the hardness of character in Kirchner's paintings of fashionable women in the streets of Berlin.

One factor that perhaps contributes to the idea that perspective does show things as they "really" are is the fact that it provides explicit and definite rules for the projection of a scene onto the artist's panel. Perspective is a *construzione legittima* and that licenses the judgment that one rendering is correctly done and another not. No judgment of that kind applies within the practice of other artistic styles. There is no such thing as "correct" painting when it comes to, say, Mannerism, Impressionism, Expressionism or Cubism. This latter is not surprising since these movements in painting got on by explicit rejection of one or more of the canons of the High Renaissance and did not seek to replace them with any alternative method rule-governed in a comparable way. None of this, however, says anything about the issue in question one way or the other. With respect to particular cases we can always ask whether *this* painting captures the look of its subject or not and whether

---

21 Translated by Eithne Wilkens and Ernst Kaiser. I am indebted to Heidi Rauscher Tilghman for calling my attention to this passage and its aptness to Kokoschka's painting.

this one does it better than that one. But to ask in general whether the perspective painting of the Renaissance represents the look of the world more accurately than does Impressionism, Expressionism or some other movement is not to ask a question at all. This, however, is not the end of the confusion in the business.

IV

Samuel Y. Edgerton, Jr. has tried to make sense of Panofsky's notion of psychophysiological space—I assume this to be the space of which we perceive the "actual subjective visual impression"—by describing it as:

> the kind of space we see empirically, without theological preconceptions or mathematical structure; it is neither homogeneous, infinite, or isotropic ... . In this kind of space the moon, for example, is perceived not as a huge body hundreds of thousands of miles away or as a divine being, but rather as an ordinary physical object about the size of a basketball which, if it were to fall, would drop within a few yards of the observer.[22]

Edgerton's point in this passage is to draw attention to Panofsky's notion that there is an important distinction between some kind of primitive, or at least everyday and unreflective, perception of things, i.e., "the kind of space we see empirically," and the constructions or interpretations that mathematics and science put on things that go in part to make up the "symbolic form" of an age.

There are several points in this passage that want discussion. Consider first the moon. Does the moon look the size of a basketball that could drop a few yards away? "How big does the moon look?" is an old conundrum to which there are a thousand answers from tea cup to wash tub to ever so big. One can say almost anything and likely will on different occasions. How big it looks may be simply a matter of how it strikes you. Sometimes when it is directly overhead it may impress you as no bigger than a tea cup, but when you see it rise above the horizon it can seem immense. If you watch the moon come up behind the town there is no tendency to say it might drop a few yards away. "How big does that look?" is often asked in a situation where one is called upon to make an estimate for some practical purpose, whether it will go through the door, say. The question of how big the moon looks certainly does not occur in any situation where one might be called on to estimate dimensions. Nothing is at stake when the question is asked and nothing governs the appropriateness of the answer.

Edgerton speaks of the "kind of space we see." This suggests that space is something we can see or can look at. The word "space" comes into our language in a number of ways, but I don't think that the word ever enters as the name of something in any philosophically significant way.

"Space" has an obvious and important use in geometry, but there is an ambiguity in its use that the discussions of art historians generally do not recognize. "Space"

---

22 *The Renaissance Rediscovery of Linear Perspective* (New York, 1975), p. 161.

can refer to a geometry considered as a formal axiomatic system whose primitive terms need not have any physical interpretation or it can refer to a system under some physical interpretation and its resulting description of the world. In Euclidean space parallel lines are always the same distance apart and that can be understood on the one hand as either an axiom of the system or a theorem deducible from the axioms or, on the other hand, under an appropriate physical interpretation as a claim about the physical behavior of rays of light.

The word, of course, has a use in describing styles and conventions in painting—we started there, after all—where we speak of the three-dimensionality of Renaissance space by contrast with the flatness of earlier Byzantine space or the distortions of Mannerist space and so on. And then there is that space into which astronauts venture and which is the final frontier where future explorers dare to boldly go where no man has gone before. More prosaically, "space" is usually a synonym for "area" or simply "room." "There was a large open space behind the fire house where we kids used to play ball" or "there isn't enough space in here to swing a cat."

Now to homogeneity, infinity and isotropism. Part of the art-historical story is that the scientific and philosophical changes in thinking about the world that took place from the Middle Ages to the Renaissance had great consequences for art. The Aristotelian picture of the world that dominated medieval science, philosophy and theology described the world as finite and space was not thought of as a container, even one of limited size, in which anything could conceivably be anywhere.

Is this psychophysiological space homogeneous? To describe space as homogeneous is to say that it is everywhere the same and when the notion is applied to geometry we assume it to mean that the postulates and theorems of the system are supposed to have universal application. But when Euclidean geometry is given a physical interpretation and used to describe astronomical relationships space turns out not to be homogeneous. Physical space is not everywhere Euclidean and in the neighborhood of large gravitational forces physicists must have recourse to Riemannian or some other non-Euclidean geometry.

If astronomical space is not homogeneous, is our "empirical space" homogeneous? It is not clear what this means. Does it mean that space everywhere *looks* the same? How is the word being used here? If we mean by "space" things like that open space where we used to play ball, then that field was certainly not homogeneous. It wasn't really level and there was grass on only part it. There are no theoretical implications in that, however, and if something else is meant, we don't know what. What would it be like if our ordinary perception was homogeneous? Until that is made clear we don't know what it is that psychophysiological space is not.

Is our empirical space infinite? Mathematical space is infinite in that there is nothing in the axioms that entail a limit to the length that can be assigned to a line segment or that the value of a function cannot be calculated for arguments that approach infinity. Under some physical interpretation, however, there may always be empirical limitations to measurement and the calculation of significant values. Whether or not physical space is infinite is an abstruse question at the outer fringes of physical theory and if it is intelligible it is so only to those who understand such theory. The corresponding question about our "empirical" space is probably not intelligible to anyone. Does it mean that we can or cannot see infinite distances? If we deny that empirical space is infinite does that mean simply that in the ordinary course of our lives when called upon on to describe distances and dimensions we inevitably do so in terms of not very large numbers?

The assertion that perceptual space is neither infinite, isotropic, nor homogeneous may come to no more than the observation that in the ordinary course of our lives we neither describe nor manipulate things in terms of some system of geometry. Most of us, in fact, are ignorant of geometry and even the best of us make no appeals to geometry when buying our groceries, calling our chickens, or enjoying the sunset or moonrise. We may do well do regard Edgerton's remarks as grammar, that is, as calling our attention to the fact that the language of geometry does not always enter into the ways we talk about things.

Edgerton interjects a note of another kind into his account of psychophysiological space which hasn't anything to do with geometry. Not only is this space non-mathematical, but it is one in which the moon is not seen as a divine being. We must assume this single example is meant to stand in for a number of others. But what others and how many? Probably anything that has religious significance, seeing God in clouds or hearing him in the wind, the sort of thing done by an untutored mind. But in the present instance that can only be brought off by a tutored mind; untutored minds see only ordinary physical objects. Does it also include seeing emotional or human character in things, the clouds as threatening or a tree lifting its leafy arms in greeting if not in prayer, for example? We are not told.

The thrust of this section has been to reinforce the suspicion that the notions of perception around which so much of the discussion of perspective have revolved are the products of conceptual confusion. The space that is supposed to be seen in primitive, unreflective fashion before the imposition of any "symbolic form" has been given no coherent description. If there is confusion here, there is equally confusion in Gombrich's contention that there is no innocent eye and that all seeing entails interpretation (all seeing is seeing-as). It makes sense to say that we see—interpret, if you would—the cloud as a whale, but there is nothing that we can intelligibly say is seen as the cloud.[23]

V

At this point I propose that we abandon as philosophically hopeless the question whether perspective represents the true look of things and put another kind of question in its place, a question that has artistic if not epistemological or metaphysical interest. What can be done artistically with geometrical perspective that cannot be

---

23 The kind of position taken by Gombrich is effectively demolished by Wittgenstein in Part II, section ii of *Philosophical Investigations*. See also the discussion of that section in B.R. Tilghman, *But is it Art?* (Oxford: Basil Blackwell, 1984), Ch. 6.

done, or done so well, in other painterly practices? I want to make some suggestions about that.

The ancients described poetry as the imitation of men in action, but it remained for the Renaissance to challenge the ancient ascendancy of poetry and make painting equally worthy of theoretical discussion. Horace's line *"ut pictura poesis,"* "a poem is like a picture," was frequently invoked as a slogan on behalf of this new concern for painting. If a poem is like a picture, then a picture is like a poem in being an imitation of men in action; witness also the importance that Alberti placed on the *istoria* of a painting. That this was not what Horace had in mind is no matter. The task of the painter thus became the technical one of representing his figures so that who they are and what they are doing is made clear to the spectator.

Understanding the actions of men, that is, what they are doing, entails being aware of such things as bodily movements, postures and expressions, what is said, what is thought, felt, and intended. To this we can add social status and relations with others, not to mention some portion of the social and cultural background that provides the conceptual space in which all the others can exist.

The epic poet, the dramatist, and the novelist must provide descriptions of some number of these factors in order to imitate the actions of men. In Book XXII of *The Iliad*, for example, Homer describes how Achilles had chased Hector thrice around the walls of Troy before Hector finally turned to face his pursuer: "Enough, O son of Peleus!/Troy has view'd/Her walls thrice circled, and her chief pursued./But now some god within me bids me try/Thine, or my fate: I kill thee or I die ... ." [Pope's translation.] To understand what is going on here we must understand the events of the war with Troy, the standing of both Hector and Achilles within their respective camps, the wrath of Achilles and the death of Patroclus, not to mention the whole *ethos* of heroic warfare. Then, of course, there is the confrontation and combat between the two heroes. What figures here is not only the relative social positions of Hector and Achilles, but their relative physical positions as well. The line "I kill thee or I die" is a challenge to Achilles only because it is uttered in the face of Achilles. If we imagine it said in the privacy of a bed chamber it could equally be a coward's fantasy, a rehearsal for a confrontation to come, perhaps a resolution finally to bring off that confrontation or even a rehearsal for an upcoming production of the Trojan Civic Theater.

Gombrich connects certain Greek developments in art, namely a more naturalistic and expressive representation of figures beginning in the sixth century, with a consciousness of narrative such as is found in the stories of Homer. He says " ... when classical sculptors and painters discovered the character of the methods of representing the human body—and indeed more than that."[24] He goes on to say that "Narrative art is bound to lead to space and the exploration of visual effects ... ."[25] I am not concerned either to affirm or deny Gombrich's historical thesis that Greek concern for space in the visual arts developed out of an awareness of narrative.

---

24 Gombrich, p. 129.
25 Gombrich, pp. 137-8.

Gombrich says that narrative art is *bound* to lead to space. The word "bound" that I have emphasized suggests that the connection between the two may be considerably more than mere historical sequence. Why is narrative art bound to lead to space and the exploration of visual effects? There is, I want to note, the possibility of a logical or conceptual connection between the two that would exist regardless of historical developments in Greek sculpture and painting. To understand this we must remind ourselves of all those things involved in the description and understanding of human action mentioned above. What is required for such description and understanding is a context in which the action can be placed. This is what the example of Hector is intended to show.

What I especially want to call attention to is the importance of the representation of spatial relations between figures. These relations must be made clear if the figures are to become proper actors in a pictorial narrative drama, an *istoria*. It has been claimed that the Greeks were never able to construct either a pictorial or sculptural space in which human relationships and interactions could be convincingly represented.[26] It is not my intention to judge the merits of this opinion of Greek art, but if the Greeks did fail in this it is undoubtedly true that the Renaissance frequently succeeded in doing it very well by means of the new developments in geometrical perspective. The new techniques permitted each figure to be given a definite size in relation to all the others and placed in the painting in a definite position with respect to all the others. From many such paintings a three dimensional model could be constructed from which all spatial ambiguity is removed and that would allow us to see the characters of the narrative as if on a stage as they confront now this one, turn away from that one or conspire behind the back of yet another. Now the painter, should he choose to paint that incident, can make it explicit, by the relative positions of the two, that Hector is challenging Achilles and that the distance between them will shortly be only a sword's length.

I do not want to insist upon my account as the correct one of the unique virtues of painting in Renaissance geometrical perspective. I might have got that wrong and wiser heads may set me straight. I do, nevertheless, want to insist upon the move of substituting the one question for the other. The question of whether or not geometrical perspective represents the world as it really looks is a philosophical blind alley that we get into from a conceptual wrong turning. Yet the question directs attention to the fact that the Renaissance introduction of perspective marks a significant moment in the history of painting. The real question is to figure out what that significance is.

---

26 See Michael Podro's account of Karl Schnasse's view of Greek sculpture in *The Critical Historians of Art* (New Haven and London, 1982), p. 42. See also William M. Ivins Jr., *Art and Geometry: A Study in Space Intuitions* (New York, 1964).

Chapter 11

A Conceptual Dimension of Art History

E.H. Gombrich's investigations into the history of art have led him to discuss several topics that have absorbed the attention of philosophers, especially the notions of human action, intention and emotion. In the art of painting these notions intersect in very interesting ways, and it is through an understanding of them that we can gain insights into the problems faced by artists in their task of representing the human figure and into the problems faced by historians, critics and spectators in their practices of understanding and appreciating what artists have done. I will focus attention primarily on two of Gombrich's papers, "Ritualized Expression and Gesture in the Arts" and "Action and Expression in Western Art," but also mention two others, "Moment and Movement in Art" and "The Evidence of Images."[1] In these essays the representation of human action and much that surrounds it is discussed. My aim in this essay is not necessarily either to question or disagree with anything that Gombrich has done, but is rather to reveal a dimension of the topics he treats that is not generally noticed and that I hope will shed some light on the nature of the work that he has done in art history.

The concepts of action, intention and emotion are logically interconnected. We can see this by recalling the ways in which we describe actions, that is, what people do. A man, for example, sits down to write a lecture, stoops to pick up a tennis ball, or flirts with a woman.[2] The descriptions of the actions include the intentions with which they are done. This inclusion is necessary in order for us to understand what is being done. I see the man yonder and notice that his legs are bent and his arm is extended so, but I can't make out what he is doing. The tennis ball has to come into the picture in order to complete the description.

Emotions are not only reactions to circumstances, as when one becomes angry, afraid or falls in love; they can also provide reasons and motives for action, they can characterize how an action is done and they can characterize people themselves. One can strike a blow out of anger, bar the windows out of fear, send flowers out of love,

---

1   The first three of these essays are collected in E.H. Gombrich, *The Image and the Eye*, (Ithaca, 1982). "The Evidence of Images" is in Charles S. Singleton (ed.), *Interpretation: Theory and Practice* (Baltimore, 1969). I am indebted to Richard Woodfield for calling my attention to this last essay.

2   I have deliberately borrowed three of John B. Watson's examples of behavior that he believes are free from intrusions of the "mental." It is more than ironic that he must describe behavior in terms of the intention with which it is carried out, especially after ruling out any appeal to "purpose." See *Behaviourism* (Chicago, 1957). (The book was originally published in 1924.)

one can stoop to retrieve the tennis ball angrily, fearfully or even lovingly, and an individual can be quarrelsome, timid or loving by temperament.

These logical connections between these concepts have consequences for the understanding of painting. The antique tradition of art inherited by the Renaissance defines it as "the imitation of men in action" and it is the painterly representation of human action that concerns Gombrich. It follows, then, that painting must make clear the character, intentions, and emotions of its figures if the action it represents is to be understood. Our understanding of what is going on in a painting must be parasitic upon our understanding of what is going on in our commerce with people in the course of our lives.

Gombrich makes a distinction among the kinds of gestures and expressions that are characteristic of human emotion. He describes these as "symptoms" and "symbols."[3] A symptom is a natural expression of emotion, such as spontaneous laughter, a cry of pain or throwing up a hand to ward off a blow. A symbol, by contrast, is a conventional or even ritualized gesture. Putting the hand on the heart is such a ritualized convention of sincerity. The two are not thought of as mutually exclusive, but as ends of a spectrum. Clapping the hands is an example of a social convention for expressing approval of a performance, and may be done quite perfunctorily and simply "out of politeness," but once this convention has taken hold it can also be a genuine and spontaneous reaction to a masterful performance. Many conventionalized gestures have been borrowed for use in painting and have become, in effect, conventions of painting. The Christian gesture of blessing with a hand with two fingers extended is one such.

The use of the terms "symbol" and "symptom" in the description of the relation between emotion and its various expressions points toward a view of that relation whose ancestry in art theory can be traced at least as far back as Xenophon's report of the conversation between Socrates and the painter Parrhasios.[4] Parrhasios does not understand how emotions can be represented in painting, because they are invisible. Socrates reminds him that emotions are displayed in a person's postures, gestures, facial expressions, and the like; the artist can certainly paint these. Renaissance literature on painting from Alberti to Le Brun is full of remarks to the effect that the task of the painter is to represent the inner emotions and character of the figures in the painting by the outward appearances that the inner states are supposed to cause. Gombrich quotes Leonardo to the effect that the most important thing in painting is to show the movements that *originate* from mental states (my emphasis).[5]

This traditional distinction in artistic theory between the inner and the outer is reflected in Gombrich's description of natural and spontaneous emotional reactions as "symptoms." To speak of them as symptoms suggests that the emotion itself is an inner state of which the visible bodily manifestations are at best bits of evidence

---

3   "Ritualized Gesture and Expression in Art." p. 64

4   Xenophon, *Memorabilia*, 3, 10, 1-5. Gombrich refers to this in "Action and Expression in Western Art," p. 85.

5   "Ritualized Gesture and Expression in Art," p. 68.

from which the true condition of a person must be inferred. To the philosopher this inner/outer, emotion/symptom distinction strongly suggests a commitment to the kind of philosophical dualism that makes a theoretical distinction between mind and body.

The philosophical thesis of mind/body dualism can be stated quite simply. Thoughts, feelings, intentions and everything that we are inclined to label "mental" are non-physical entities known only by the one who experiences them. Only I can feel my pains, think my thoughts and know my intentions. Your mental states are not available to me and mine are not available to you. Our bodily postures and movements that are publicly observable are only contingently related to the inner mental states of which they are presumably symptoms or for which they are presumed to be evidence.

The immediate consequence of this dualism is skepticism with respect to other minds. If this theory is true, we can never know what another person is thinking or feeling, because it is theoretically impossible to establish any correlation between outward bodily behavior and inward mental state.

Given that the traditional aim of art was to imitate people in action, that is, to show us what they are thinking, feeling and doing as well as what is happening to them, painting must accomplish this aim by representing, among other things, the gestures, postures and facial expressions of the figures. Gombrich's emphasis on this representation is, of course, exactly right. How else could human character and feeling be shown? For many, however, the ghost of dualism still hovers over our thinking about this, and we are nagged by the question, "How can bodily postures and gestures—including the painted representations of them—reveal human character and feeling?"

At this point it will be useful to take another look at Socrates's response to Parrhasios when he said that human emotions are displayed in the face and in attitudes of the body. There is a temptation to construe this talk about facial expressions and bodily attitudes as references to one half of mind/body dualism. Whatever philosophical theory of the mind that may have lain behind what Socrates said, we do not have to understand his words as implying any form of dualism, or any other theory, for that matter. Let me suggest that we construe them as what Wittgenstein calls grammatical remarks, that is, remarks that remind us how the words of our language are used.

Taken in this way, Socrates's words remind us that the attitudes of the body that concern us are not the behaviorist's "colorless bodily movements" to be described in the vocabulary of physics and physiology, but are, instead, the gestures, expressions and actions of people, to be described in the full vocabulary of human character and emotion. It is the face itself that is described as angry or sorrowful, the gesture itself that is described as fearful or emphatic and it is the whole bodily attitude that is aggressive or submissive. As Wittgenstein said, "The human body is the best picture of the human soul."[6] This is meant as a grammatical remark and is part of an

---

6   Ludwig Wittgenstein, *Philosophical Investigations*, 2nd edn, G.E. Anscombe. Trans. (New York, 1958), p. 178.

explicit rejection of dualism. It is in the light of this remark of Wittgenstein's that it is possible to understand Socrates in the way that I have suggested. Socrates can be taken as telling us, in effect, that the human body is the best picture of the human soul. Mind/body dualism with its attendant skepticism and "other minds" problem is intellectually incoherent. I will assert this dogmatically as an assumption of the discussion that follows and leave it to the reader to seek its justification in other places.[7]

Although some of the theorizing on the practice of painting in the Parrhasios-Leonardo-Gombrich tradition can suggest philosophical dualism, the philosophical theory can play no role in the *practice* of painting, just as it can play no role in our dealings with people in the stream of life. There is no logical room for theoretical skepticism in the stream of life. It makes no sense to wonder whether we can ever know what another person is thinking or feeling. If art is the imitation of life and of people in action, then there is no logical room for theoretical skepticism in painting, either. It would be a conceptual mistake to suppose that painters must limit themselves to the representation of what is visible, that is, gestures, movements, facial expressions, and the like, because they cannot represent the real emotions and intentions which are believed to lie invisibly behind them. The representation of the body is not something painters must resort to *faut de mieux*.

There is, to be sure, a common-or-garden variety of skepticism that is logically independent of philosophical dualism and its theoretical skepticism about other minds. In particular cases we can be unsure of what a person is thinking, feeling or intending, for we are fully aware that people can conceal their thoughts and feelings and that they can lie to us about these things. In the stream of life it makes perfectly good sense, in certain situations at least, to doubt what a person says and to wonder what a person is really up to.

There is no logical room in art, however, for even this "garden" variety of skepticism to get a foothold. It makes no sense to ask whether the kneeling figure of the Magdalene with her attendant skull and crucifix is truly repentant or only putting on an act, say, to ingratiate herself with the other Mary, or whether the girl in Zurbaran's execrable *The Virgin as a Child* is only affecting a pious face to please the nuns. Why this kind of skepticism makes no sense with respect to art is easy to understand. At one point Wittgenstein asks:

> Why can't a dog simulate pain? Is he too honest? Could one teach a dog to simulate pain? Perhaps is possible to teach him to howl on particular occasions as if he were in pain, even when he is not. But the surroundings which are necessary for this behavior to be real simulation are missing.[8]

---

7   See, for example, David Cockburn, *Other Human Beings* (Houndsmill, Basingstoke, 1990), and B.R. Tilghman, *Wittgenstein, Ethics and Aesthetics* (Houndsmill, Basingstoke, 1991), Chap. 5.

8   PI, §250.

There are people who are too open and honest to lie. It may never occur to them to do it, or if they try, they can't do it convincingly. Their whole manner and expression betrays them. Wittgenstein, of course, wants us to realize that it makes no sense to speak of a dog lying. The conceptual surroundings for dissimulation are simply not there.

The figures in a painting cannot lie either; but it is not because they are too honest. The conceptual surroundings for intelligibly ascribing a lie include such things as the possibility of discovering ulterior motives, overhearing sinister conversations, facing the culprit with the truth and the like. All that would have to entail acquaintance with the figures in a life outside the painting, and this is where we bump against the limits of intelligibility. It makes no sense to question whether the figures in a painting are really feeling what they are painted as feeling.

While there is no place for skepticism about how it really is with a figure in a painting, pretense and dissimulation can, of course, be shown in a painting. Giotto did it in a masterly fashion in his Arena Chapel panel of the kiss of Judas, where Christ looks directly into Judas' face as if to say, "I know exactly what you are doing." Rembrandt also succeeded magnificently in a similar task in his painting of Peter's denial of Christ.[9]

Although the aim of painting is to represent human feeling and action, it faces certain problems in doing so, and Gombrich has called attention to some of these. There is too much about people that painting cannot represent. Art cannot, for example, represent speech, and so poor St. Sebastian cannot tell us how much it hurts, but neither can it show the head nodding or shaking, a sudden blush or eye movement. It thus lacks "most of the resources on which human beings and animals rely in their contacts and interactions,"[10] that is, the resources that we need to understand how it is with another. Leonardo advised artists to make careful observations of the actual gestures that people make in everyday life. Gombrich notes, however, that such observation could not produce great works of art, because "Life in movement is just too rich and too manifold to allow of imitation without some selective principle."[11] Consequently painting must rely on a somewhat restricted range of conventional and ritualized gestures already familiar to its audience in order to help make clear what the figures are about.

The resources, in all their richness and manifoldness, that we need to understand other people need further comment. I would like to look at it this way. Leonardo's gestures of everyday life can, of course, be captured by the draughts person. Too often, unfortunately, these gestures appear to be, as many would say, without meaning. What the notion of meaning comes to here, I suspect, has something to do with description. A sketch, or snapshot, of a gesture (posture, face, etc.) taken *sur le champ* may not permit us *to describe* and hence understand the gesture as

---

9   See Gombrich's account of the Rembrandt's painting in "Action and Expression in Western Art," pp. 98-9.

10   "Action and Expression in Western Art," p. 78.

11   "Ritualized Gesture and Expression in Art," p. 70.

one of anger, resignation, emphasis or whatever. The problem that Gombrich has pointed out is partly a conceptual problem concerning the application of appropriate descriptions.

There is not much logical room in painting for the understanding of even those nuances that can be represented by the lift of an eyebrow or the curl of the lips. Appreciating and understanding nuances as expressions of thought and feelings often depends upon the kind of close knowledge of an individual that includes an awareness of his or her characteristic and habitual ways of reacting to situations, as well as the observation of patterns of behavior manifested over time. Art and life are importantly different in this respect. Since it makes no sense to speak of encountering the figure in the painting apart from the represented scene, there is nothing that can be called becoming more fully aware of his mannerisms, his characteristic ways of acting, his likes and dislikes, or anything of that sort.

The question for Gombrich in its most general form is to determine what the relation is between the gestures performed in real life and those represented in art. More specifically, however, the question is this: If we are to understand what is going on in a painting, or sculpture for that matter, the figures must make use of ritualized gestures. In life, ritual can take the place of genuine feeling. In art the representation of ritual can become an empty formula. The problem for the artist, therefore, is how to use the conventional gestures to express genuine feeling. This, I think, is a practical problem and not a theoretical one, at least not one with any philosophical overtones. It is a matter of the artist's sensitivity and skill. Some can do it and some cannot. Zurbaran fails with his *The Virgin as a Child* and Rembrandt succeeds with his *David in Prayer*, to invoke two of Gombrich's examples.[12] There seems little else to be said.

Gombrich's answer to the general question about the relation between the gestures of life and the gestures of art is twofold. On the one hand, the artist, as already pointed out, must make use of ritualized gestures whose significance has been conventionally established. On the other hand, these gestures must be understood in an appropriate context in order to realize their full significance for the action being represented. It is in this contextual requirement that the principal conceptual dimension of Gombrich's work is found. An appropriate context is necessary for the intelligible application of descriptions of people's actions and reactions. Contexts enter into Gombrich's work in two different ways. These two ways can be illustrated by the example of his discussion of Rembrandt's *St. Peter's Denial*.

He contrasts the Rembrandt with a mosaic of the same scene in S. Apollinaire Nuovo.[13] In the earlier work the maid extends her hand in a conventional speaking gesture and Peter recoils and raises his hands in another conventional gesture. The gestures and postures are stylized and theatrical—"theatrical" in the sense of being broad and exaggerated in the way that is necessary if they are to be recognized from the cheap seats where nuances simply cannot be seen. Gombrich says that the

---

12 Ibid., pp. 72-3.
13 "Action and Expression in Western Art," pp. 98-9.

gesture of Rembrandt's Saint Peter raising his hand is much less unambiguous than in the mosaic. He says that: "taken in isolation the figure may simply be shown to speak or even make an inviting gesture asking one of the other figures to come forward. But the figure is not in isolation and thus Rembrandt compels us to picture the whole tragic scene in our mind." The figure is not in isolation, and Rembrandt compels us to picture the whole tragic scene. It is in terms of this remark that we can understand the two ways in which context plays a role. The figure is not in isolation, in that it is shown in relation to and reacting to the other figures in the painting and it is not in isolation in that it is part of a representation of an episode in a larger history that both precedes and follows the moment.

Whatever an emotion is—and it is not necessary for us to decide that—it is not, as William James had it, an inner turmoil of physiological reactions and the sensations produced by them. There are, to be sure, physical and physiological reactions characteristic of emotions, but for these to count as *emotional* reactions they must be seen in appropriate contexts; the individual must be reacting *to* something. This is sometimes put by saying that emotions have objects. This is another grammatical remark. Fear, for example, is always fear *of* something and anger is always anger *at* something or someone. A person's reactions, facial expressions, gestures and so on can be recognized as manifestations of a particular emotion only when understood in relation to a possible object of emotion.[14]

It is his failure to provide any context and hence any object of emotion that explains why Le Brun's attempt to teach aspiring artists how to represent the emotions by the examples of his notorious drawings of what he imagines the proper facial expression for each to be cannot possibly work. Several of the faces seem quite interchangeable; "fright" and "anger" for two, and without some indication of what the expression is a reaction to, one can only shrug one's shoulders.

Such a context is certainly not lacking in Rembrandt's painting. Peter is clearly reacting to the woman and the two "tough soldiers," as Gombrich describes them. There is, nevertheless, something lacking for understanding. What is it about these people that produce Peter's reaction? If we compare this painting with any number of versions of the *Pietà* we can see what is lacking. A *Pietà*, whatever else it may be, is a representation of a woman grieving over a dead man. Since the woman's expression is focused on the dead body it can usually be recognized unambiguously as grief; it is clear what produces her reaction. To understand that the expression is one of grief the spectator does not have to know any more than that grief is a characteristic human response to death; the knowledge that the dead man is Christ and the woman, Mary, his mother, does not have to enter into it; the juxtaposition of the two is enough. The juxtaposition of Peter and the others, however, is not enough.

---

14 The grammatical, or conceptual, aspect of emotion is argued for in A.I. Melden, "The Conceptual Dimensions of Emotion," in Theodore Mischel (ed.), *Human Action* (New York and London, 1969) and B.R. Tilghman, "Emotion and Some Psychologists," *Southern Journal of Philosophy*, 3:2 (1965).

To understand what is going on in Rembrandt's painting we must know that this is Peter, that it is Christ in the background, looking over his shoulder at him, and that the others have just accused him of being one of the followers of Jesus. In other words, we must know something of the whole story of which the painting portrays only one incident. This is an example of the second of the two ways in which context enters into the understanding of emotion and action in painting.

I said earlier that our understanding of what is going on in a painting must be parasitic upon our understanding of what is going on in our commerce with people in the course of our lives. In the course of our lives we must often know, as it were, the "whole story" in order to understand what people are doing and how they are reacting in various situations. As an illustration of this, let us consider the incident mentioned earlier, represented in Giotto's Arena Chapel fresco of the kiss of Judas. Christ is shown looking directly into the eyes of Judas as he delivers the betraying kiss. The eyes say, in effect, "I know exactly what you are doing." We understand what Judas is doing because we know the story. Had we been spectators of the actual event we would have had "to know the story" too, in order to understand the kiss as dissimulation. That is, we would have had to know something about Jesus and Judas, the situation with the authorities, Judas' dealings with them, and so on. Giotto's accomplishment lies in the way he portrays the gaze of Christ, that makes clear to us, who understand, the depth of his discernment. As spectators to the original we could well have noticed something unusual in the way that Jesus looked at Judas, but recognized it as seeing through the disciple's motivation only after we had learned more about what was going on.

Gombrich has devoted considerable attention to the way that the "whole story" enters into our understanding of paintings. He questions distinctions such as Lessing's between the arts of time and the arts of space, but sees a problem in how images of allegedly "arrested" action, such as paintings or even photographs, can appear to proceed from what has gone before and to presage what will come after. He makes an appeal to what psychologists have supposed to be explanations of these alleged facts in order to justify the claim that there is no such thing as an identifiable *point* in time that a painting or photograph can be said to capture.[15] The psychological machinery that is claimed to be responsible for our perception can be exchanged for the grammatical point that pictures are usually seen and understood as illustrations of a *story*.

The fact that we understand paintings as illustrations of stories makes clear the nature of at least one aspect of the interpretation of paintings and explains why there is frequently a problem about interpretation. One task of interpretation is to determine what the story is that is being illustrated, and that involves identifying who the figures are, what they are doing, how they are reacting, and so on. This task is sometimes made easier by the fact that the painting is part of a history already familiar to us, as is the case with Rembrandt's painting of Peter's denial. It would be possible to read the painting in a different way; Peter is not denying Christ and proclaiming his own

---

15 These matters are discussed in "Moment and Movement in Art."

innocence, but instead is expressing horror at the false accusations that the people are bringing against Christ. This is consistent with the figure of Christ looking back: he is expressing thanks for this bit of support that he knows will be of no avail in the end. This is, of course, not the way to understand the painting, because it demands that we tell another story, and we already know what the real story is.

Sometimes, however, we don't know what the story is, and consequently we can't know what is going on in the painting. The logical interconnections noted earlier between concepts of action, intention and emotion come into play here. To understand what people are doing, what their intentions and emotional reactions are, often demands a wider acquaintance with the history of their projects and relations. Where that wider history is not known the art historian must try to construct a tale that will make sense of it all. Gombrich discusses a number of fascinating examples involving elaborate inferences and hypothetical constructions that art historians have employed to try to wrest sense out of various recalcitrant paintings.

In order to know what people are up to we must know something of their intentions and projects, and this involves knowing a story about them. The identification of a person, however, does not have the same conceptual ties to action and intention. We can identify people and the representations of them in art without knowing what they are doing.

This conceptual point, as well as the other conceptual point, that what is going on in a painting can be described in more than one way, depending upon the narrative that surrounds it, can be brought home by means of a joke that is really a conceptual joke. A humorous caption has been supplied for Albrecht Dürer's *The Knight, Death, and Devil* that reads "Dragon? Ain't no Dragons 'round these parts."[16] There is no problem about the identification of the figures. We know that here is an anonymous knight, Death and a devil, but there are controversies about just what is going on.[17] The joke line imposes a certain perspective on the engraving although it is a crazy one.

In one reading suggested by this line, Death becomes a curious yokel. This interpretation, however, does not take account either the hourglass or the figure of the devil. That could be easily remedied by assuming that we are in the presence of a Monty Python skit. The mad man of the woods carries an hour glass instead of a pocket-watch, but can't keep count of how many times he has turned it. And as for the devil, you can find anything in Monty Python's woods. The Python people once complained of the commercial editing of their television shows, which interrupted the flow of the comedy. A remark was made to the effect that if you are going to milk humor out of a non sequitur, then there is going to have to be something for it not to follow from. Anything can be found in Python country; the devil figure is a visual *non sequitur*.

---

16 Bob Reisner and Hal Kapplow, *Captions Courageous* (London and New York, 1958). Gombrich refers to this book in "Action and Expression in Western Art," p. 86.

17 Gombrich discusses varying interpretations of Dürer's engraving in "The Evidence of Images," pp. 98-102.

I have tried to show that our understanding of what people are doing in paintings is based on our understanding of what real people are doing. This is the foundation of much of Gombrich's work in the interpretation of painting. I have also tried to show that not all of the conceptual connections that link the notions of action, intention and emotion in life have application to art, and that it is this lack of application that is responsible for many of the problems about the interpretation of particular works of art.

Chapter 12

Language and Painting, Border Wars and Pipe Dreams

I

Philosophers of art as well as art critics and art historians, not to mention artists themselves, are wont to construct theories about art or, in some cases, to borrow other peoples'. These theories, even when advanced by those who are not professional philosophers, nevertheless tend to be philosophical in character. While philosophers usually construct theories of art in general, the side of criticism has been inclined to theories of the particular arts, literature, painting, and so on. In recent decades theories about language have been given pride of place in critical and art historical inquiries under the assumption that the arts themselves are forms of language or closely related to language. It is then assumed that a proper theory of language will take us some distance toward an understanding of the nature of the arts. The influences in this direction have largely derived from Ferdinand de Saussure, and to some extent C.S. Peirce, as filtered through structuralism and deconstruction. Interestingly enough, it is language that has been the primary focus of twentieth-century Anglo-American "analytic" philosophy to which one would have to add the powerful influences of Frege and the Viennese positivists. It was thought by this latter movement that only through a proper understanding of language and the distinction between sense and nonsense could a proper understanding of the traditional problems of philosophy be reached. It would have been inconceivable to these philosophers to think of art as a language, although they were sometimes much concerned with the logical nature of the language used in aesthetic judgments and descriptions.[1] The roots of most critical theory, however, have been in the continental tradition of de Saussure and his posterity, rather than in analytical philosophy which by and large has been opposed to that tradition.

I want to do three things in this chapter: provide a critical examination of the idea that art, especially painting, is a form of language; look at some of the things that have been said about supposed relations between words and images that depend

---

1 One exception to this may be Nelson Goodman (*Languages of Art*, Indianapolis and New York, 1968) who says that paintings, along with the words of language, musical notations, architectural drawings, etc., have denotations. He makes clear, however, that what he calls "allographic" nature of pictures makes them very different from language. Sorting all that out is a task for another occasion. Other aspects of analytical philosophy and its relation to aesthetics are discussed in B.R.Tilghman, *But is it Art?* (Oxford, 1984).

upon thinking of images (paintings) as language; and end by considering certain discussions of paintings of René Magritte where some of the consequences of thinking of art as language can be seen at work. Throughout all this, my discussion will be informed by Ludwig Wittgenstein's conception of philosophy and what he has to tell us about language.

Before examining theories of art as language it will be well to begin with some general considerations about theories. The contention that art is a kind of language has been given a veneer of plausibility because its proponents have bought into a kind of theory about language in general. Theory, after all, is the philosopher's stock in trade. When the philosopher seeks to understand some field of interest, be it knowledge, ethics, science, mathematics, politics, or whatever, he most often supposes that a proper understanding of that field can only be provided by a theory of it. This is certainly true when philosophers come to look at art. Philosophers of art, especially in the twentieth century, have often argued that a theory of the arts is required to identify works of art and to distinguish them from other things, to explain our responses to art and the nature of our aesthetic judgments and, in addition, have sometimes argued that a satisfactory theory of art should provide criteria and standards of artistic value as well.[2]

There are a great many things we are prepared to call theories, and it is by no means certain that there is a common thread that unites them all. For all that, I think that our notion of theory seems most at home in the natural sciences and it is by looking at some aspects of scientific theories that we can get a basis for a better understanding of what has been wanted by theorists of the arts. Classical Newtonian mechanics may be taken as a paradigm of a scientific theory. One of the great accomplishments of this theory was to show that a number of apparently disparate phenomena of motion could be understood as essentially connected. The motions of falling bodies, of pendulums, projectiles and planets, can be shown to be so connected because they can be explained by the same general laws. Newtonian mechanics is completely general, that is, it purports to apply to all objects (masses) whatsoever. Consider the second law: $f = ma$. The law states a functional relation between force, mass, and acceleration. For this law to be anything more than a universally quantified statement containing variables whose values remain unspecified, certain things have to be done. Acceleration is defined as change in velocity with respect to time (dv/dt) and velocity is defined as change in space with respect to time (ds/dt). In order to give the quantified variables values, then, there must be ways of measuring s, t, and m. One learns these various techniques of measurement in learning physics. The theories of science are clearly tied to scientific practice and can mean nothing in abstraction from their use in that practice. It happens to be the case that classical mechanics applies to an extraordinarily wide range of objects and although one is tempted to say it applies to all masses whatsoever, that is not quite right. Classical mechanics begins to break down at the sub-atomic level, and also goes awry at

---

2   I have discussed some of these theories and their problems in *But is it Art?* (Oxford, 1984).

velocities approaching the speed of light and in the presence of large gravitational masses. Learning physics is in part a matter of learning the limitations of particular theories and the range of phenomena to which they can properly be applied.

The point of these remarks is to stress the importance of practice in understanding science. Scientific theories are not simply abstract formulations—although some of them can be formulated abstractly—but get their sense and importance within a particular region of human activity. To know science is not simply to know that there is such a functional relation between force and acceleration, but is also to know how to use that function to describe and explain particular phenomena. There may be a moral to be drawn from these observations about the various theories that historians and critics of the arts have offered about their subjects.

If we are to understand and explain the physical behavior of objects, be they gears and connecting rods or the planets of our solar system, theory is required. We could not design machinery or build bridges without the theory of mechanics. We have to pause to ask whether or not theory is required to understand an art such as painting and, more specifically, whether a theory of language is required to understand and explain art.

Now on to the theory that art is a language. A recent text gets underway with this idea:

> A picture is worth a lot more than a thousand words. No amount of words can describe an image or an object exactly, whether it is a picture, a sculpture, or a work of architecture. This is because words constitute one kind of language and imagery another, thereby creating a need for translation.[3]

So it is said that the visual arts constitute a language and because it is a different kind of language it is supposed to follow that words cannot describe works of visual art exactly. Let us look at the two contentions in this passage, that words cannot describe art exactly and that art is a kind of language. It is often a useful tactic in a philosophical investigation when faced with the thesis that something is not the case to ask for a detailed statement of what is being denied. Therefore with respect to the first contention, we have to ask what it is that words cannot do. To economize I will speak only of pictures. What would it be like to describe a picture exactly? We must imagine some uses of "exactly." It is quite possible to place a sufficiently fine grid over a picture so that the contents, the color, say, of each square of the grid can be specified and we might say that in this way we could provide an exact description of the picture. The binary code for a computer image does much this sort of thing, and might be described as a symbolic equivalent of a picture. I tell a friend that there is a painting in the museum that he must see because it is so bad. He is to look for the picture of the Virgin as a child who is shown praying, but her pious expression is so

---

3 L.S. Adams, *The Methodologies of Art: An Introduction* (New York, 1996), p. xiii.

obviously phony that she can only be trying to work the nuns at the convent school.[4] Later he says that I described the picture exactly.

Theorists would doubtless reject these examples as not at all what they had in mind. What, then, do they have in mind? Since they have specified no criterion of exactitude we do not know what would count for them as an "exact description" and, since we don't know that, we can't understand the contention that words cannot describe a picture exactly. It sheds no light at all on how we do in fact talk about and describe pictures nor on the point of doing so.

Perhaps the claim is in part a reflection of the fact that there are times when we want the real thing and not merely a description of it. Extant examples of ancient Greek painting are almost nonexistent and although Pliny has left us a host of descriptions, it is not the same as being able to see, appreciate, and study them for ourselves. Painting is by no means the only thing of which this is true. You tell me how hilarious it was when Aunt Mabel slipped on the banana peel, guffawing all the while, but I cannot appreciate the recital as I would have appreciated the event itself. In neither of these cases is the shortcoming of the description a function of its belonging to a different "language" than the thing described. I suggest this is partly a matter of our reactions to things. We may find the account of Aunt Mabel's embarrassment amusing, but this is not to find the event amusing. Likewise we may have many responses to and views about Pliny's descriptions, but these are about the descriptions and not the paintings. Let us suppose we could produce a notational equivalent of a painting of the sort suggested earlier which, for the sake of argument, we can call a "translation" from the "language" of painting into another system. In such a case our responses to the notational representation will not be the same, could not be the same, as our responses to the painting itself. It would make no sense to speak of the description as visually balanced, as cubist in style, or garish in color. Perhaps the best that could be hoped for here is that by some new and improved technology an exact facsimile of the painting could be produced from the description which we could then talk about and appreciate as we do the original.

The second contention is that words and imagery constitute two different kinds of language. At first glance there is something wildly implausible about describing art as a language at all despite such familiar, and borrowed, language-describing expressions as, "This artist has something to say," "He made a statement with that painting," and "She exploited the vocabulary of cubism in her work." The things that artists are doing under these descriptions do not seem much like what we are doing when we have something to say in the departmental meeting, make a statement to the police, or employ the vocabulary of the gutter. In response to someone's contention that art (painting, etc.) is a language one obvious *reductio* is to ask that person to say something in art. How do you say "Where is the toilet?" in art? Like as not the response will be that art is not that kind of language. But what kind is it? And what is meant by a kind of language? Are there different kinds of language? There are several different ways of classifying languages, e.g., Indo-European/Altaic,

---

4   The painting I have in mind is Zurbaran's *The Virgin as a Child*.

inflected/uninflected, and so on. Those distinctions, however, do not seem to be what is wanted, but it is by no means clear what is wanted.

When it is said that art is a language we must bring to this claim our understanding of what a language is, otherwise we could not understand what is being claimed. A language is such a thing as English, French, or German, therefore if we are to say that art is a language we must suggest that art is something like English, French, or German. I suppose it must follow from that that a particular work of art is like a sentence within the language of art. To add to the implausibility of thinking of art as a language we must note that art has neither a syntax nor a semantics, two features that seem essential to language. Syntax is required to distinguish meaningful expressions from mere sequences of words, that is, sense from syntactic nonsense, and a semantics is required to provide a notion of truth and to distinguish true statements from false ones and thereby make one kind of connection between language and the world.

It may seem that there are painterly analogs of the true/false and sense/nonsense distinctions in language. We can speak of a painting as a true likeness of a person or accurate portrayal of some thing or event. The ability to lie is characteristic of a language speaker. It might be said that a painting can lie to the extent that it purports to be an accurate portrayal when in fact it is not. A Spanish courtly painter of centuries past could have described his work as a lie when self-interest dictated that he portray his royal subjects as rather more attractive than the ugly creatures actually were. If we think of painting as documentation, then there are circumstances where it makes sense to describe a painting as true, false, or a lie. Some times accuracy of portrayal is relevant to the appreciation of a painting and sometimes it is not.

Can a painting also be nonsensical? Syntactical nonsense occurs when a string of words is not properly ordered, but the question is whether there could be an analogous breakdown of pictorial ordering. There are times, however, when surprising sense can be made of what seems utter nonsense, if only one can exercise enough ingenuity. Wittgenstein once offered "Milk me sugar" as an example of syntactical nonsense,[5] but one wag imagined being accosted by a cow who said, doubtless in a sultry voice, "Milk me, Sugar." It is instructive that the result of this ingenuity is a joke. It is difficult to imagine unequivocal examples of paintings that are nonsense. There can certainly be unusual juxtapositions of objects in paintings that could never be found in reality such as the miniature steam locomotive emerging from an ordinary parlor fireplace in Magritte's *Time Transfixed*. Surreal juxtapositions can be intriguing, amusing, suggestive, but not necessarily nonsensical. Like as not some story could be devised to account for it. Perhaps we can call a painting nonsense in which a number of unrelated figures are scattered about the canvas randomly with no coherent organization or design, but then we should never underestimate the ingenuity of some latter day critics. Wittgenstein has a remark that does suggest the possibility of one kind of pictorial nonsense:

---

5   Ludwig Wittgenstein, *Philosophical Investigations*, 2nd edn, trans. G.E.M. Anscombe, Oxford: Basil Blackwell, 1958), §498.

It looks as if we could say: "Word-language allows of senseless combinations of words, but the language of imaging does not allow us to imagine anything senseless."—Hence, too, the language of drawing doesn't allow of senseless drawings? Suppose there were drawings from which bodies were supposed to be modeled. In this case some drawings make sense, some not.—What if I imagine senseless combinations of words?[6]

Some of Escher's drawings with their impossible perspective are obvious examples of drawings from which nothing could be constructed and in that respect would be nonsense.[7] The nonsense here is a function of "that respect." I am given what purports to be the technical drawing for a piece of machinery and I remark, "This makes no sense; nothing could go together like this." In this case the sense of the picture is a function of the use to which we wish to put it. We intend to use such drawings in the construction of machines, but this one can't be so used. Other drawings cannot be so used either, but that may be because they show only a single elevation or are insufficiently detailed and not because they make no sense; they are simply incomplete. Wittgenstein has given us here one specific example of where the sense/nonsense distinction can intelligibly be applied to pictures. It is only by a metaphorical extension that we might speak here of syntax in a diagram and, once more, it need not have any artistic relevance.

A theory must provide a completely general account of its subject matter, and thus a theory of painting as language must provide a general account of its language-making features including semantics and syntax. The application of these notions to pictures where we have seen that they are intelligible, however, are to particular cases in this and that respect and by no means can be made to apply across the board. These particular cases, we have noted, may or may not have relevance for the artistic value and appreciation of painting. We should be suspicious of any attempt to insist upon general accounts of the distinctions in abstraction from particular circumstances and to suppose that there are such things as principles of semantics and syntax for pictures and images analogous to those for natural languages.

II

The primary force behind the thesis that art is a kind of language derives from Fernand de Saussure. De Saussure thought of language as a code for expressing thoughts.[8] Language itself is said to be a system of signs and a sign is defined as a union of meanings (concepts) and what he calls sound-images; both of which are said to be psychological entities. In the familiar jargon the concept is the signified

---

6   PI, §512.

7   Samuel Y. Edgerton, *The Heritage of Giotto's Geometry* (Ithaca and London, 1991, ch. 8) has shown several seventeenth-century Chinese woodcuts illustrating translations of Western mechanical treatises. The Chinese artists did not understand the western conventions of technical drawing and their versions of the drawings are thoroughly impossible.

8   Fernand De Saussure, *Course in General Linguistics* (Charles Bally and Albert Sechehaye eds, trans. W. Baskin (New York, 1959), p. 16.

while the sound-image is the signifier. With this goes a picture of what happens when two people talk with one another. In the brain of one a concept is associated with a sound-image. A spoken word, which is an instantiation of a sound-image, is then produced that is heard by the other and which triggers in the hearer the reverse process whereby a sound-image is created that is associated with the same or a very similar concept. De Saussure is sanguine about the general success of this process of communication for he says that, "Among all the individuals that are linked together by speech, some sort of average will be set up: all will reproduce—not exactly of course, but approximately—the same signs united with the same concepts." [de Saussure, p. 13.]

He envisaged semiology as a general science of signs. Customs and rites, for example, are listed as systems of signs along with language. This science "would show what constitutes signs, what laws govern them." [de Saussure, p. 1.] Just as Newton's mechanics explained a disparate range of phenomena by bringing them under a common set of laws so presumably the imagined science of semiology will show that a range of phenomena that apparently have nothing in common really do have significant common features by subsuming them under the single genus of signs. The assumption that sets this web of notions into play is clearly the idea that thoughts exist in logical independence of any particular expression of them. It follows that anything whatsoever could become associated with a thought and thereby be an expression, that is, a sign, of that thought and thus the way is opened to suppose that works of art as well as what we say in our natural languages belong to systems of signs. In this respect painting is not essentially different from English and we might as well say that painting is just as much a language as is the tongue of Chaucer and Donne.

There is more than one confusion in all of this. De Saussure's picture of human communication taken on its own terms commits us to complete skepticism about what anyone is saying. Since signs (concepts and associated sound-images) are internal psychological entities there is no way that I can know what signs are present in the brain (mind?) of another and de Saussure can have no grounds whatsoever for his contention that "all will reproduce ... the same signs united with the same concepts." The theory grounds the words of our language in presumed psychological events which are private to the one who has them. Meanings are thus necessarily private and language turns out to be "private language." De Saussure has fallen victim to the hoary other-minds problem. The essential objection to de Saussure, however, is not simply that his theory leads to complete skepticism, but that the picture of thoughts and communication upon which it is based is incoherent.[9]

I have been following Wittgenstein in describing de Saussure's view as a "picture." A philosophical picture is basically a misleading analogy. It takes as a model a use of language that is perfectly intelligible and then seeks to transfer it to a situation where it has no application. De Saussure pictures communication as

---

9   The incoherence of the picture of mental events as "private objects" and the attendant idea that our language is therefore a "private" language is made clear in PI, §§ 253ff.

like sending a telegram. A message, such as, "Arriving on the six o'clock train," is encoded into the dots and dashes of Morse code and then decoded at the other end to retrieve the original message. The thought plays the role of the message and language plays the role of the Morse code. It has to be shown that the model of telegraphic communication has no application to conversation.

There is only a contingent connection between the messages we send over the wires and the code in which they are sent. That is to say, we can easily imagine using other electronic codes. There is, nevertheless, serious confusion in the idea that the connection between thoughts and the language that is supposed to be an expression or encoding of them is only a contingent one. The telegraph clicks express the message that I am arriving on the six o'clock train. To push the matter into de Saussure's domain we have to ask what the thought is that is expressed by the message. This thought has to exist apart from any expression of it, so it won't do to say that the thought is that I am arriving at six for "I am arriving at six" is only another expression of the thought. No matter how we try to get at the thought we arrive only at expressions of it, but this should not be taken as a failure to come up with the thought itself. The word "thought" does not function as the name of an object or event, not even a mysterious private one. Its use always involves an expression of what is thought. Thoughts, unlike objects, are individuated and identified by their expressions. We can put this by saying that the connection between a thought and its expression is a necessary and internal one rather than a contingent and external one.

An interesting consequence of this is that many thoughts can be had only by language users. I intend to catch that train and want to be met. To have these thoughts, intentions, and desires, I must be able to use the telegraph, have a wife at the other end, not to mention participate in all the other human practices that surround railroads and their schedules, family life, and so on. Wittgenstein has an intriguing passage that speaks to this:

> A dog believes his master is at the door. But can he also believe his master will come the day after tomorrow?—And what can he not do here?—How do I do it?— How am I supposed to answer this?
>
>   Can only those hope who can talk? Only those who have mastered the use of a language. That is to say, the phenomena of hope are modes of this complicated form of life. (If a concept refers to a character of human handwriting, it has no application to beings who do not write.) [PI, p. 174.]

Note that to believe his master will come the day after tomorrow the dog would have to have some knowledge of the calendar and days of the week.

De Saussure's picture[10] of how words get their meanings and how communication takes place has some of the appearance of a genuine scientific theory. Unlike a genuine

---

10 Interestingly enough, de Saussure has an actual picture, a simple drawing, of two heads with lines connecting the two brains (de Saussure, p.11). One can't help but see these as two telegraph offices and the wires between them.

scientific theory, however, the terms of the theory have no application. Nothing can count as an example of either a signifier or a signified and these notions can play no role in our understanding of language. The problem here is deeper than mere lack of verifiability for its assumptions about thoughts and their expressions makes the fact that we can talk to one another unintelligible. Faced with de Saussure's nonstarter we have to look elsewhere to understand language and communication, not to mention painting.

III

Stripped of all the psychological baggage that makes nonsense of the signifier/signified notions, de Saussure's view of how words get their meanings seems to come down to something like this. The meaning of a word is what is associated with, that is, what it refers to, regardless of what the referent might be. The important thing is that a word gets its meaning by standing for something. In this theory, words are thought of as signs and we must suppose that they are thus one with billboards, stop lights, darkening clouds, and a host of other things. Now apply that idea to paintings. Paintings represent things, and it is tempting to say that in that way they refer to them. Given that temptation we may as well say that in that respect pictures are like the words of our language, not to mention advertising hoardings, traffic lights, and all the rest. They are presumed to acquire their "meaning" in just the same way. It is the implications of this that I want to pursue.

If a general theory of signs is to have explanatory value, it must show that there is a unity among the range of apparently disparate things it is willing to call signs. That unity must be found in the relation between the "sign" and what it means, refers to or stands for. That relation must be the same for all "signs." The assumption that there is such a unity must be challenged and I propose to do it by making use of some of the things that Wittgenstein says about language.

Wittgenstein wants us to realize that the words and expressions of our language have many different uses. Early on in *Philosophical Investigations*, he calls our attention to the fact of those many uses and stresses the point that speaking a language is a human practice and part of what he calls a form of life. In a series of remarks from §11 on, he compares language to a set of tools and reminds us that just as the tools in a tool box have different uses, so do words. In another analogy, they are said to be like the handles in a locomotive cabin which are manipulated in different ways to different ends (§12). He adds "When we say that 'Every word in language signifies something' we have so far said *nothing whatever*; unless we have explained exactly what distinction we want to make [§13]." Think of the distinction between genuine words and jabberwocky ("tove" doesn't mean—refer to—anything) or nouns and, say, prepositions In §23 he gives us some examples of the many different uses language has: giving orders and obeying them; describing the appearance of an object; constructing an object from a description (a drawing); reporting an event; speculating about an event; forming and testing an hypothesis;

presenting the results of an experiment in a diagram; making up a story; play-acting; singing catches; guessing riddles; telling a joke, solving a problem in practical arithmetic, translating from one language to another; asking, thanking, cursing, greeting, praying. He compares the myriad aspects of language to games and speaks of "language games." The game analogy calls attention to two things. Just as the moves in a game are governed by rules so there are rules and regularities in our use of language. Secondly, playing a game is an activity and using language is an activity—a series of activities—embedded in human life.

He then gets to the philosophical meat of what he has been suggesting to us about language:

> Here we come up against the great question that lies behind all these considerations.—For someone might object against me: "You have taken the easy way out! You talk about all sorts of language-games, but have nowhere said what the essence of a language-game, and hence of language, is: what is common to all these activities, and what makes them into language or parts of language ... ."
>
> And this is true.—Instead of producing something common to all that we call language, I am saying that these phenomena have no one thing in common which makes us use the same word for all,—but that they are *related* to one another in many different ways. And it is because of these relationships, that we call them all "language." [PI, §65.]

Let us follow Wittgenstein's lead and look for elements common to different language games. What, for example, do telling jokes and saying prayers have in common? It is not at all clear what would serve as an answer. These are activities embedded in very different facets of our lives. Wittgenstein has given us every reason to believe that a general theory of language and what words mean or, by implication, a general theory of signs that encompasses language—not to mention art—is a fantasy. The assumption on which a general theory of language would have to be constructed is that all human activities and practices have something in common. There is no reason to believe that there is any such common feature or features nor have we any idea of what might be a candidate for such a feature—and consequentially that there is any set of general laws that will make clear what is common to all the human practices in which language figures and in which what we are willing to call signs play a role. It is difficult to see how any envisioned theory would contribute to a better understanding of human life with its myriad activities and practices.

What is true of language is also true of what we ordinarily think of as signs—when we are not in the grip of semiotic theory. To understand this we need to remind ourselves of the many different roles that signs play in the activities of our lives. The red traffic light is a signal to stop backed up by the traffic laws. The bent arrow warns of a curve ahead. The darkening clouds are signs, evidence, that a storm is likely. The roadside billboard touting THE WORLD'S LARGEST BALL OF TWINE bespeaks no legal penalty for not stopping and neither warns of nor is evidence for anything, but rather seeks to persuade you to stop and pay your money. None of these signs have anything in common, but work in many different ways. We do, of course, say that these signs all mean something or signify something, but recall Wittgenstein's remark that, "When we say that 'Every word in language signifies something' we have so far said *nothing whatever*; unless we have explained exactly what distinction we want to make," and see how it can also apply to signs. It is important to keep in mind that the words "mean" and "signify" themselves have different uses. To break the hold of the idea that when we say that all signs have signification that we have said something important, we must remember the many different roles that signs play in our lives and activities. Then we may realize the pointlessness of insisting on a common denominator as well as the emptiness of saying that they all mean something.

Just as theory of mechanics establishes connections between apparently disparate physical phenomena so a general theory of signs seeks to do the same thing with the phenomena of language, signs, art, and so on. Against Wittgenstein's reminder that the meaning of words and signs is embedded in human activities and practices, a theory of signs would have to show that there are elements common to all the vast multitude of human practices. To put that in particular terms, one would have to show that saying a prayer is at bottom like both telling a joke and obeying the speed limit, not to mention understanding a painting. We should conclude from this that the thesis that art is a kind of language—a thesis connected with a general theory of signs—tells us nothing about art in general or painting in particular.

IV

The view that painting is a kind of language and its corollary that it is a different kind of language has introduced considerable obscurity into the discussion of particular works of art. This is certainly true in the case of René Magritte's intriguing painting, *The Betrayal of Images*, a realistic painting of a pipe which has beneath it the legend, "Ceci n'est pas une pipe." This painting, as well as some other Magritte's, has been thought to raise puzzling questions about the relation between language and painting, words, and images. For some Michel Foucault is a key figure in this alleged puzzlement. Gary Shapiro, in his account of ekphrasis, speaks of Foucault:

> noting the different registers of the linguistic and the visual; neither can be reduced to the other. ... This becomes clear in Foucault's essay on René Magritte, *This is Not a Pipe*, in which he argues that painting has overcome the code, traditional, at least since the fourteenth century, that prohibited interchanges between the linguistic and the visual. There he complicates the genre of ekphrasis, the verbal description of a visual work, by writing of a painting that, on his reading, has already entered into the linguistic realm.[11]

This, however, is not quite what Foucault says. His clearest statement seems to be this:

---

11 Gary Shapiro, "French Aesthetics: Contemporary Painting Theory," Michael Kelly, ed., *Encyclopedia of Aesthetics*, vol. 2 (Oxford, 1998), p. 235.

Separation between linguistic signs and plastic elements; equivalence of resemblance and affirmation. These two principles constituted the tension in classical painting, because the second reintroduced discourse ... into an art from which the linguistic element was rigorously excluded.[12]

As near as can be made out, this seems to tells us that in some unspecified way verbal descriptions and painting were not supposed to mix, but traditional representational art usually presents us with scenes that we can identify and describe, for example, here is Abraham getting ready to sacrifice Isaac, or this is the swan about to get it on with Leda, and so pictures and words really have been mixing all along. Perhaps the point is that Magritte's work is supposed to bring this issue, if it is one, to a head.

James W. Hefferman, after defining ekphrasis as *"the verbal representation of visual representation"*[13] goes on to add in the spirit of Shapiro's remark about Foucault, "because it verbally represents visual art, ekphrasis stages a contest between rival modes of representation: between the driving force of the narrating word and the stubborn resistance of the fixed image."[14] In this view, words and visual art are both modes of representation; one might as well say both are languages. Not only are they thought to be languages, but they are also thought to be rivals in some sort of competition. We may suppose that the competition is to see which does the best job of representation.

In 1927 Magritte published an essay entitled "Les Mots et Les Image"[15] in which he points out by means of little sketches a number of relations that words and pictures may have. A word may serve to identify the object pictured, a picture may replace a word as in a rebus, and so on. In each instance the assumption seems to be that just as words name things so pictures represent things. It has been noted that there are striking similarities between what Magritte says about words and de Saussure's theory of language, although there is no reason to think that Magritte was aware of the latter's work. Frederik Leen, however, reminds us that "it is significant to know that his word paintings were conceived in an intellectual context which was becoming increasingly aware that our knowledge of the world is subject to the idiosyncratic character of language."[16] This intellectual context includes Peirce, Frege, and the Wittgenstein of the *Tractatus Logico-Philosophicus* as well as de Saussure. Leen goes on:

> In his word paintings, Magritte shows that the contents of works of art cannot be determined by the actual limitations of word and image as conventional sign-systems, nor by their

---

12 Michel Foucault, *This is not a Pipe*, J. Harkness, ed. and trans. (Berkeley, 1982) p. 53.

13 James A.W. Hefferman, *Museum of Words: The Poetics of Ekphrasis from Homer to Ashberry* (Chicago and London, 1993), p. 3.

14 Hefferman, p. 6.

15 A translation of this article is in *Magritte: 1898-1967*, (G. Ollinger-Zinque and F. Leen, eds, Ghent, 1998).

16 Ollinger-Zinque and Leen, p. 27.

dependence on an object. ... . Artists are not obliged to focus on the usual dependencies between these systems as this would simply be to affirm the existing order. That is why Magritte was so keen to foment border disputes between word, image and reality.[17]

Here again, the theory that art is a kind of language comes into play with its corollary assumption that the two are rivals and engaged in "border disputes." There are, to be sure, circumstances in which it is intelligible to consider the relative merits of words and pictures in doing certain jobs. A picture, plan, or diagram is essential for, say, assembly instructions (place tab A in slot B) where a verbal description would be lengthy, complex, and confusing. Another circumstance is propaganda where a picture of the atrocity may be more effective in arousing passions than a description of the event. Neither of these cases, however, have anything to do with art, and it is by no means clear what the rivalry is when it is a matter of the art of painting nor what is the traditional code that prohibits interchanges between the linguistic and the visual that presumably makes a border dispute possible. Is it simply the conventional Renaissance practice of not painting words into pictures like the banners common in medieval painting?

Perhaps the assumptions at work have something to do with Renaissance and early modern disputes about the relative merits of poetry and painting. Such disputes can arise only on the assumption that painting and poetry are trying to do essentially the same thing, and then it is a matter of which one does it better. What they both were thought to do, of course, is to imitate nature. Leonardo says this:

> Painting serves a nobler sense [sight] than poetry and represents the works of nature with more truth than poetry ... . And if you, poet, wish to confine yourself exclusively to your own profession in describing the works of nature, representing diverse places and form of various objects, you will be out-distanced by the painter's infinitely greater power.[18]

Apart from the fact that the old theory of the arts as imitation inherited from antiquity was still very much alive and well in Leonardo's thinking, what is important to note is the assumption at work in all of this that both poetry and painting have something important in common, but it is not the common element assumed by a general theory of signs.

In a later century, Lessing would suggest a different way of getting at this common element that may seem closer to the posterity of de Saussure:

> If it be true that painting employs wholly different signs or means of imitations from poetry,—the one using forms and colors in space, the other articulate sounds in time,—and if signs must stand in convenient relation with the thing signified, then signs arranged

---

17 Ollinger-Zinque and Leen, p, 25.

18 Leonardo da Vinci, *Paragones*, trans. I.A. Richter (London, New York, Toronto, 1949), p. 53, §22.

side by side can represent only objects existing side by side ... while consecutive signs can express only objects which succeed each other ... .[19]

Lessing classifies signs as either arbitrary, such as the letters and words of our language, or natural, such as pictures.[20] Pictures are said to be natural signs because they are supposed to look like what they are pictures of. Generally speaking and in most familiar circumstances, anyone can tell what a picture is of, such as a man, a dog, a horse, or, in an essentially Christian culture, the Virgin Mary. On the other hand, not everyone (non-English speakers, for example) can tell what the word "man" means. Note that when we come to describe the difference between the two kinds of "signs" it seems natural for the vocabulary to change. The painted image is a "picture of" while the word "means." The use of the word "sign" to cover both words and pictures suggests that "picture of'" and "means" refer to the same relation. And, as we have seen, that is not the case.

To add to what has been said earlier, it is useful to remind ourselves of the different ways that "to mean" can be employed and the different ways the meaning of a word is explained. Sometimes we explain the meaning of a word by a synonym, sometimes by a description, by an illustration, or example and sometimes by the grammatical role it plays in sentences. It is tempting to suppose that the relation between a word and its meaning on the one hand and a picture and what it pictures on the other must be different because pictures resemble what they are pictures of while words do not resemble the things they refer to. We should fight temptation here by asking what it is that words do not do. That is, what would it be like if a word did resemble what it means? In concrete and calligraphic poetry words can be printed in shapes that picture objects, but the thesis demands that we imagine all words in all cases resembling their referents. We have no idea what that would be like.

In view of the many different ways the word "sign" is used, it has to strike us as odd, if not downright crazy, to think that in the painting of the Holy Family before us this figure is a "sign" of the Virgin Mary in the same way that the familiar female outline is a sign for one side of the public toilets in the airport. Let yourself be struck by the oddness of thinking of the figure in the painting as a "sign" of the Virgin as if we had a relation like that of the other sign and the ladies' room: here the sign, there the facility. The painting is not a "sign" of the Virgin Mary, in the painting it is the Virgin Mary. Her picture can, of course, be used as a sign, pointing the way, say, to the shrine, but that is not how the painting works.

Lessing's concern in Laocoon—and this is also true of Leonardo—is with how a painter is to draw on a story for his subject. He thinks of paintings largely as illustrations of episodes in stories and painters then have the task of which episodes

---

19 G.E. Lessing, *Laocoon*, E. Frothingham, trans. (New York, 1957), XVI, p. 91.

20 Our language is arbitrary in that it is a matter of history that we have the alphabet, grammar and vocabulary that we do; these could have been different. Our use of this language, however, is not arbitrary. To be understood we have to make use of its resources as it is. That is glory for you.

to select, what details to include, how best to render the expression of the figures, and the like. His own views about how painters should carry out that task and whether he got it right are not here to the point. What does want noting is that he seems to start out with something like an incipient "theory of signs" that presumably is to give theoretical underpinning to his view of the proper work of painters as opposed to poets. When we look at what Lessing actually does, however, we see that the arbitrary/natural sign business is so much baggage and plays no role in his strictures about how painters should or should not draw on the subjects of poetry. Everything he says about the two arts can be said without that theoretical baggage. Lessing's incipient "theory of signs" works no mischief in what he actually does. This may not be the case, however, for more recent work in art theory; some of the accounts of Magritte are my case in point.

V

I want to go back to the sentence "Ceci n'est pas une pipe." What is it doing in Magritte's painting? Foucault was sufficiently puzzled by this to write an essay about it. Foucault says "The statement is perfectly true, since it is quite apparent that the drawing representing the pipe is not the pipe itself."[21] And again:

> The drawn form of the pipe is so easily recognized that it excludes any explanatory or descriptive text. Its academic schematicism says very explicitly, "You see me so clearly that it would be ridiculous for me to arrange myself so as to write: This is a pipe. To be sure words would draw me less adequately than I re-present myself."[22]

We may also be inclined to agree with Foucault that what the painted legend says is too obvious to need saying; of course the thing is not a pipe, it is only a picture of one. We must challenge that inclination. Wittgenstein will be our guide in this.

It is well known that Wittgenstein spoke often of meaning as use. He said that for a great many cases the meaning of a word is its use in the language [PI, §43]. There are disputes about how this is to be understood. Our question, however, concerns not the meaning of the single word "pipe," but rather the sense of the whole sentence, "This is not a pipe." To illustrate the kind of thing that Wittgenstein is talking about with respect to use consider the following passage:

> "After he had said this, he left her as he did the day before."—Do I understand this sentence? Do I understand it just as I should if I heard it in the course of a narrative? If it were set down in isolation I should say, I don't know what it is about. But all the same I should know how this sentence might perhaps be used; I could myself invent a context for it [PI, §525].

---

21 Foucault, p. 19.
22 Foucault, p. 25.

To understand the importance of use we must realize the importance of the context in which a sentence is used. Imagine Wittgenstein's sentence occurring in different works of literature, a story, novel, or play with different characters in different situations. Perhaps the story is about Tarzan and Jane, Willy Loman and his wife, or Bluebeard and his latest wife. Alternatively, imagine different things the speaker might be doing with the sentence: telling a tale for our amusement, reporting the latest neighborhood gossip, or providing a sample sentence for grammatical analysis. The context also includes such things as the tone of voice in which it is spoken as well as accompanying gestures which help to establish the remark as serious, joking, ironic, or the like.

Another passage is especially to my point:

> Just as the words "I am here" have a meaning only in certain contexts, and not when I say them to someone who is sitting in front of me and sees me clearly,—and not because they are superfluous, but because their meaning is not determined by the situation, yet stands in need of such determination [PI, §348].

We may be inclined to say that those words are superfluous, that is, it is only too obvious that I am here and so it does not need saying. To suppose this, however, is to treat the expression as if its meaning is perfectly clear. Wittgenstein's point, by contrast, is that its meaning is not clear at all, but stands in need of some determination. In this respect it is like the sentence from the previous passage; we understand it to the extent that we know how it can be used and we can invent contexts for it. Here are two such possible contexts that can determine a sense. The boss has called me to his office. I sit down and say, "You wanted to talk to me. I am here." After a long and arduous journey I sit down before my true love's fireside and say, "At last, I am here."

Discussions of Magritte's paintings that include words seem to assume that these words have a definite sense. Frederik Leen describes the words as "captions" but then points out that the captions and images cannot be connected by any associations. "Nor," he says, "is it the case that the labels have been mixed up—no matter how you rearrange them, the puzzle never falls into place."[23] It would appear that we have to go on a hunt armed with theories about words and images to discover what it all means. Let us apply what we have learned from Wittgenstein and note that in the absence of any clear contextual determination we simply do not know how the expressions are being used, if they are being used at all and not simply idling or "on holiday." Perhaps this is what Foucault is getting at when he speaks of "the impossibility of defining a perspective that would let us say that the assertion is true, false or contradictory."[24] Contrary to Foucault, however, we have seen that we can easily imagine "perspectives," contexts, that would give the sentence a use although

---

23 Frederik Leen, "A Razor is a Razor," in Ollinger-Zinque and Leen, p. 20.
24 Foucault, p. 20.

we must keep in mind that whatever we imagine is in no sense a "discovery" of what Magritte was really about.[25]

Leen's assumption that there is a puzzle comes from supposing that Magritte was engaged in breaking down the borders between words and images. That Magritte was breaking down borders may mean no more than the fact that he wanted to paint words into his pictures. Critical theorists, however, cannot have in mind anything that simple. For them the very idea of there being borders between words and images depends upon theories about "signs" that tumble language, art, and everything else into the same hopper. We have every reason to believe, however, that these are only philosophical confusions. We have no notion of what such a border is nor where the two are supposed to come into competition. This talk of borders obscures the relations that actually obtain between painting and language. I have in mind such things as how a title can make clear what a painting is about, how information can serve to put a painting in an appropriate art historical context and how certain descriptions can help us to see what is in a painting. Although Leen says that Magritte was raising questions about the "borders" between words and images, he would have been wiser to say that he thought he was raising these questions. He cannot be described as actually doing that since no sense has so far been given to talk of such borders. I have tried to point out several objections to the idea that art is a language, albeit a different kind of language that is thought to be incommensurate with what we ordinarily think of as language yet is in some kind of competition with it. The assumption that it is a language derives ultimately from de Saussure's semiotic theory. In the first place that theory is based on an incoherent philosophical psychology. In the second place, unlike language, paintings have neither syntax nor semantics. Lastly, its notion of signs confuses and confounds a multitude of diverse human practices and the attempts to apply it to the understanding of particular works of art leads to thinking of painters as engaged in projects to which no sense has been given.

Philosophical theories about art and language are of no help in understanding Magritte, or anything else, as I am inclined to believe. To understand and appreciate painting we must rely on our own sensitivity and experience with art rather than theories. What, then, are we to make of Magritte? Perhaps some remarks that he made in a letter to Foucault contain a suggestion. After some unclear assertions about thought being invisible and resembling "by being what it sees, hears, or knows; it becomes what the world offers it," he says "What does not 'lack' importance is the mystery evoked in fact by the visible and the invisible, and which can be evoked in principle by the thought that unites 'things' in an order that evokes mystery."[26] The key here is the word "mystery." Let us understand mystery, not in the detective story sense where there is always an answer to whodunit, but in that other sense of the

---

25 As a possible circumstance suppose that the blowdown valve activated by the Escape key on the new steam powered computer bears more than a passing resemblance to the vicar's old briar. The article in *Popular Science* teases us with an illustration telling us that it is not a pipe.

26 René Magritte, "Letter of May 23, 1966" in Foucault, p. 57.

word in which we encounter something inexplicable and in the face of which we can only wonder. In a Magritte painting the connection between the image and whatever words are found there may be just such a mystery, a mystery to which a solution is not to be sought. It is quite enough that it intrigue us. We should not, however, rule out the alternative that Magritte is simply having his fun with us.[27]

27 I am indebted to James Hamilton, Michael Turvey and Richard Allen for helpful comments.

Chapter 13

Literature, Human Understanding and Morality

The ancients characterized poetry as the imitation of men in action. They had in mind such things as epic, dramatic and dithyrambic poetry, all forms of literature that tell a story. There is no problem in adding novels and short stories to this roster of imitations. It is hard to see what else such literature could be but imitation, that is, stories, of men in action. There are of course, a few exceptions; *Bambi* could be described as an imitation of deer in action, although deer that have the thoughts of people. Much poetry, of course, does not fit the mold. The lines "Tyger, tyger, burning bright/In the forest of the night" is not about tigers *in action*.

If we are to understand literature as the imitation of action, then we must approach literature with a prior understanding of human action. The kind of prior understanding relevant here is nothing that has to be articulated in our ordinary day to day dealings with people, for in this everyday traffic it simply shows itself in how we go about our business. We have, for the most part, no difficulty in understanding the people we encounter and what they are doing and, consequently, for the most part, we have no difficulty in understanding what the characters we encounter in literature are doing. There is, to be sure, the occasional Hamlet who may or may not be putting on an antic disposition and about whose behavior we may be unsure.

The topic of human action, whether in life or in literature, immediately leads us to the topic of morality. Aristotle said, and I think quite correctly, that "an action implies personal agents who necessarily possess certain distinctive qualities of character and thought; for it is by these that we qualify actions themselves ... ."[1] Morality is not only a matter of action, but of character and thought as well where the latter notion comprehends a person's motives, intentions, and feelings; literature that "imitates" the actions of men must then necessarily have something to do with morality. Just as our understanding of others shows itself in our dealings with them, so our morality shows itself in our life with others and shows itself in the ways that characters in literature are represented.

Lyric poetry, by contrast with the other sort, does not deal with action, but with a view of the world or a reaction to the world. But such perspectives and reactions are themselves fraught with moral values. In this connection we can think of Wittgenstein's remark that "The world of the happy man is a different one from that

---

1 *Poetics*, VI.

of the unhappy man"[2] and cite as examples Wordsworth's heart leaping up when he espies a rainbow in the clouds or a field of daffodils on the one hand and on the other the atmosphere that Poe creates about the dank tarn of Auber.

I said that at least in our daily lives we understand other people and their actions "for the most part." We must now look at some of those situations where we do not understand others in order to see how such failures affect our understanding of literature. Let's begin by remarking that the notion of action has conceptual ties with numerous other notions. Aristotle makes this clear when he speaks of a person's actions being qualified in terms of his character and thought. The gospel story describes the Good Samaritan as having compassion for the injured man and we also can describe his deed as a compassionate one. This reference to character and thought, however, can suggest to the philosophically minded all the old skeptical problems that make up the traditional mind-body problem. We can be tempted into supposing that we can never really know the thoughts, feelings, and intentions of another. For all we know the Good Samaritan did not act from compassion at all, but was really out to get good marks from future generations of Sunday school children.

That we may fail to understand other people because of this kind of philosophical skepticism can be dismissed right off. One of Wittgenstein's concerns in the *Philosophical Investigations* is to expose the confusions in this traditional "other minds" problem with its claim that our mental life is in some metaphysical fashion essentially hidden from others. It does not follow, however, that because there is no metaphysical problem of other minds that the thoughts and feelings of another cannot sometimes be hidden from us. The difficulties we have in understanding other people are practical rather than theoretical. A person may not chose to tell us what is on his mind, we may not know him well enough to recognize his characteristic ways of acting and expressing himself, or we may not be sufficiently familiar with the situation in which he finds himself. In Part II of the *Investigations* Wittgenstein calls our attention to another kind of practical difficulty:

> We also say of some people that they are transparent to us. It is, however, important as regards this observation that one human being can be a complete enigma to another. We learn this when we come into a strange country with entirely strange conditions; and, what is more, given a mastery of the country's language. We do not *understand* the people. (And not because of not knowing what they are saying to themselves.) We cannot find our feet with them.[3]

The following two examples may help make clear the kind of failure to understand that Wittgenstein is calling attention to. In his sociological study of the English village he calls Akenfield, Ronald Blythe recounts his conversation with a Welsh clergyman who, although he has worked in the village for some years, still found

---

2   Ludwig Wittgenstein, *Tractatus Logico-Philosophicus*, trans., Pears & McGuinness, (London. 1961), 6.43.

3   Ludwig Wittgenstein, *Philosophical Investigations*, G.E.M. Anscombe (trans.), (New York: 1958), p. 223.

himself a stranger. The man told Blythe that "Behind the progress there lies the great imponderable of the East Anglican character, something to which I now know I shall never have the key. I have spent most of my time searching for the point of contact."[4] In Conrad's *Heart of Darkness* Marlowe describes the trip in the steamer up the African river and the people seen in the villages along the banks:

> The steamer toiled along slowly on the edge of a black and incomprehensible frenzy. The prehistoric man was cursing us, praying to us, welcoming us—who could tell? We were cut off from the comprehension of our surroundings; ... . It was unearthly, and the men were—No, they were not inhuman. Well, you know, that was the worst of it—this suspicion of their not being inhuman. It would slowly come to one. They howled and leaped, and spun, and made horrid faces; but what thrilled you was just the thought of their humanity—like yours—the thought of your remote kinship with his wild and passionate uproar.

Marlowe's view of the people on the bank is not like the view it is possible to have of the cavorting of a group of animals. We don't know what the creatures are doing, but this ignorance need not be disturbing. We may be curious to know, if only in a detached kind of way, what the animal scientists make of it. The savages on the bank, however, are not animals—not *inhuman*—and that is where the thought of the kinship enters. They must in some way be like us and therefore we ought to be able to understand them; indeed, since they are human, it is incumbent upon us to do so. It is obviously incumbent upon the clergyman of Akenfield to understand his parishioners, not only because of his position as minister, but simply because they are the people with whom he lives and works. It is incumbent upon Marlowe and his party to understand the Africans, not only because they must eventually deal with them, but also simply because they are fellow human beings. And yet the possibility of understanding may be frightening to Marlowe because he sees in their howling and leaping aspects of his own, and our, humanity that he rather not recognize.

So far I have tried to suggest three themes: literature is about men in action; human action and morality are internally related to one another and people can be enigmas to other people. I want now to investigate what these three themes can show us about literature and our understanding of it.

I will begin by characterizing literature as a reminder of what it is like to be a human being. This remark must not be misunderstood. We do not read literature to find out what it is like to be in some abstract sense a human being as we may read *Anna Karenina* to find out what it is like to be an adulteress nor like we read P.C. Wren to find out what it was like to be in the Foreign Legion. Neither is it is at all the same thing as reminding ourselves what it is like to be a bat—"There I was, hanging upside down in the cave and thinking about how I could scare that girl by

---

4 Ronald Blythe, *Akenfield: Portrait of an English Village* (London, 1969), p. 69.

flying in her hair."[5] Being a human being is not an occupation or social position into which literature may open a window. That literature can be such a reminder is to be understood as a grammatical remark. To the extent that literature imitates men in action its descriptions must make use of the concepts appropriate to human beings and what they do. The understanding of a person's action, what that person does, necessarily involves understanding his thoughts, feelings, motives, intentions, and all the rest and literature must make use of the vocabulary appropriate for describing these things.

How else could a story be written other than in the vocabulary of human thought and action? It would make an interesting exercise—though doubtless one in futility— to imagine a story written only in the vocabulary of the behaviorist's "colorless bodily movements" or only in terms of the brain states of the eliminative materialist.[6] Even B.F. Skinner quite forgets his own theories when in his one excursion into literature, *Walden Two*, he describes how Burris comes to visit the Walden Two community and is met by Frazier: "He shook my hand warmly, and as I introduced my companions, he greeted each of them with a smile which succeeded in being friendly in spite of an intensely searching glance." Warm handshakes, friendly smiles, and searching glances are certainly not the stuff of behaviorist theory. Even more philosophically interesting perhaps is the use of the language appropriate to human beings in circumstances where its application seems more than questionable because the subjects are not human beings. In the last act of Karel Čapek's play *R.U.R.* the two latest model robots, Helena and Primus, are apparently on the road to becoming something very much like human beings. They begin to behave in ways quite uncharacteristic of robots. Each expresses a willingness to die for the other; they find the sunrise and birdsongs beautiful; Primus tells Helena she is beautiful and Helena says, "I feel so strange. I do not know what it is. I have lost my head. I feel an aching in my body, in my heart, all over me." Quite apart from the unanswered questions about how they came by the biological apparatus that will permit them to go off as a new Adam and Eve to repopulate the world, we want to know how they suddenly were able to speak of feelings and of beauty all by themselves, as it were, without the necessary community to provide the preparation and teaching. An important philosophical implication of this curious play is its use as a reminder of what is required by way of background to make our language possible and to give it application. Such a background is, of course, missing in the case of robots.

I want now to turn to a literary example where I shall try to show that there may be a serious difficulty in understanding what the characters are doing. My example is Sophocles' *Oedipus Rex*. When Oedipus discovered that his actions had fulfilled the predictions that he would kill his father and marry his mother and then found Jocasta,

---

5   Not at all, I am sure, what Thomas Nagel had in mind. Cf. B.R. Tilghman, "What is it Like to Be an Aardvark?," *Philosophy* (July 1991).

6   It would be unkind to suggest that the brain states of someone else would make a more interesting story.

his wife/mother, had hanged herself, he blinded himself in a manner graphically described by a messenger:

> For the King ripped from her gown the golden brooches/ That were her ornament, and raised them, and plunged them down/ Straight into his own eyeballs, crying "No more,/ No more shall you look on the misery about me,/ The horrors of my own doing! Too long you have known/ The faces of those whom I should never have seen,/ Too long been blind to those for whom I was searching/ From this hour go in darkness!" And as he spoke,/ He struck his eyes—not once, but many times;/And the blood spattered his beard,/ Bursting from his ruined sockets like red hail. [1268-79][7]

And to cap off that gruesome episode Oedipus exiled himself from Thebes!

How are we to understand this behavior on the part of Oedipus? Why did he blind himself? The immediate answer, of course, is because he had found out that he had killed his father and married his mother. But is not his reaction to that news a bit extreme? After all, he did not know that the man he killed at the crossroads was his father. Oedipus was a young prince of the blood in a rough and barbaric age; he had been forced off the road and was only defending himself. How else could he be expected to behave? It might be added that old Laïos had never been a father to him anyway; he was the one who had him put out to die as an infant. And Oedipus surely did not know that the woman he married was momma. His deeds were all quite unintentional and were the very ones he had been doing his best to avoid. There appears to be a vast disproportion between what Oedipus had done and his self-inflicted punishment. From our perspective we may well wonder what could have got into him.

To put this problem of understanding Oedipus and his motives into better focus let us construct a kind of parable and think ourselves back to those days of yore when the west was wild. We shall imagine a young lad, the son of a prosperous rancher and his wife, who grows up learning to ride, to rope, to handle a six-gun and generally to exemplify all the virtues we associate with that period in the American past. We may, if you wish, add something about the mutterings of an old indian medicine man which may or may not have had something to do with what happened. Whether it was out of superstition or merely a desire to see more of the world and to seek his own fortune, our lad saddled up Old Paint one day and rode away from home.

At one point in his wanderings he entered a narrow defile in a canyon when he encountered several horsemen riding rapidly toward him. They shouted for him to get out of their way in blasphemous terms and threatened bodily harm. The pride and courage with which he was raised would permit him to brook no such insult. Guns were drawn, but our hero was faster and a better shot than his opponents and he disposed of them in short order. Had he lived into the middle of the next century, he would have been pleased to see John Wayne doing the same sort of thing.

After a time he arrived at the town of Rattlesnake Gulch and found it being terrorized by a vicious outlaw and his gang. There was the inevitable confrontation

---

7   The translation is that of Dudley Fitts and Robert Fitzgerald.

in the saloon and the shoot out in the street. The town was now free of the outlaw and our protagonist became the local hero. It seems that the town's sheriff had recently been killed and the job was offered to the lad. The old sheriff had left a widow who seemed to go with the job. Although she was an older woman, there were some good years left in her and she was soon married to the newcomer. Years went by, there were children and the new sheriff continued to serve well and gain everyone's respect.

Then, as you may already have guessed, it all came out. The details of how everything was revealed need not detain us, but the town was abuzz with the scandal. The wife was ostracized at the Baptist Church and the children couldn't face their schoolmates. What was our hero to do? What paths of action were open to him? One thing we could not imagine him doing is putting out his eyes. Clearly there was no future in Rattlesnake Gulch for him. What he did do, as a matter of fact, was to slip down to the depot and catch the first train headed west to yet unsettled territory where he could change his name, make a new start and, as Mark Twain says somewhere, chalk the whole thing up to profit and loss.

Why didn't Oedipus behave more like our westerner? It had to be more than clear that he could not hang on to the job of king anymore, but couldn't he have abdicated with as little fuss as possible and gone somewhere else? There is one detail in Sophocles's play that is absent in my parable. There is some kind of dreadful plague in Thebes. The Chorus describes it vividly:

> Thebes is tossed on a murdering sea/ And cannot lift her head from the death surge./ A rust consumes the buds and fruits of the earth;/ The herds are sick; children die unborn,/And labor is in vain. The god of plague and pyre/ Raids like detestable lightning through the city,/ And all the house of Kadmos is laid waste,/ All emptied, and all darkened; Death alone/ Battens upon the misery of Thebes. [23-30]

It is an unusual state of affairs when crops are diseased, cattle sicken, children are stillborn and these misfortunes descend upon the city all at the same time. It is the obligation of Oedipus as king of Thebes to discover the cause of this general calamity and take steps to correct it. Just as his subsequent actions ought to strike us as curious, so should the way he went about determining the cause. Any of us would have called on the Environmental Protection Agency or The Center for Disease Control, but Oedipus chooses to send Creon to consult the Oracle! The cause is not, as those among us who don't know the story might be inclined to suppose, water or atmospheric pollution or biological warfare being waged by an enemy. Instead it turns out to be the presence of the killer of old King Laïos in the city. Most of us knew that, of course. My intention, however, is to point up the oddness in this fact. How could the mere presence of the regicide have this kind of influence?

The explanation is to be looked for in certain Greek religious beliefs about how the world worked, beliefs that may appear quite primitive, but apparently were still alive and reasonably well in the fifth century when the great tragedies were written. These beliefs assume that when a person performs certain kinds of actions that person becomes religiously polluted. It is almost as if this species of pollution is akin to a disease that infects that one, something akin to a communicable disease that can affect other people. When Oedipus became polluted because he committed both parricide and incest, two of the offenses that cause religious taint, his very presence had the consequence of infecting the whole of Thebes; he had become, in effect, a kind of Typhoid Mary.[8]

The religious wrongdoing that was believed to produce pollution is not to be assimilated to our notion of moral wrongdoing. For one thing, the role of intention is very different. That one did not intend to commit the deed in question does not prevent or lessen the degree of the pollution. Pollution can only be removed by ritual cleansing which would require some kind of officially sanctioned rite of purification or catharsis. There have been what I take to be misunderstandings of the idea of pollution and its relation to our contemporary moral sensitivity. Laura Jepsen, for example, agrees that Oedipus has become religiously polluted and says, "Oedipus ... feels himself polluted and the polluter of all who come into contact with him."[9] (Never mind that Oedipus doesn't just *feel* himself polluted, he *is* polluted and knows it.) She goes on:

> It was possible for a Greek of Sophocles' time to believe that certain conduct made a man physically unfit for human society, and yet to absolve him of moral blame. According to primitive ethics, which regards only the external act without taking cognizance of the internal act of will, the case of Oedipus constitutes a ritual defilement. But a more advanced ethics, taking into account the intention of the doer, and distinguishing between deeds done with open eyes and deeds done in ignorance, would recognize Oedipus as morally innocent.[10]

Although it is possible to construct a picture of what is going on in Sophocles as illustrating a movement from a primitive kind of morality in which the only thing that counts is the deed done to a more advanced morality in which intention becomes a more central criterion of moral worth, this is not the only way to read Sophocles. The other side of the coin of ritual pollution is ritual purification or catharsis. It is likely the case that a person's motives and intentions played a role in determining his eligibility for purification.[11] If this is right, then intention was already a feature of the "primitive" morality of pollution and the plays reveal only the going, traditional, religious/moral climate rather than pointing to new moral horizons.

---

8   This situation may suggest what Frazer says in the *Golden Bough* about kingship and the well being of the community depending upon the well being of the king. If the king is afflicted, then the community suffers. Given the problems with Frazer's position, however, I would not want to press this analogy.

9   Laura Jepsen, *Ethical Aspects of Tragedy: A Comparison of Certain Tragedies by Aeschylus, Sophocles, Euripides, Seneca and Shakespeare* (Gainesville, 1953), p.44.

10 Jepsen, pp. 44-5.

11 My understanding of the notions of pollution and catharsis together with the roles they play in Greek tragedy owes much to Gerald F. Else, *Aristotle's Poetics: The Argument* (Cambridge, Mass., 1963).

To understand the role of intention and its mitigating function in this Greek scheme of things we must understand what Aristotle calls "hamartia." This term has generated a great deal of scholarly controversy and has been variously translated to mean character failure ("tragic flaw") or some kind of mistake or error. Laura Jepsen understands "hamartia" as "a defect of a noble quality, a deviation from Aristotle's middle-of-the-road doctrine."[12] She applies this understanding to Oedipus:

> The impetuosity which characterized Oedipus antecedent to the drama is exactly that which he manifests in the tragedy and which brings about his downfall. If he had not had the resolution to probe to the bottom of questions, he would never had gone to Delphi to discover his parentage. If he had employed greater restraint, he would never have slain Laius at the crossroads.[13]

And then in a comparison of Oedipus and Othello she adds that "In each case an uncontrolled passion induces the hero's downfall."[14] Let us note in passing that it is a bit much to demand greater restraint on Oedipus' part at the crossroads. Should we assume him willing to be insulted and run off the road? Hardly what would have been expected of a prince of the blood in that age.

More to my point, however, is Jepsen's claim that there would have been no tragedy had Oedipus not been so rash as to pursue the inquiry into his origins. This overlooks the circumstance that gets the whole thing going, the plague in Thebes. As king it is Oedipus' obligation to discover the cause of the misfortune and take steps to remedy it. Since the cause of the plague is the presence of the killer of Laius, Oedipus must find out who that is. It is, of course himself and therein is the terrible irony of the drama.

It is worthwhile pausing to ask what would have happened had Oedipus not been so resolute in pursuing the inquiry and had let the sleeping dog lie. The plague, of course, would have continued and probably gotten worse and Oedipus himself no doubt would have sickened in some revolting way. That seemed to have been the way religious pollution worked. In Aeschylus' *Libation Bearers* Orestes explains the consequences that would have befallen him had he not carried out Apollo's demand that he kill his mother and her lover Aegisthus:

> Else with my very life I should atone/ This deed undone, in many a ghastly wise./ For he proclaimed unto the ears of men/ That offerings poured to angry powers of death,/ Exude again, unless their will be done,/ As grim disease on those that poured them forth/ As leprous ulcers mounting on the flesh/ And with fell fangs corroding what of old/ Wore natural form; and on the brow arise/ White poisoned hairs, the crown of this disease. [276-82][15]

---

12 Jepsen, p. 32.
13 Jepsen, p. 38.
14 Jepsen, p. 47.
15 The translation of E.D.A. Morshead.

True, what Orestes describes is the consequence for not having done something rather than for having done something, but it does help to emphasize that pollution involves much more than feelings, personal conscience and moral relations within a community. It is this something more, a very physical more, that tends to get overlooked in so many discussions of Greek tragedy.

Martha Nussbaum points out, contrary to Jepsen and others, that Aristotle's "hamartia" is "some sort of mistake in action that is casually intelligible, not simply fortuitous, done in some sense by oneself; and yet not the outgrowth of a defective disposition of character."[16] It is well understood by a number of scholars that "hamartia" is no "tragic flaw" in an otherwise heroic character, no vaulting ambition o'er leaping itself nor destroying green-eyed monster. Nussbaum says that "Oedipus's shortness of temper is not the *cause* of his decline; but it is one thing about Oedipus that makes him a character with whom we can identify."[17] There is something very right about this characterization. Oedipus' short fuse does make him a more interesting person and certainly adds spice to the drama, but the extent to which we can "identify" with Oedipus remains to be examined.

She goes on to point out that "hamartia" can refer to more than one kind of error. It can indicate a momentary departure from a person's usual character such as when Neoptolemus lies or to actions taken under unusual pressures as are Agamemnon's. In the case of Oedipus, however, the mistake is a failure to recognize who he is dealing with. He does not know the man encountered where the three roads meet is his father and he does not know that Jocasta is really his mother. The kind of recognition involved here is the awareness of certain kinship relations, specifically that this man is his father and this woman his mother. Oedipus' ignorance of the kinship relations leads him to commit both parricide and incest which are offenses that are surely chief among the "dread deeds" that Aristotle speaks of and that, in the Greek view of the world and religion, cause the pollution that infects the doer of such deeds.

It is at this point that the true difficulties of understanding *Oedipus* as well as other of the tragedies begin to emerge. In one of the most insightful and level headed accounts of Greek tragedy Brian Vickers notes that

> [h]uman behavior in these plays is not of some special, uniquely "Greek tragedy" kind. It concerns those fundamental human passions which are reflected to a greater or lesser degree in the literature of all nations at all periods. In Greek tragedy people love and hate as we do; they protect or destroy as we do; like us, they deceive each other, abuse language or beliefs to suit their own ends. They are no less concerned than we—or our descendants, hopefully—with personal integrity, justice, and political health.[18]

---

16 Martha C. Nussbaum, *The Fragility of Goodness: Luck and Ethics in Greek Tragedy and Philosophy* (Cambridge, 1986), p. 383.

17 Nussbaum, p. 387.

18 Brian Vickers, *Towards Greek Tragedy: Drama, Myth, Society* (London and New York, 1973, corrected edn 1979), p. 3.

This makes very clear that Greek tragedy is indeed an imitation of men in action. Human action surely does involve love and hate and all the rest. Would it be human action if it didn't? It would be difficult to imagine a race of people who did not love or hate "as we do" and we wonder what other ways there might be to love or hate. The characters in the tragedies are thus presumed to be, like Nussbaum's Oedipus, those with which we can identify. While it is important to be reminded of what goes to make up human action and that these elements are common to all people, a problem nevertheless remains in the understanding of those actions with which Greek tragedy is concerned. What are the objects of love and hate in the Greek drama? What is it that the characters seek to protect or destroy? What are the ends for which they deceive? It is with these questions that we have our problems.

What makes the dramas get on is neither fate, some curse nor its characters being playthings of the gods. Misfortune is brought on by a person's own actions. Vickers makes this clear:

> If we consider the use of the concepts of pollution and purification in Greek tragedy we will occasionally see the more external concept of the "stain" as being something which has been handed down in a family, from generation to generation, as a consequence of some curse, or inherited blood guilt. Both categories can be found in the *Oresteia* and *Oedipus Tyrannus*, but ... as submotifs which do not in any way eliminate human responsibility for action.[19]

The submotif, I take it, is not the pollution itself, which is surely a principal motif, but rather how the pollution comes about. That is, whether it is the result of an individual's action or handed down through a family. In either case, Vickers wants to say, it ultimately rests upon the free action of some individual, be it the present character or some ancestor. If an action is not free, then presumably the agent cannot be held responsible for it. This leads Vickers to say:

> I think we need to stress that, since freedom means—at the very least—that I am able to act and control my actions with full knowledge of who I am, so that my intentions (whether fulfilled or not) derive from a coherent connection between my present and my past—then Oedipus is not free ... . his lack of freedom in the past needs to be emphasized since it is the assurance of his innocence in the present.[20]

Obviously this alleged lack of freedom is intended to apply only to the actions that have some connection with those parts of his life about which he is ignorant. It surely doesn't apply to how he wanted his eggs that morning. Even so, this seems a curious notion of freedom. Oedipus' innocence is assured by his ignorance of the situation, not by any lack of freedom. This ignorance cannot, of course, be the kind which results from negligence (if only he had been a bit more careful he could have had his security people run a background check on Jocasta ...). The drama has to

---

19 Vickers, p.147.
20 Vickers, p. 499.

assume that there was no reasonable way that he could have known the truth until it was too late.

Why did Oedipus suffer? The plain answer is that he killed his father and bedded his mother. Our sense of justice notes, however, that he did these things quite unintentionally and while he surely should feel bad about it all, there is no reason he should be made to suffer. The reason he is made to suffer is because in Sophocles' world that is what happens when you do the things that Oedipus did and the reason it happens is because that is just how that world works. In this scheme of things contracting religious pollution is not at all unlike contracting a disease because you came into contact with the wrong bacteria. Our ordinary notions of moral blame have no application here.

I want to contend that it is difficult, if not impossible, for us to "identify" with Oedipus. Identifying with someone, we may assume, is a matter of having some understanding of that person's situation, motives, reactions, thoughts, feelings, and the like. Furthermore, this understanding must be something more than a mere intellectual awareness that he is, say, concerned with this, that, or the other. It must also entail something like an empathic appreciation of that concern; one must have some sense of what it is to have that kind of concern. In this way one can identify with Othello because we know something of jealousy and hence can be shown what it may be like to be mastered by that passion and we can identity with Anna Karenina because we know sexual passion and be brought to realize how someone can be ruined by it. In the case of Oedipus, however, we do not know what it is like to be horrified by religious pollution or the prospect of it. That something we do, however innocently, can so pollute us is not one of our fears.

Aristotle spoke of pity and fear as the preeminent tragic emotions. One way of understanding that remark is to suppose him to have meant that we would pity anyone who had become religiously polluted and then fear that, despite our best efforts, it could happen to us. Although a Greek audience may have been able to fear that, *we* cannot fear it for to do so requires participation in a moral and religious world that we do not inhabit.

I have tried to suggest that just as there are people with whom, in Wittgenstein's expression, we cannot find our feet, so there is some literature with which we cannot find our feet. Some of the Greek drama is like that. The ritual incantations tossed back and forth between Electra and Orestes when they steel themselves to the murder of their mother have a hint of Conrad's prehistoric man cursing, praying—unearthly, but certainly not inhuman. There is kinship with this wild and passionate uproar although it is a remote one. We know we are in the presence of something deep and terrible and yet we are cut off from it; what access we have seems to be by way of a scholar's footnotes. The single touch of familiar humanity in that drama is provided only by the old nurse, the ancestral Eve of generations of literary characters.

My test case has been *Oedipus*, but I have not argued that we are cut off from all appreciation of that play or of Greek drama in general. We can appreciate the skill with which the drama is constructed, how the plot moves to its resolution and how the dramatic conflicts are represented. What we cannot appreciate, I want to say, are the religious concerns that motivate the whole thing. There is an important sense in which we cannot find our feet with Oedipus.

Chapter 14

Reflections on Aesthetic Judgment

Understanding the nature of aesthetic judgment has been a problem for philosophers. I use the word "judgment" here in the broad sense that includes not only assessments of value, but descriptions and characterizations of many sorts. The range and variety of these judgments has not, I think, been properly appreciated. Many have been struck by the areas of wide disagreement in aesthetic matters and have found this distressing. What David Hume said about this is as good a place as any to begin. In the second paragraph of his essay, "Of the Standard of Taste," he remarks on the disagreements to be found in judgments of beauty and deformity and says:

> Every voice is united in applauding elegance, propriety, simplicity, spirit in writing; and in blaming fustian, affectation, coldness, and a false brilliancy. But when critics come to particulars, this seeming unanimity vanishes; and it is found, that they had affixed a very different meaning to their expressions. In all matters of opinion and science, the case is the opposite.[1]

There is an assumption about language and meaning in this passage that needs examining and that I believe has infected more recent examinations of aesthetic judgment.

The talk of affixing different meanings to these expressions is reminiscent of the idea that the words are essentially names and get their meaning from what they refer to. One person says this is fustian and someone else says no, it is not, but this other is fustian. It is tempting to suppose that in a case like this there are two conflicting opinions about the meaning of the word "fustian," one thinks that it means a thing like this, while the other believes that the word means a thing like that. Here we may be inclined to say that there is no real dispute between the parties and to take a sometime popular "semantic" stance and dismiss the dispute as merely a quibble about words. The implication seems to be that agreement about the meaning of the words would lead to agreement about the truth of the judgments. That, however, cannot be the way to look at it. It is surely not right to say that the critics had affixed different *meanings* to their expressions; it is likely all would agree with the dictionary explanation that fustian is a matter of pompous banality. The disagreement comes in with respect to what is regarded as a case of fustian. What one takes to be a grand

---

1 The situation Hume describes with respect to science I would venture to affirm may have been the result of the lack of a uniform terminology in the eighteenth century so that in certain cases the same thing was called by different names, e.g., dephlogisticated air vs. nitrogen.

passage, another may dismiss as pompously banal. This disagreement is not about the meaning of a word, that is, it is not a "semantic" one, but is, instead, about how one understands and appreciates the character of the passage. What may not have been noticed is that very similar considerations can apply to our judgments of people. Where one may see, say, exemplary generosity, another may find only wasteful extravagance. Hume's own examples are interesting. He says that Homer's general precepts will never be controverted, but when he "draws particular pictures of manners and represents heroism in Achilles and prudence in Ulysses, he intermixes a much greater degree of ferocity in the former, and of cunning and fraud in the latter, than Fenelon would admit of." Any such dispute between Homer and Fenelon is not about the meaning of "heroism" and "prudence," but the range of application of those words, including the nature of the deeds done and perhaps also the character, motives and perspective of the agent, as seen from the moral perspective of the one who judges. Although Hume's essay is almost entirely about literature, what he says can easily be adapted to the visual arts as well where design, color, composition, spatial organization, dramatic character, and a host of other features come into play in place of the literary qualities of elegance and spirit in writing.

We should pause here to note that such judgments, whether aesthetic or of human character, are made neither in isolation nor to be regarded in isolation, but must be understood in a wider context, a context that includes the people, their characters, and histories, involved in the conversation in which the judgment is made. Consider the one who swears this piece of fustian to be a truly noble work. What other judgments would he make and what might it show about his own character and work? When Maria in Shakespeare's *Twelfth Night* reports the general opinion of Sir Andrew Aguecheek as a fool, a great quarreler and a coward, Sir Toby blusters in response, "By this hand, they are scoundrels and subtractors that say so of him" [I, iii] and thereby displays his own character as being of much the same stripe. The importance of this for aesthetic judgment remains to be shown.

The fact that there seems to be much more disagreement in aesthetic matters than in any number of other activities of life, together with the fact that there are apparently no settled methods for resolving these disputes, have provided challenges for philosophers. It is easy to suppose that aesthetic judgments are in some way anomalous and not quite like what proper propositions ought to be like. This has led some to suppose that trying to make aesthetic judgments respectable is a hopeless matter altogether. Thus it can be thought that if our talk about art and aesthetic matters is to be worth our while, then that talk should be shown to be respectable, and one way of doing that is to try to show that aesthetic judgments are not essentially different from statements about the performance of, say, fighter aircraft. This is the project of aesthetic realism.

Aesthetic realism makes two central claims. One is that there really are aesthetic properties in the world to be detected and characterized, and the other is that aesthetic judgments about them are genuine assertions that are either true or false. Realism thus purports to provide a foundation for aesthetic judgment, a foundation presumably based on the nature of things. Eddy Zemach describes aesthetic realism as "the view that aesthetic sentences have genuine truth-values: they are true if and only if the aesthetic properties they ascribe to things really characterize those things."[2] Realism also puts emphasis on the rational justification of such descriptions and on the evidence that is to provide that justification as well as upon commanding assent to those assertions.[3] There are several things about this view that I find very odd.

In the first place there may be something amiss in talking about the existence of properties, aesthetic or otherwise. Does it make sense to ask whether a property exists? Upon the report that 'twas brillig and the slithy toves were doing whatever they purportedly do, some of us may be inclined to ask whether or no there really is a property of slithyness. We who are familiar with the peregrinations of Alice certainly don't want to respond that there is, but at the same time it may be misleading to say that there isn't. It could be said simply that "slithy" is a nonsense word and doesn't mean anything at all. Does that come to the same thing as saying that there is no such property? Compare asking whether or not there is the philosopher's property of being grue. "Grue" is also a "made-up" word, but there is a description that goes with it. The question is not whether there is or isn't such a property, but whether or not anything has the property. There is, of course, no description that goes with "slithy" (I put no trust in Humpty Dumpty's explanation) and no ostensive demonstration either and thus no question about anything being or not being slithy. If it makes sense at all to ask about the existence of a property, it is very different from asking about the existence of an object.

Suppose, for the time being, that it does make sense to ask whether or not aesthetic properties really do exist. The realist claim that they do would then be intelligible. In that case the counter-claim that aesthetic properties do not exist would be equally intelligible. What would things be like in this latter circumstance? We might suppose that if they did not exist, then no composition would ever be balanced and no colors ever harmonize, contrast, or clash, and so on. "Composition," however, is an aesthetic term and there would be nothing to call a composition. If colors lacked those properties, the world would certainly be most dull and drab. "Dull" and "drab" are also aesthetic descriptions and if there are no aesthetic properties, there is nothing for them to describe. We could not even bemoan the aesthetic lack. I suppose we would have to imagine a world in which the aesthetic use of language is entirely withdrawn from circulation and that would entail not only that aesthetic judgments are stricken from the rolls, but also that all the aesthetic practices in which those judgments are embedded are removed from human life. There would thus be

---

2   Eddy M. Zemach, *Real Beauty* (University Park, 1997), p. x. My account of aesthetic realism also makes reference to the views expressed by Philip Pettit, 'The Possibility of Aesthetic Realism,' in *Pleasure, Preference, and Value: Studies in Philosophical Aesthetics*, ed. Eva Schaper (Cambridge, 1983) and Marcia Eaton, "The Intrinsic, Non-Supervenient Nature of Aesthetic Properties," *JAAC* (Fall 1994).

3   The point about evidence and rational justification is stressed by Marcia Eaton.

no painting, music, poetry, interior decoration, concern for the clothes one wears, and who knows what else.

If aesthetic realism is true and aesthetic properties really do exist, we would have to ask how many of them they are. There is scarcely a word in English that cannot on one occasion or another be pressed into doing aesthetic duty. Is there, then, an aesthetic property corresponding to each of them? I shall not press this point.

Aesthetic realism never says in so many words that its target is the possibility that aesthetic properties do not exist. Its stated target is non-cognitivism, that is, any theory such as relativism, emotivism or prescriptivism that would have aesthetic judgments refer to, express, or encourage only "subjective" reactions. It may be implicitly assumed that non-cognitivism entails the nonexistence of aesthetic properties. If the claims of aesthetic realism can be shown to be true, that there really are aesthetic properties to be recognized and judgments about them have truth values, then all forms of non-cognitivism will be exposed as false.

Zemach's criticism of non-cognitivism takes a curious turn at one point. He describes one form of prescriptivism that "construes aesthetic sentences as exhorting us to engage in (what Wittgenstein calls) some "fine shades of behavior."[4] If this is intended as a report of what Wittgenstein says, it is quite wide of the mark. Wittgenstein never exhorts anyone to engage in shades of behavior, fine or otherwise. It is, rather, fine shades of behavior that serve as expressions of a person's aesthetic understanding and appreciation. He offers the example of whistling a tune with the correct expression as showing a person's understanding of a theme. We can also imagine how the understanding of the spatial composition of a painting can be expressed by hand gestures, the understanding of a poem by how it is read, and so on. Of this more later.

The principal impetus for non-cognitivism, I have noted, comes from the fact of widespread aesthetic disagreement and the apparent lack of a decision procedure to settle aesthetic disputes. Realism accepts this fact about disagreement and then has the task of showing how it is nevertheless consistent with realism. One common explanation for disagreements in many ordinary and everyday judgments is that such judgments can be correctly made only under standard conditions of observation and one of the parties to the dispute may not be favored by those conditions. An obvious example is judgment of color, which requires not only normal eyesight, but also proper light to tell what color something really is. Zemach wants to say that the business of standard conditions of observation applies to aesthetic judgments as well.

Zemach says that "SOC (standard observations conditions) are defined as the conditions in which things appear as they are. How things are (in any world) is stated by our theory, so what are SOC for objects of kind K with respect to F-ness depends

---

4 *Real Beauty*, pp. 18-19. Zemach references the phrase "fine shades of behavior" to Wittgenstein's *Lectures and Conversations on Aesthetics, Psychology and Religious Belief.* The expression does not appear in that book, but is found in *Philosophical Investigations*, p. 207.

on what our theory says about Ks."[5] The reference to theory here requires comment. Theory is, of course, required to make sense of many scientific observations. To identify these lines on a photographic plate as indicating the activities of certain atomic particles requires both laboratory expertise and knowledge of a theory, that is, atomic theory. To recognize these chairs as Chippendale or this painting as Mannerist requires a certain expertise in furniture styles or art history—and, presumably, knowledge of a theory. What theory? And what is the theory required to see that the objects are really chairs? Here again is the curious, but philosophically widespread idea, that the ordinary day-to-day dealings that make up our lives involve theories. What seems quite appropriate to scientific activities goes queer with respect to tables and chairs, cabbages and kings, not to mention poems and paintings.[6] Fortunately it is not necessary to untangle all the confusions wrapped up in this talk of theory to get at relevant issues about aesthetic judgment.

If we are to make anything of aesthetic realism we must get clear about what counts as standard observation conditions in aesthetic and artistic matters. It is obvious that normal eyesight and proper light are required to appreciate and judge painting, normal hearing to listen to music, and knowledge of the language to understand poetry. These factors won't go very far, however, in explaining disagreement in any interesting cases. A person's bad eyesight doesn't so much explain why we disagree about the painting so much as it disqualifies him from taking part in the discussion. Moreover those factors are constant in all cases; we can, as it were, divide through by them. The interesting issues come up when we try to uncover what else goes into Zemach's SOC. Here is one listing:

> ... SOC for literature must include sensitivity to language and style, ability to detect nuances and follow suggestions, life experience, musical ear, psychological sophistication, attention to plot and manner of narration, sensitivity to recurring motifs, broad liberal education, familiarity with the history of the culture, acquaintance with other works of the artist and the period, information about events known to educated people in that society, etc.[7]

We may assume that SOC for painting are analogous. There is another category of SOC that Zemach calls time-sensitive properties (TP). He says that "to see something as original, as conservative, revolutionary, classic, surprising, conventional, etc., we must tacitly position ourselves in a certain historical time or use that time as a reference point."[8] We can often cite one or another of these various factors to explain

---

5   Zemach, p. 54.

6   "To buy a friend a present, you want to know what aesthetic features that person identifies and appreciates; you need an aesthetic theory in whose terms a gift can be described and match with the friend's aesthetic taste." [Zemach, p.58.] It takes a philosopher to suppose you have to have a theory to know what she likes.

7   Zemach, p. 88.

8   Zemach, pp. 77-78. Pettit [pp. 30-31] makes a similar point when he says that for an object to be seen correctly it must be "positioned" correctly.

why someone failed to understand or appreciate a work of art. One of the sources of humor in Aristophanes' play *The Frogs*, scholars tell us, is his parody of the styles of Aeschylus and Euripedes. For those of us who do not read classical Greek the jokes are unavailable since these parodies cannot come across in translation. Most of us cannot position ourselves fully to appreciate the play. The critics and public who mocked the Post Impressionists early in the last century surely had not "positioned" them correctly—they tried to "position" them with both the artists of the later Renaissance as well as the contemporary salon, that is, they tried to see Cézanne and company as doing the same sort of thing as the "old masters" and their contemporary imitators—and so failed to see the point of what they were up to. The things that are listed under these headings are indeed factors that play a role when we make aesthetic and artistic judgments as well as assess the judgments of others. Whether or not these factors belong in the same basket with matters of eyesight and hearing as well as whether it is helpful, or even intelligible, to think of them as anything like the standard conditions of observation that function in science and some other affairs are other matters altogether.

Zemach says that while aesthetic qualities are real, their ontological status is that of being supervenient; aesthetic properties are said to be supervenient upon nonaesthetic ones. A look at this notion of supervenience will, I think, make clear at least some of what is really going on in the business of aesthetic realism. Aesthetic qualities, he says, "supervene upon nonaesthetic ones because we observe the former by observing the latter through a special medium: desire."[9] Desire apparently includes anything having human character and interest so that "Aesthetic sensitivity requires an ability to see things as having interest-determined properties ... ."[10] He notes that "Even abstract art is thoroughly anthropomorphic: a visual or melodic line is seen as striving, ascending, climbing, ... ,"[11] and the list goes on. On these same pages he says such things as "Some aesthetic properties, the expressive ones, require that we see the things that have them as manifesting an attitude to a satisfaction or frustration of desire." And again, "Aesthetic sensitivity requires an ability to see things as having interest-determined properties ... ." What is striking about this notion of supervenience is that it is spelled out in terms of *seeing* one thing *as* another. The repeated use of the expression "seeing as" strongly suggests that talk about supervenience is really talk about what Wittgenstein has taught us to understand as aspect perception. The thesis that an aesthetic property supervenes upon a nonaesthetic one would appear to be essentially the thesis that the property is an aspect and that the thing can be seen aesthetically.

This suggestion is reinforced by Philip Pettit when he points out that like judgments of color, aesthetic judgments are perceptual, but unlike judgments of color they are said to be "perceptually elusive." He explains this by saying that "visual scrutiny of a picture, necessary though it may be for aesthetic knowledge, is

---

9   Zemach, p. 95.
10   Zemach, p. 106.
11   Zemach, p. 105.

not always sufficient to guarantee it ... . One may look and look (at a painting) and not see its elegance or economy or sadness ... ."[12] He goes on to adduce the duck-rabbit figure as an example of something that is perceptually elusive. The duck-rabbit, of course, is the very figure that Wittgenstein uses to bring out much about the notion of aspect perception.

If this suspicion is correct, as I believe it is, then the notion of supervenience and its ontology, at least in the context of aesthetics, can be set aside for aspect perception. The view is then delightfully ironic since Wittgenstein makes clear that aspects are not properties.[13] There is the further suspicion that realism is trivial: aesthetic properties are simply aspects and the question of whether aesthetic properties really exist is simply the question of whether or not we can see appropriate aspects. Looked at in this way Zemach's standard conditions of observation cannot be causal conditions for judgment, as adequate light and normal eyesight are for color perception and resulting judgments of color, but rather are conditions of intelligibility, e.g., only if a person is acquainted with, say, period styles in art is it intelligible to say that he sees this painting as closer to the mannerist tradition than to the baroque.

Wittgenstein says:

> The substratum of this experience (of seeing one thing as another) is the mastery of a technique.
> But how queer for this to be the logical condition of someone's having such-and-such an *experience*! After all you don't say that one only "has toothache" if one is capable of doing such-and-such.–From this it follows that we cannot be dealing with the same concept of experience here. It is a different though related concept. [PI, p. 208]

Wittgenstein makes clear that the investigation of these various concepts of seeing is not a causal, but a conceptual one and Zemach's SOC surely belong to the conceptual background that makes aesthetic judgment intelligible.

We can recognize a certain overlapping between Zemach's SOC and the requirements that David Hume, in the "Standard of Taste" essay, lays out for the ideal critic: "strong sense, united to delicate sentiment, improved by practice, perfected by comparison, and cleared of all prejudice ... ." It is, he says, the joint verdict of such critics that is the true standard of taste and beauty. This leads to an interesting speculation. It would appear that any particular case of divergence from the taste of the ideal critic can be put down to a deficiency in one or more of the relevant factors affecting taste. Should that deficiency or failure be adjusted for, one would suspect that there ought to be agreement in judgment. Thus we can imagine the possibility of assigning to each person an aesthetic handicap, or possibly a taste quotient, so that when the taste quotient was factored in or the handicap added there would be substantial agreement in everyone's aesthetic judgments. I see no reason why

---

12 Pettit, p. 26.

13 " ... what I perceive in the dawning of an aspect is not a property of the object, but an internal relation between it and other objects." [Ludwig Wittgenstein, *Philosophical Investigations*, 2nd edn (New York, 1958)] p. 212.

Zemach's theory would not entail a similar consequence. A false aesthetic judgment is presumably the result of a failure of one or more of the SOC to be satisfied, and should those failures be rectified all judgments ought to come out on the mark.

What I have just said may be a parody, but it is a parody intended to draw attention to two things about aesthetic realism. One is that for the realist agreement in matters aesthetic is a consummation devoutly to be wished and the other is that there is something about the view that suggests that aesthetic judgment depends at bottom on an intellectual awareness that certain things have certain properties. If it is primarily a matter of recognizing the presence of properties, then it would seem to open the possibility that one could be quite indifferent to them. Just as one can identify various species of motor cars without having any particular concern for them, so it would appear that one can note that this line is graceful or that these colors contrast with one another without ever being struck by, or impressed by, any of this, in a word, without any of what we think of as characteristic aesthetic reactions.

The notion of aesthetic properties as supervenient demands a clear distinction between aesthetic and nonaesthetic properties as there must be something for aesthetic properties to be supervenient upon. It is doubtful that a general distinction can be made between what is aesthetic and what is not. If we turn our attention, however, from the "properties" themselves to aesthetic descriptions and the language in which we couch them we will notice that a particular word can sometimes carry aesthetic weight and sometimes not. Color words are like that. One may report as a simple matter of fact that the Chinese vase in that display case is red. Another time, in pointing to the same vase, one may exclaim "Look at that *red*!" as an expression of how one has been struck by the color. The tone of voice with its emphasis is one of those fine shades of behavior that manifests one's aesthetic appreciation and response. There are a multitude of words in our language that have both aesthetic and nonaesthetic uses. I would think that what should concern us is not so much a sorting of properties, the aesthetic ones here and the nonaesthetic ones over there, along with a corresponding sorting of the terms that denote them, but rather keeping an eye out for when a word is being used to do aesthetic duty and when it is not. The exploitation of an aesthetic/nonaesthetic distinction as a building block of aesthetic theory is, I suggest, fruitless and of little interest. The important task is to gain an understanding of the ways in which aesthetic judgments actually work and the roles that they play, especially in our traffic with art.

Marcia Eaton, as part of her objection to the idea of supervenience, makes a somewhat different use of the duck-rabbit. She says that in aesthetics "Agreement is possible because evidence is forthcoming, where the evidence consists of pointing to intrinsic properties via statements that members of the same community understand."[14] As an analogy to illuminate aesthetic judgment she refers to both a picture of a cow and to the duck-rabbit. She says that there can be evidence that the cow is of a certain breed and that the figure is a duck. She adds, however, that the evidence in neither case will guarantee that there will be agreement about the breed

---

14 Eaton, p. 394.

or its being a duck. Aesthetic judgment is said to be like that, there is no guarantee that there will be agreement, but there is evidence.

There is more than one thing amiss here. The conformation and coloring of the cow in the picture can indeed be evidence that the beast is of that breed, and if the picture is sufficiently detailed those details can add up to a guarantee that it is one. The picture can always be compared to the real thing. A lack of agreement in this case brings the charge of ignorance or stupidity. The cow picture, however, is not an ambiguous figure like the duck-rabbit. When one points out that these lines must be taken as the bill and the eye as looking in this direction, one is not marshaling evidence for duckness, but trying to get another to see the picture as a duck. In this latter case it is not a matter of identification, but of perception. A failure to see the duck aspect is not the result of either ignorance or stupidity, but is perhaps due to a lack of imagination or what Wittgenstein calls aspect blindness.

It is a passing strange kind of evidence where there can be no guarantee of agreement. Evidence can suggest that the airplane crashed when the pilot ran out of fuel. Inspection of the wreckage can verify that and everyone who counts would have to agree. Understanding a painting, for example, is not like that. There can, of course, be evidence for its attribution, iconography, or subject matter, but hardly for the balance of its composition, the appropriateness of the treatment of the subject, or for it being perhaps overly sentimental. While we can cite the keys as evidence that this figure is St. Peter, the features that we cite to bring someone to appreciate the composition or the appropriateness of the dramatic subject matter do not work like evidence. They are, instead, guides to alter one's perception in order to bring one to see the thing in a certain way. To bring one to realize that this picture is sentimental kitsch may require a rather radical readjustment in his view of the world. What is vitally important is how a person reacts to all of this and how the resulting judgment is anchored in that person's character and connects with other aspects of his life.

As was made clear earlier, the aesthetic realist understands the alternative to realism to be subjectivism in any of its many forms. These, however, are not the alternatives for both are to be rejected. Enough has been said about realism and a quick glance at subjectivism should be enough. Consider a sentence such as "Reubens was a great painter." The sentence could be used to report a widely held view as on, say, an examination in some humanities course where students are asked to identify various historical figures. "A great painter" may be marked correct for Reubens, but not for Milton. Imagine now someone of wide acquaintance with art and deeply sensitive to it. After gazing at Reuben's *Descent from the Cross* in Antwerp he exclaims "God, but Reubens was a great painter." This exclamation is not the "Wow!" of emotivism, which could always be an untutored "wow!", but rather in this case is precipitated out of a background of knowledge and experience. His reaction to a Rossi, we may assume, is somewhat more restrained. It would be a travesty to describe him as voicing a purely subjective and personal opinion.

The variety and diversity of aesthetic judgments and the uses to which they can be put ought to be bewildering to anyone who seeks a common denominator or general theory to account for them all. We speak of the aesthetic character of nature—the beauty of flowers, the majesty of mountains, the sunset colors, and all of that. Then there are aesthetic considerations for the household—the appropriateness of styles of furniture, the color of the walls and the draperies, the arrangement of objects on the mantle or the bookshelf, the "art" that is hung on the walls, usually more for its decorative effect than its artistic value. And then there is *art*, painting and sculpture that should be taken seriously and is not there just because it "looks pretty" or complements the sofa. With respect to a painting we can speak of its design, composition, color harmonies, and so on, but also, and more especially, of its human and dramatic qualities. It is on these latter that I wish to concentrate.

Phillip Pettit had described aesthetic judgments as "perceptually elusive" and that term is not inapt. He cited the duck-rabbit as an example of something that is perceptually elusive. That figure, however, will not go very far toward shedding light on aesthetic perception and judgment. Very few paintings are visually ambiguous in that way. We must remember that after introducing the whole business of aspect perception with the example of seeing a likeness, as between two faces, he goes on to use the picture of that curious creature to call attention to more of the conceptual complexities of seeing and seeing aspects. He goes on to talk about seeing aspects of organization, experiencing the meaning of a word, using words in secondary senses, and then of what he calls imponderable evidence. One place in which perceptual elusiveness can be manifested is in understanding other human beings and their expressions. Wittgenstein talked about the idea of imponderable evidence with reference to the genuineness of a person's expression although it can certainly be applied to the understanding of expressions in general. This is by no means the notion of evidence that Eaton believes figures in rational justification. An example can be found in Balzac's *Les Chouans*, a novel of the royalist uprising in the Vendée during the French revolution. Balzac describes an encounter between several people who, although barely acquainted, are suspicious of one another's intentions. The young and beautiful Mademoiselle de Verneuil has just intervened to prevent the republican military commandant from questioning a young man whom he suspects of being a royalist. Madame de Gua, who represents herself as the young man's mother, observes the incident:

> [Madame de Verneuil] turned toward the young man to whom, in the intoxication of triumph, she threw a look in which malice was mixed with an amorous expression. Both their brows lightened; joy colored their agitated faces, and a thousand contradictory thoughts stirred in their souls. By a single look madame de Gua appeared to attribute rather more love than charity to the generosity of mademoiselle de Verneuil, and certainly she was right. The pretty traveler blushed and lowered her eyes in divining everything that was said in that one look from a woman. (My translation.)

I strongly suspect that it required a woman to divine what was in that other woman's look. Although Balzac does not describe their reactions, it is more than likely that the men were unaware of any special significance in the look of Madame de Gua, if they noticed it at all. It is this kind of subtlety of glance along with such things as gestures and tones of voice that Wittgenstein would include in what he calls imponderable evidence.

There are questions of reading character in art that parallel Wittgenstein's questions about genuiness of human feeling. In his discussion of Van Loo's *St. Augustine Disputing with the Donatists* Michael Fried cites more than one critic who is struck by how one of the secretaries who are shown recording the proceedings has stopped writing and turned toward the saint because he is so taken with the force and power of Augustine's argument.[15] It strikes me, however, that there is a different way to understand what is going on. Perhaps there is no special significance in the secretary's pause; he is just waiting for Augustine to come to a stopping place so he can record the thought coherently. We can well imagine people present at the debate itself who may have reacted in these different ways and so formed quite different judgments about the secretary. We, who have only the painted secretary to respond to, will form different judgments about the painting. Someone may find the painting to be less significant than those critics that Fried quotes. A case like this shows how seeing things and reacting to them on the basis of imponderable evidence can make a difference in our understanding of works of art.

Much in aesthetics and art is, indeed, "perceptually elusive", but in a far deeper and more complex way than is imagined by Pettit and the aesthetic realists. Aesthetic and artistic appreciation and judgment can run deep in human life where it makes connections with wider human relations and morality. There is much in that wider human life that is "elusive," if not always perceptually so. There are a myriad of uncertainties in our dealings with others and we often have nothing to go on but imponderables. Aesthetic realism does not do justice to this. It is by no means obvious that agreement in art and aesthetics is the consummation that so many devoutly wish. Diversity in taste and appreciation is sometimes to be valued. To be sure, there are occasions in which agreement, or at least some measure of it, is important, the selection of civic monuments and art for public spaces are obvious examples. Nor should we forget what is at stake for married couples when it is a matter of interior decoration and appropriateness of clothing. There is, nevertheless, one very important reason for seeking aesthetic, especially artistic, agreement. It can connect us with our own history and culture and, in addition, it can connect us personally with one another so that in our shared appreciation of art we can appreciate not only the works of art, but one another. None of this seems to enter into aesthetic realism's account of judgment.

It is no help at all in understanding our relations to art and our judgments about it to insist that aesthetic qualities really exist. At worst its intelligibility is questionable and at best, it amounts to saying no more than what we all know: that there is such a thing as aesthetic appreciation and judgment. To make the question about the existence of aesthetic properties intelligible it should be restated as a question about the use of aesthetic terms as well as the life in which they function. Do they function

---

15 Michael Fried, *Absorption and Theatricality: Painting and Beholder in the Age of Diderot*, (Chicago and London, 1980), pp. 19-20.

like so many familiar descriptions, e.g., "It is red," "its top speed is 350mph," or do they work like exclamations and exhortations, "Wow!", "Ugh!", and their ilk? The answer, I suggest, is neither.

Index of Names

Index of Subjects